STALIN'S 'WONDER TANK'

STALIN'S 'WONDER TANK'

THE TRUTH BEHIND HITLER'S NEMESIS, THE SOVIET T-34 TANK

DMITRY ZUBOV

FRONTLINE
BOOKS

STALIN'S 'WONDER TANK'
The Truth Behind Hitler's Nemesis, the Soviet T-34 Tank

First published in Great Britain in 2025 by
Frontline Books
An imprint of Pen & Sword Books Ltd
Yorkshire – Philadelphia

Copyright © Dmitry Zubov

ISBN 9781399066754

A CIP catalogue record for this book is available from the British Library.

Typeset by Lapiz Digital
Printed and bound in the UK by CPI Group (UK) Ltd, Croydon, CR0 4YY.

MIX
Paper | Supporting
responsible forestry
FSC® C013604

The Publisher's authorised representative in the EU for product safety is Authorised Rep Compliance Ltd., Ground Floor, 71 Lower Baggot Street, Dublin D02 P593, Ireland.
www.arccompliance.com

For a complete list of Pen & Sword titles please contact

PEN & SWORD BOOKS LIMITED
47 Church Street, Barnsley, South Yorkshire, S70 2AS, England
E-mail: enquiries@pen-and-sword.co.uk
Website: www.pen-and-sword.co.uk
or
PEN AND SWORD BOOKS
1950 Lawrence Road, Havertown, PA 19083, USA
E-mail: uspen-and-sword@casematepublishers.com
Website: www.penandswordbooks.com

CONTENTS

List of Plates vi
Introduction viii

Chapter 1   Stalin's Militarism 1
Chapter 2   Vickers and Christie 34
Chapter 3   The American Ancestor of the T-34. 65
Chapter 4   The T-34 is a By-product of Stalin's Repressions 103
Chapter 5   Tank of the 'New Type' 158

Conclusion 216
Notes 220
Bibliography 231
Index 236

LIST OF PLATES

1.   Production of 'Sormovo's freaks' at Krasnoye Sormovo Shipyard No. 112.

2.   Vladimir Lenin delivers a speech on Red Square, Moscow, 7 November 1918.

3.   'Parade of Steel and Motors', 9 February 1934.

4.   Top commanders of the Red Army in 1927.

5.   Captured Renault FT-17 tank at the Krasnoye Sormovo Locomotive Factory in Nizhny Novgorod.

6.   British Mark V tanks in service with the Red Army.

7.   Tests of the prototype T-24 medium tank, 1931.

8.   Head of the Red Army's Mechanisation and Motorisation Directorate (UMM) Innokenty Khalepsky.

9.   Prototype of the TG tank.

10.   Vickers 12-ton Medium Mark II tank during tests near Moscow.

11.   'Revolutionary Military Council'. Painting by Isaac Brodsky.

12.   T-17 tankette.

13.   Head of Armaments of the Red Army Ieronim Uborevich.

14.   Former officer of the Russian Imperial Guard Mikhail Tukhachevsky.

15.   The chieftain of Soviet military industry, Gregory (Sergo) Ordzhonikidze, speaks.

16.   Christie tank No. 2051 being tested. Moscow region, May 1931.

17.   The doomed 'wrecker' Afanasii Firsov.

18.   The big Kiev manoeuvres (military exercises of the Kiev Military District troops), September 1935.

19.   BT-7 wheel-and-track tank, Kharkov 1936.

20.   The 'Red Marshal' Mikhail Tukhachevsky.

21. Prototype of the T-29 wheel-and-track tank, 1937.

22. BT-5-IS wheel-and-track tank. Thanks to the removed armour plates, the design of the three-axle drive can be seen.

23. Real friends: Joseph Stalin and Kliment Voroshilov.

24. Study of a tank engine by cadets of the Military Academy of Mechanisation and Motorisation of the Red Army 'Stalin' (VAMM). November 1940.

25. Director of the Factory No. 183 Ivan Bondarenko.

26. Colonel General Dmitry Pavlov.

27. A prototype drawing of the BT-20 (A-20) wheel-and-track tank. March 1938.

28. Chief Designer of the Factory No. 183 Mikhail Koshkin.

29. T-32 (A-32) prototype tank, loaded with ballast, simulating the weight of additional armour. Autumn 1939.

30. T-34 tank No. 1 departs from Kharkov to Moscow.

31. One of the first mass-produced T-34 tanks.

32. An abandoned Stalin's 'wonder tank'.

INTRODUCTION

' . . . I really hope that you will finally be able to do something about Sormovo's freak, which our tankmen are afraid to fight on'

The degree of failure of the Soviet tank industry in the early summer of 1943 was so egregious that the top management of tank factories could not hide this fact from Stalin. Concerned about the constant problems with the production of tanks, the 'Red Tsar' wrote in one of his letters to his devoted servant, the People's Commissar of the Tank Industry, in June 1943: '. . . and in conclusion, Comrade Malyshev,[1] I really hope that you will finally be able to do something about Sormovo's freak, which our tankmen are afraid to fight on'.

The abusive nickname 'Sormovo's freak' was what Stalin called the T-34-76 tank, which had been produced in large quantities at Krasnoye Sormovo Shipyard No. 112 since the autumn of 1941. The rude and poorly educated 'Red Tsar' liked to come up with abusive nicknames for his subordinates and related objects. At the same time, he did not hesitate to use the rudest expressions even in official correspondence with his servants. But in this case, Stalin was not the author of the abusive expression 'Sormovo's freak'. He only used the results of the creativity of the Red Army soldiers. The Gorky-made T-34 tanks were named 'Freak' by their crews and Red Army commanders. They had sufficient reasons for this in the form of egregious vices, namely cracks in the armour and the constantly breaking transmission. At the same time, it is surprising that the monstrously cruel Stalin, who killed millions of Soviet citizens for no reason, resigned himself to the mass production of entirely defective military equipment. He did not order the immediate execution of all those involved in the creation of 'Sormovo's freaks'. Instead, the bloodthirsty Red Tsar, in a letter to his servant, once again modestly hoped to eliminate the glaring shortcomings of the T-34 tank. The reason for such a strange change in the character of the bloody tyrant is that in 1943 it was a different Stalin!

The 'Red Tsar's' confidence in his infallibility had been significantly shaken by Hitler's insidious attack and the endless crushing defeats of the Red Army that continued throughout 1941 and 1942. After these defeats, the morally broken Stalin, in letters to his servants, instead of categorical orders accompanied by direct threats of shooting the guilty, began to use the peaceful, and even respectful words 'I ask', 'I hope', and 'I suggest'. In 1943, the 'Red Tsar', crushed by Hitler, no longer asked his servants stupid questions about the reasons why his beloved T-34 tank was being produced at a shipyard located 1,000km from the nearest sea. He was no longer interested in where several huge tank factories, specially built in the 1930s by American architects, had disappeared to. In response to numerous complaints from Red Army commanders about the monstrously low quality of the T-34 tanks, Stalin was forced to throw up his hands and powerlessly rely on the 'skill' of his top managers who ran the Soviet tank industry. It so happened that on 22 June 1941, the 'Red Lord', who had previously easily dismissed and executed his generals and ministers, became dependent on the servants who saved his 'Red Empire' and him personally from death. However, as soon as the capricious 'military fate' finally turned away from Hitler and the situation on the Eastern Front changed in favour of the Red Army, the former rude and cruel Stalin returned. As early as 1944, arrests, torture, and executions of Soviet citizens would once again become an integral part of life in the 'Red Empire'.

The Birth of the T-34 Myth

Soviet propaganda turned the T-34 into one of the most recognisable symbols of the Red Army. A huge number of pretentious books and films are dedicated to this, Stalin's 'wonder tank'. All Soviet and many Russian historians categorically call the T-34 the best tank of the Second World War. At the same time, they refer to the 'authoritative' opinion of Heinz Guderian and other German generals. Many Western researchers are joining this chorus of outright Stalinist propaganda, who are persistently trying to find the non-existent advantages of this very mediocre tank. The legendary sloped armour, diesel engine and wide tank tracks of the T-34 are presented as purely Soviet innovations, which the 'talentless' German tank designers tried in vain to copy when creating the Panther.

The myth of the 'invincibility' of the T-34 hides behind its fake facade the acute facts of the total inefficiency of this creation of the miserable Stalinist industry. The reality of the summer of 1941 showed that it took the Wehrmacht only a couple of months to turn Stalin's tank armada into a pile of scrap metal. Moreover, the Germans, carried away by the success of Blitzkrieg, did not notice that in addition to 12,000 'obsolete' tanks with thin armour, about 1,200 of the newest T-34 tanks were also destroyed. Hitler's generals remembered Stalin's 'wonder tank' only after the pace of the tank wedges' offensive slowed down. Following the stupid orders of their Führer, the Germans got bogged down in endless operations to cover their flanks from the mythical counter-attacks of the Red Army, which by that time had actually lost its combat capability. To hide the consequences of Hitler's incompetent command, the German generals had to explain the collapse of Operation Barbarossa by the incredible resilience of Soviet soldiers, the Russian Winter, and finally the 'terrible' Russian T-34 tank, which destroyed their victorious plans. Stalin's incompetent generals, who abandoned their huge but completely unprepared army to the mercy of fate, also do not like to recall the colossal losses of T-34 tanks. The Mechanised Corps, grandiose in number of tanks, which, according to Stalin's 'ingenious' plan, was preparing to conquer the whole of Europe, simply disappeared, crushed by the Wehrmacht. A huge amount of destroyed, immobile and simply abandoned military equipment became a picturesque backdrop for the photographed German soldiers. By November 1941, Stalin, who had recently owned a huge number of heavy KV and medium T-34 tanks, was forced to tearfully ask the Allies for urgent supplies of British and American tanks to defend Moscow.

These facts motivate us to turn to the real story of the creation, production and combat use of Stalin's 'wonder tank'. Under the numerous layers of Soviet secrecy, myths, propaganda and outright lies, a bitter reality is revealed. The T-34 tank was not a masterpiece of Soviet engineering, but represented a set of far from the newest and far from the best design solutions borrowed by Soviet designers from the West. Produced by unskilled workers in an incredible hurry, the tank was very often an easy target for the Panzerwaffe and a mass grave for brave Soviet tankmen. This book is an attempt to convey to Western readers the objective circumstances of the creation of Stalin's much-loved T-34 tank. Unlike many books about the creation of armoured fighting vehicles, this book focuses on human relationships. According to the author, analysing the motives of the main characters is the key to understanding the reasons for creating this tank. In modern literature devoted to the creation and use of armoured fighting vehicles, this important human aspect is usually ignored or presented in a distorted form. The book contains a number of widely used psychological terms and interpretations necessary for analysing the actions of the characters. However, readers are not required to have special competencies in order to understand the ideas outlined by the author.

A detailed description of the design of Soviet tanks was not the priority of this book, but the technical aspect is presented in sufficient detail to understand the essence of the history of the creation of the T-34.

The author is also interested in analysing the organisation of the Soviet military industry and management at specific military plants, in particular at the Kharkov Locomotive Factory (KhPZ). This aspect allows us to better understand the specifics of the development and production of Soviet tanks.

This book reflects only a small part of the extensive history of the creation, production and combat use of the T-34 tank. There is no doubt that many books can and should be written about this tank. However, in the author's subjective opinion, this small book represents a new perspective on the subject and quite fully reflects the essence of Stalin's 'wonder tank'.

Chapter 1

STALIN'S MILITARISM

'Parade of Steel and Motors'

February 9th 1934, Moscow, Red Square.

On a cold winter morning, a grand military parade is taking place on the main square of the Soviet Union. The cadets of the Soviet higher military schools are the first to march across the paving stones covered with a thin layer of snow. Then, in the same close columns, numerous soldiers and officers of the Red Army are marching in precise steps: infantrymen, sappers, snipers, pilots and sailors. Then the combined detachments of the best OGPU troops,[1] the armed railway guards and the Moscow militia march. The foot columns are followed by cavalry squadrons, units of the ridiculous horse-drawn machine guns ('tachanka') and numerous artillery pieces of various types towed by horses. According to the plan of the experienced directors of the militarised play, this order of military units in 1934 repeated the events of the first military parade of the Bolsheviks, which took place on 1 May 1918.

That year, the Bolsheviks, who had recently seized power in the country as a result of a military coup, were far from the grand scale of the Stalinist parades of the 1930s. Lenin had objective reasons to doubt that the Red state he had created could last long enough. In addition to powerful external enemies, among whom were all the major states of the world, the Bolsheviks had numerous internal enemies. Moreover, a significant part of them were recent allies in the revolutionary struggle. In 1918, Lenin did not have the strength to openly fight against numerous enemies. For this reason, the Red government moved in great haste, little different from a cowardly flight, from the brilliant European Petersburg to provincial Moscow. This city, which had long since lost its role as the capital, had an important advantage

1

due to its location in the safe centre of the European part of a huge country. On 12 March 1918, by Lenin's will, Moscow became the capital of Red Russia.

Red Square was poorly suited for military parades at that time. It was a dirty, neglected space surrounded by the Kremlin's medieval walls and ornate buildings built in the Russian Revival style. Access to the square by large masses of troops and especially military equipment was restricted by dilapidated buildings. However, in 1918, the pragmatic Lenin chose Red Square without hesitation for the first demonstration of the military might of the Red Army. Lenin's successor, who succeeded him in 1924, steadfastly observed the traditions of military parades. However, despite the emphasised respect for the events of the recent past, Stalin made significant amendments to this main Bolshevik ritual. They reflected the drastic changes that had taken place in the Soviet Union over the long years of its rule.

In 1930, huge financial resources were allocated in a country suffering from permanent famine to carry out a large-scale reconstruction of Red Square, sacred to Stalin. Instead of a broken cobblestone pavement, beautiful paving stones made of the strongest basalt appeared. These, specially made for Red Square, could withstand the passage of the tracks of the heaviest tanks of that time without damage. The muddy puddles that had been hastily filled with sand by Red Army soldiers before the parades in the 1920s had disappeared forever. The predicted service life of the basalt pavement, even with the continuous movement of tanks on it, was a thousand years! The improvised cemetery of the fallen revolutionary heroes, which appeared on Red Square back in 1917, was also put in order. In the centre of the reconstructed Bolshevik necropolis, on Stalin's orders, a majestic Mausoleum was built, lined with giant blocks of rare granite. On the underground level of this strange structure, which resembled an Egyptian pyramid, lay a sarcophagus with the mummy of Vladimir Lenin. The transformations also affected the architectural ensemble of Red Square. The Monument to Minin and Pozharsky[2] was moved closer to the Cathedral of Vasily the Blessed. Kazan Cathedral and Resurrection Gate, which restricted access to the parade of military equipment, was ruthlessly demolished.

The main participant of the Bolshevik ritual, the Red Army, underwent the same total reconstruction. Its creator, the People's Commissar for Military and Naval Affairs (Minister of War) Leon Trotsky who hosted the first parade on 1 May 1918, was declared an enemy after Stalin came to power. After a dramatic power struggle, Trotsky was removed from all positions and sent into exile. On 6 November 1925, Kliment Voroshilov, who was slavishly devoted to

Stalin, was appointed official commander of the Red Army. From the moment of his appointment in 1925 until 1 May 1941, all military parades in Red Square were commanded only by Voroshilov.

Instead of cavalry squadrons, numerous military equipment, primarily tanks of various types, became the main character of the Stalinist parades of the 1930s. The first tank, a captured French Renault FT-17, drove through Red Square on 1 May 1919. It had been captured by Red Army soldiers at the Russian Civil War front near Odessa. The tank was named 'Kremlin' and was sent to Moscow as a gift to Lenin. Hundreds of tanks had already participated in the Stalinist parades of the 1930s. In this type of military equipment, the progress of Stalin's militarisation was particularly noticeable. The Soviet military industry, created almost from scratch, was able in 1934 to produce hundreds of tanks for the hastily modernised Red Army.

On 9 February 1934, the author of these changes, Joseph Stalin, stood on the podium of the Mausoleum. He watched with interest the grandiose military performance unfolding in front of him. This small, moustachioed man, dressed in a modest military overcoat, did not fit the traditional image of the Russian 'Tsar'. There was nothing to distinguish him from the group of servants standing nearby. However, the Bolshevik leader's outward expressionlessness could not hide Stalin's megalomania, which was being broadcast in the Soviet Union at the state level. A striking evidence of the quasi-religious cult of worship of the 'Red Tsar' is his giant image placed on one of the buildings forming Red Square. Stalin is depicted in the portrait as a handsome black-moustached man with a kind expression on his face. Next to the image of the 'Red Lord' is the same huge portrait of the founder of the 'Red Empire', Lenin. This combination of two Bolshevik 'icons' demonstrated to the viewers of the military parade the legitimacy of the transfer of power from the deceased leader of the Bolsheviks to the living 'Red Tsar'.

Meanwhile, the most impressive mechanised and actually Stalinist part of the parade was unfolding on Red Square. Ahead of the giant wave of roaring engines and rumbling tracks of mechanical monsters, numerous columns of trucks with infantry in the back followed. Then there were hundreds of artillery tractors towing artillery pieces of various types. Finally, the main characters of the parade, tanks, clanked onto Red Square. Leading the columns of Stalin's armoured mechanical monsters was a giant T-35 five-turret tank with a red flag mounted on it. This 60-ton 'land battleship' remained the largest production tank in the world throughout the 1930s and symbolised the military might of the 'Red Empire'. Next, the three-turret T-28 tanks crept confidently, second in size and weight only to the five-turret giants. Behind them moved columns of T-26 light tanks, the most numerous tanks of the Red Army. Against the background of the giant T-35s and T-28s, groups of miniature T-27 tankettes, which also participated in the demonstration of the power of the Red Army, seemed like swarms of metal 'insects'.

The mass-produced tanks with hybrid drive in the USSR attracted the special attention of numerous spectators of Stalin's parades of the 1930s. The wheel-and-track BT-2 and BT-5 'wonder tanks' caused waves of delight and surprise to a large audience. They raced across the square at great speed, showing the advantages of the Soviet tank industry that were unattainable for other countries. Stalin is particularly proud of the columns of T-37A light amphibious tanks. These small tanks with very thin armour could overcome rivers and lakes inaccessible to traditional armoured fighting vehicles without preparation.

The grand parade that took place on 9 February 1934 was special for Stalin. The main organisers of the pompous event made every effort to ensure that this event was noticed and remembered by both Soviet citizens and invited foreigners. The very fact that the parade was held not on 1 May or 7 November, which were customary for the main Bolshevik rituals, but on 9 February, was surprising. The number of participants in this militaristic performance attracted even more attention from the audience. The Red Army command brought 42,000 soldiers and officers to Red Square. The number of armoured fighting vehicles participating in the parade was also a record. On that day, 525 tanks and hundreds of other military vehicles passed through the central square of the Soviet Union. The parade lasted more than three hours!

In the totalitarian Bolshevik state, the change in the traditional date of the military parade, combined with the grandiose scale of the tank demonstration, could only happen at the behest of Stalin. What was the reason that the bloody tyrant so grossly violated the sacred Bolshevik ritual? What was Stalin in a hurry to communicate in such a symbolic form to his country and the world around him by inviting a record number of Soviet and foreign correspondents to Red Square?

The formal reason for this unusual parade was the end of the 17th Congress of the All-Union Communist Party (Bolsheviks), which took place in Moscow from 26 January to 10 February 1934. At this pompous Bolshevik event, Stalin had to evaluate the results of the total Industrialisation of the Soviet Union initiated by him in 1929.

The consequences of Stalin's brutal interference in the life of a vast country were very ambiguous. In the period from 1929 to 1933, several large factories were built in the USSR, the equipment for which was entirely purchased abroad. These flagships of Stalinist industry produced thousands of military vehicles, planes, and tanks. However, the quality of the products produced by the factories, including tanks, was extremely poor.

Since the funds needed to build the flagships of Stalin's industry were literally taken away from the peasants, the grandiose industrial 'revolution' turned into a massive famine in 1932–3. An artificially created disaster has engulfed vast territories of the USSR. According to various sources, from three to eight million people died from the consequences of Stalin's criminal policy. On Stalin's orders, the horrific humanitarian and demographic consequences of Industrialisation were carefully concealed. Only successes were publicly demonstrated. Every year, Stalin's sycophantic servants prepared impressive reports on the growth of Soviet industrial production for their 'Red Tsar'. These boastful reports were then published in all Soviet newspapers. The pompous parades and total propaganda of the extraordinary industrial successes of the early 1930s deceived not only naive foreign correspondents, but even the pathologically suspicious Stalin. By the beginning of 1934, the intellectually limited 'Red Tsar' finally believed in the victory of Industrialisation. Such a change in the previously darkly anxious mental state of the Soviet leader had a huge impact on the internal and foreign policy of the USSR. For a short time, Stalin's obsessive mania for finding external and internal enemies subsided. The massive repression inside the country suddenly weakened. Many of those sentenced to long terms of imprisonment in Stalin's Gulag as 'wreckers' and 'enemies of the people' in the early 1930s were pardoned. The main Stalinist executioners from the OGPU suddenly began to doubt the need for mass executions of enemies of the Soviet government. There were also unprecedented events in foreign policy before 1934. Propaganda rhetoric had significantly softened. The streams of lies that inspired the Soviet people with the idea of a hostile environment of the USSR, dreaming of militarily capturing the world's first state of workers and peasants, have subsided. The results of this amazing 'liberalisation' were summed up by Stalin himself in his speech at the 17th Congress of the All-Union Communist Party (Bolsheviks) on 26 January 1934.

In the first part of his speech, the 'Red Tsar' solemnly proclaimed the victory of Industrialisation initiated by him and outlined even more ambitious plans for the industrial development of the USSR for the second five-year plan.

In the second part of his speech, referring to foreign policy issues, Stalin spoke in an unexpectedly peaceful tone about the European neighbours of the 'Red Empire'. Even more surprising was the announcement by the 'Red Tsar' of the USSR's intention to join the League of Nations. This step testified to his desire to end the external isolation of the Bolshevik state.

The delegates of the congress greeted Stalin's words with deafening applause. The 'Red Tsar' had no reason to doubt the full loyalty of the delegates of the party congress. All of them passed through the thin 'filter' of Stalin's personnel policy. On the part of the delegates, there was not a single attempt to criticise the activities of the Bolshevik leader, which led to the deaths of millions of Soviet citizens. As a result, all the 'successes' of Industrialisation and Stalin's plans aimed at accelerating the development of the USSR's military industry were unanimously approved by the Congress delegates. Later, this pompous Bolshevik event was called the Congress of Winners in the propaganda newspapers.

Stalin enjoyed his power. He believed that under his wise leadership, the Soviet Union had transformed from a backward agrarian country into a powerful economic, industrial, and military power ready to join the League of Nations. Stalin's general optimism about the success of Industrialisation, demonstrated at the parade, became the basis of state propaganda policy. The day after the parade, *Pravda*, the main Bolshevik newspaper, published a long article. In it, the pretentious demonstration of the triumph of Stalinist Industrialisation was boastfully called the 'Parade of Steel and Motors'.

However, the reality was far from the enthusiastic slogans of the Bolshevik newspapers. The pathos of the 'Parade of Steel and Motors' hid the gigantic vices of the Stalinist empire. Despite the brilliant demonstration of its capabilities on Red Square, Stalin's 'wonder tanks' had not been tested in combat conditions. Even in peacetime, the operation of armoured fighting vehicles in military units revealed a lot of design and production shortcomings. Moreover, the problem of the quality of Stalin's tanks could not be hidden even at carefully prepared parades. Tanks often broke down before reaching Red Square. Sometimes annoying incidents in the form of unexpectedly immobilised armoured fighting vehicles happened right in front of Stalin standing on the podium of the Mausoleum. Correspondents of the British newspaper *The Times*, in their generally laudatory report on the 'Parade of Steel and Motors', pointed out the fact of serious breakdowns of several types of armoured fighting vehicles, including one tank. In such cases, Stalin only frowned as he watched tractors, specially prepared for such unpleasant incidents, try to quickly remove the immobilised tanks from Red Square. Engine fires were an even more dangerous manifestation of the poor quality of the products of the Soviet tank industry. This happened especially often with the BT-2 and BT-5 high-speed wheel-and-track tanks. However, in 1934, the optimistic 'Red Lord' still believed the words of his servants. They promised to immediately eliminate all the shortcomings of the mass-produced tanks and create even more advanced models. It was for this reason alone that many top Red Army commanders, managers of Stalin's industry, and designers of military equipment were still alive.

In 1937, just three years after the 'Parade of Steel and Motors', Stalin's faith in the 'wonder tanks' mass-produced by the Soviet industry would be seriously undermined. The experience of military use of T-26 and BT-5 tanks in the battles of the Spanish Civil War ended in complete failure. The disadvantages of mass-produced Stalinist tanks would prove so fatal that information about it will finally reach the 'Red Lord'. Under the pressure of reality, the pretentious myth about the effectiveness of the Soviet tank industry will burst like a soap bubble. The consequences of the wrath of the 'Red Lord' will be terrible. In 1936–8, two-thirds of Soviet tank industry managers and armoured fighting vehicles designers would be shot for 'deceiving' Stalin. An inescapable Moloch of repression ouched those who, until recently, applauded the victorious speeches of the red tyrant. Eighty per cent of the delegates of the Congress of Winners, in honour of which an unusual parade was organised on 9 February1934, will be executed at the NKVD firing ranges. The 'wonder tanks' (T-35, T-28, BT-5, T-37A), which until recently were the pride of the Stalinist parades of the 1930s, will be considered hopelessly outdated. In official Soviet documents, these owners of irreparable structural and manufacturing defects will be contemptuously referred to as tanks of the 'Old Type'.

'Lenin's Shadow'

The path to the triumph of Stalin's militarism, demonstrated at the 'Parade of Steel and Motors' ran through many strange circumstances and unlikely events. Before the 1917 revolution, the Georgian revolutionary Joseph Dzhugashvili, little known even among the Bolsheviks, had virtually no chance to play any significant role in the history of the giant Russian Empire.

Poorly educated and intellectually limited, Dzhugashvili represented the exact opposite of Lenin's closest associates. He never participated in heated party discussions where brilliantly educated Bolsheviks discussed the complex philosophical aspects of Marxism. Modest and taciturn, Joseph was poorly versed in the intricacies of Bolshevik ideology. However, he was indispensable for carrying out various practical assignments. It was precisely for these very rare qualities among the chatty but relatively harmless Bolsheviks that Joseph Dzhugashvili earned Lenin's special attention.

Admittedly, the Bolshevik leader, who chose his party comrades very carefully, did not regret his decision. It was Dzhugashvili who was able to organise the daring robbery of a bank stagecoach, carried out in Tbilisi in 1907. The explosion of the bomb and the indiscriminate shooting by the bandits led to numerous casualties, including among bystanders of the robbery. This bloodstained money allowed a bunch of loafers, led by Lenin, to live comfortably abroad for many years. At the same time, Dzhugashvili was careful enough to carry out Lenin's risky assignments with someone else's hands. He left no obvious signs of his involvement in this brutal crime.

In 1912, Joseph Dzhugashvili finally adopted the party pseudonym 'Stalin'. However, this standard solution for a state criminal hiding from the tsarist police will in no way change his position among Lenin's close circle of associates. Before the events of the Bolshevik coup of 1917, Stalin would be perceived by his party comrades as an inconspicuous but fanatically loyal leader of the Bolsheviks, 'Lenin's Shadow'.

The Servant of 'Morgoth'[3]

The collapse of the Russian Empire, mired in endless defeats on the fronts of the First World War, opened up long-awaited prospects for the Bolsheviks to seize power in the huge country. In the autumn of 1917, the evil but infinitely cowardly Lenin needed people capable of decisive action more than ever. Stalin's participation in the revolutionary events was reduced to the role of Lenin's faithful servant and assistant. He supported his 'Master' in everything and ensured his safety.

Another important associate of Lenin, Leon Trotsky, played a key role in the dramatic events of the Bolshevik coup of 1917. It so happened that it was Lenin's recent implacable opponent who not only brought the Bolsheviks to power, but also helped to keep it. A brilliant intellectual who, unlike Stalin, was not a servant but an ally of Lenin, turned out to have an undoubted military talent that was in demand in the Russian Civil War that began after the Bolshevik coup. The White Army, formed from numerous opponents of the Bolsheviks, was advancing rapidly. On 14 March 1918, under pressure of possible defeat in a brutal war, Lenin appointed Trotsky to the post of People's Commissar for Military and Naval Affairs (Minister of War and Commander of the Red Army). The new military leader of the Bolsheviks managed to convince Lenin that restoring military discipline and inviting former tsarist officers to serve in the Red Army could significantly change the balance of power on the fronts of the Russian Civil War.

In a short time, using extremely brutal measures, Trotsky was able to turn the crowds of ragamuffins who made up the bulk of the Red Army into a semblance, if still a pathetic one, of an organised military force. Former tsarist officers, who occupied almost all command positions, created a solid foundation for the future victory of the Bolsheviks in the Russian Civil War.

Trotsky's acquisition of the official status of 'War Leader of the Bolsheviks', actually the second person after Lenin in the Bolshevik hierarchy, deeply angered the jealous Stalin. As a result, all the actions of Trotsky, who very confidently placed his men in command positions in the Red Army, seemed deeply erroneous to Stalin.

Unexpectedly for party comrades, in 1918 the recent 'Lenin's Shadow' loudly declared his ambitions for the role of the second man in the Bolshevik hierarchy. The position of People's Commissar of Nationalities of the RSFSR (Minister of National Affairs), received from Lenin for his faithful service during the revolution, seemed to Stalin completely insufficient. In the conditions of the Russian Civil War, Stalin's claims to power could only be realised as commander of the Red Army. However, this place was already firmly occupied by Trotsky.

The pragmatic Lenin was also not satisfied with the excessive elevation of his recent rival in the political struggle. He understood that during the war, his power depended entirely on Trotsky's military successes. Lenin, being a great expert in manipulating his subordinates, found an original way to compensate for the increased influence of Trotsky and mitigate the resentment of his devoted servant. He decided to realise Stalin's suddenly-manifested ambitions on another, equally important, 'front', in the fight against hunger.

In the summer of 1918, southern governors of Russia, the main grain producers, were engulfed by military action. This made it much more difficult to requisition grain and other food from the peasants, which was practised by the Bolsheviks. In the chaos of the Russian Civil War, compounded by the pathological economic policies of the

Bolsheviks, food flows from southern Russia to Moscow dried up. The central Governorates of the vast country, which formed the core of the Bolshevik state, were threatened with total starvation. To solve this problem, on 28 May 1918, the Bolshevik leader appointed Stalin the extraordinary commissioner for the requisition and export of grain from the Southern Governorates with virtually unlimited powers. After receiving this important mission, Lenin's faithful servant immediately set off for the Civil War-torn south of Russia.

'Red Verdun'

On 6 June 1918, Stalin arrived in Tsaritsyn, a key city in the North Caucasus Military District, which was opposed by numerous formations of the White Army. He took the powers given to him by Lenin literally and began to act as the head of the Bolsheviks in this war-torn region. The solution of Moscow's food supply issues quickly faded into the background. Stalin focused his attention on the management of the Red Army troops in this region. Constant gross interference in military matters led to a conflict between Stalin and the commander of the North Caucasus Military District, Lieutenant General Andrei Snesarev.[4] This former tsarist officer, sympathetic to the Bolsheviks, had been appointed to this position by Trotsky. The appointment of Snesarev to the post of commander infuriated Stalin. On far-fetched suspicion of treason against the Soviet government, Stalin dismissed the Lieutenant General from office and arrested all the officers of his staff.

To replace Trotsky's henchmen, Stalin gathered around himself a group of supporters as poorly educated and incompetent in military matters as himself. In this group, former locksmith Kliment Voroshilov stood out with a special doglike devotion. It was to him that Stalin entrusted the management of the Red Army troops in this sector of the front.

This behaviour of Stalin, who in a short period of time became the sole military leader in the North Caucasus and in the Tsaritsyn region, provoked outrage from the formal commander of the Red Army Trotsky. The situation of the conflict was aggravated by the sharp deterioration of the military situation of the Bolsheviks on this front. As a result of the stupid decisions of Stalin and Voroshilov, the town of Tsaritsyn, a key Bolshevik defence point in the south, was besieged by troops of the White Army. In this crisis situation, the conflict between Stalin and Trotsky continued to escalate. The formal commander-in-chief of the Red Army, realising that the situation was close to disaster, turned to Lenin for help.

Despite Stalin's gross violation of military subordination and blatant arbitrariness, Lenin stood up for his devoted servant. The head of the Bolsheviks actually confirmed him in his self-appointed position of commander of the North Caucasus Military District. Lenin gave Stalin the opportunity to show off his military 'talents'. This decision quickly led to a sharp deterioration of the military situation in the Tsaritsyn area. Stalin's complete incompetence became apparent to the Bolshevik leadership. On 19 October 1918, Lenin, at Trotsky's insistence, was forced to strip Stalin of his military powers, and recalled his servant back to Moscow. However, it was already too late and the resignation of 'Lenin's Shadow' did not save Red Army from collapse. The defence of Tsaritsyn, which was called 'Red Verdun' because of the ferocity of the battles, ended in a shameful defeat for the Bolsheviks. Despite a significant numerical advantage in soldiers, Tsaritsyn was captured by the White Army on 30 June 1919. The city returned to Bolshevik control only in January 1920.

The main reason for the Red Army's defeat in the battles of Tsaritsyn was the monstrous military incompetence of Stalin and his henchmen. However, the self-appointed Head of the North Caucasus Military District did not acknowledge his responsibility for the collapse of the city's defences. Stalin persistently blamed his failure on Trotsky and the former tsarist officers he appointed to command positions.

The Rise of 'Sauron'

Despite a series of dramatic events involving defeats and victories, the Red Army still managed to destroy the White Army. The Bolshevik victory in the Russian Civil War made Leon Trotsky the most famous man in Red Russia. He was second only to Lenin in popularity among the population, and he was the number one person in the Red Army. However, the downside of the end of the war was the decline in the influence of the 'War Leader of the Bolsheviks'. Obsessed with activity, Trotsky literally found no use for himself in peaceful life. His insane Labour Army project, designed to use soldiers freed after the victory in the Russian Civil War as slaves, failed miserably. Thus, although at the end of 1922 Trotsky still held the position of People's Commissar for Military and Naval Affairs and Commander-in-Chief of the Red Army, his opportunities in the struggle for leadership in the Bolshevik Party decreased significantly.

Trotsky's main opponent, Stalin, on the contrary, significantly increased his influence in the Bolshevik republic after the end of the war. The military setbacks at Tsaritsyn did not affect his relationship with Lenin. Using the patronage of the Bolshevik leader, Stalin gradually strengthened his position in the party hierarchy. An important achievement was the position of General Secretary of the Central Committee of the Communist Party of the Soviet Union, which Stalin received on 3 April 1922. Using its powers, the insidious 'Lenin's Shadow', through intrigue and outright deception, took control of all the most important issues of the functioning of the Bolshevik Party, and, accordingly, the entire Soviet state. This allowed Stalin to take an important position as regent of the incapacitated Lenin, who had been painfully dying of neurosyphilis for a year and a half.

Lenin's death in March 1924 led to a new escalation of the uncompromising struggle between Stalin and Trotsky for the vacant position of the main 'Red Devil'. In this deadly battle 'Lenin's Shadow' turned out to be a more skilled player than in leading the troops. Unlike the 'War Leader of the Bolsheviks', who treated most of his party comrades with an undisguised sense of superiority, the humble Stalin was able to build strong coalitions of Trotsky's enemies. This approach became the key to his success in the difficult party struggle. Remaining in the shadows, Stalin, manipulating the numerous enemies of the 'War Leader of the Bolsheviks', was able in early 1925 to deprive Trotsky of all positions and, consequently, most of his influence in the Red Army.

Trotsky's resistance turned out to be unexpectedly weak. The one who mercilessly shot Red Army soldiers for cowardice was unable to act as decisively with his opponent in the struggle for power. Not daring to split the Bolshevik Party for the sake of defeating his main enemy, Trotsky actually resigned himself to the role of victim. Stalin was devoid of such 'shortcomings' and saw no problem in the repression and even the physical elimination of his rivals in the struggle for absolute power in the Bolshevik Party. However, it took another three years of hard struggle for the future 'Red Lord' to finally break his influential opponent. Finally, on 12 February 1929, the completely neutralised Trotsky was sent abroad. Stalin's fear of the already former 'War Leader of the Bolsheviks' was so great that Lenin's cruel successor did not have the determination to physically destroy Trotsky. Subsequently, Stalin greatly regretted his indecision and was forced to entrust the liquidation of his main enemy to loyal servants from NKVD. On 20 August 1940, Trotsky, living in Mexico, was assassinated by a foreign agent of the Soviet secret police on Stalin's orders. Up to this point, any mention of Trotsky had caused the pathologically cruel Stalin to panic and launch severe bouts of bloody repression.

New Master of Red Army

Trotsky's dismissal from the posts of People's Commissar for Military and Naval Affairs and Commander-in-Chief of the Red Army was an important victory for Stalin. However, the vast majority of the personnel of the USSR military department and the top commanders of the Red Army were people appointed by Trotsky. With the weakening power of the 'War Leader of the Bolsheviks', this was the best defence against Stalin's attacks. The Red Army was too big a force and it didn't know any other commander-in-chief besides Trotsky. In this regard, Stalin had long feared a military coup and accused his mortal enemy of seeking to establish a military dictatorship. Under these conditions, the new 'Master of the USSR' was forced to moderate his appetites for the immediate strengthening of his influence in the Red Army. When replacing the top commanders appointed by Trotsky with loyal men, Stalin had to act with great caution. After Trotsky's removal, the new 'Master of the USSR' resigned himself to the compromise figure of Mikhail Frunze as Minister of War and Commander-in-Chief. However, nine months later Frunze died while undergoing surgery for a stomach ulcer. The death was caused by a gross mistake by anaesthesiologists, who injected him with a lethal dose of anaesthesia. Although this incident was very beneficial to Stalin, the author has no precise information about his involvement in this mysterious death. However, it was he who, despite Frunze's resistance, insisted on a surgical operation by a team of doctors who made a fatal mistake during its implementation. It is difficult to find other motives for Stalin's act. All his life, he was deathly afraid of doctors, and he never agreed to any surgical operations.

Finally, on 6 November 1925, Stalin took the last step to absolutise his influence in the Red Army. He secured appointments to the positions of People's Commissar for Military and Naval Affairs and Chairman of the Revolutionary Military Council (RVS), the doggedly-devoted Kliment Voroshilov. From that moment on, Stalin's henchman began systematically eradicating any memory of Trotsky in the Red Army. Voroshilov impressed upon his subordinates that the true creator of the Bolshevik armed forces was only Stalin.

Stalin managed to resolve the important issue of trust in former Trotsky people who held all important military positions in a relatively short time. Lenin's heir also entrusted this dirty work to his servant Voroshilov. The most notorious supporters of the former 'War Leader of the Bolsheviks' were immediately removed from the Red Army. However, most of the professional military openly declared their complete loyalty to Stalin. The new Bolshevik leader felt that he needed competent military specialists who had won the victory for the Bolsheviks on the battlefields of the Russian Civil War to win future wars. Without these former tsarist officers, the Red Army risked becoming a mob of armed workers and peasants again. Thanks to this compromise, the 'Trotsky people' maintained top command positions until the Great Terror in 1937–8. Thus, despite Voroshilov's increasing influence, his power in the Red Army was significantly limited by former tsarist officers, who made up the majority of the Red Army's professionals. The incompetent and poorly educated Voroshilov supporters hated the 'Trotsky people'. Stalin skilfully manipulated the interests of the warring factions of the Red Army senior military. This made it possible to avoid uniting the military around a single leader, which was dangerous for his power.

The most difficult problem for Kliment Voroshilov was the Chief of Staff of the Red Army Mikhail Tukhachevsky.[5] He was an intellectually gifted military professional, a former officer of the tsarist army, who possessed power ambitions. Due to his special features, Tukhachevsky had the unofficial nickname 'the Red Aristocrat' in the Red Army. He openly came into conflict with the incompetent Voroshilov for the right to command the Red Army in the event of a possible war. In response, Stalin's loyal servant launched a bureaucratic war against Tukhachevsky aimed at reducing his influence in the Red Army. Voroshilov did everything possible to ensure that the Chief of Staff of the Red Army's sphere of authority began to gradually but steadily narrow. As a result of Voroshilov's intrigues, Tukhachevsky had fewer and fewer opportunities to influence the state of the Red Army. The 'Master of the USSR' did not object to these actions of his servant.

However, at the end of 1926, against the background of deteriorating relations with the West, Stalin remembered Tukhachevsky and instructed him to evaluate the capabilities of the Red Army when faced with a potential enemy. The Chief of Staff of the Red Army took the assignment extremely seriously and prepared an extensive analysis of the situation of the USSR and the state of the Red Army from the point of view of geostrategy and geopolitics. Presented on 26 December 1926 at a meeting of the Political Bureau of the Central Committee of the CPSU(b), the report 'Defence of the Union of Soviet Socialist Republics'[6] had the effect of an exploding bomb. No one except Tukhachevsky could directly tell Stalin that the USSR and the Red Army were not ready for a new war. The report provided convincing arguments for the total weakness of the Bolsheviks in the event of a possible conflict with the numerous enemies of the USSR. The Chief of Staff of the Red Army backed up his words with a huge array of evidence, which neither Voroshilov nor other top Red Army commanders could refute. For example, according to Tukhachevsky's calculations, in the event of war, the Red Army's needs for shells and ammunition will be met by no more than 20 per cent of the required amount. Stalin was very surprised by this information. He wanted to get additional confirmation of such a terrible report by Tukhachevsky.

In response to Stalin's inquiry about the state of the military might of the enemies of Bolshevism, the Red Army intelligence department informed him of frightening new facts. In case of mobilisation, the likely enemies (Finland, Estonia, Latvia, Lithuania, Poland and Romania) could deploy ground forces of more than 2.5 million men. The USSR's opponents were armed with 5,746 artillery pieces, 1,157 combat aircraft, and 483 tanks and armoured cars. In addition, Japan and Manchuria could deploy sixty-four rifle division and sixteen cavalry brigades against the Red Army in the Far East. In the Middle East, fifty-two rifle divisions and eight cavalry brigades could act against the USSR from Turkey, Persia and Afghanistan. In addition, the Chief of Staff of the Red Army, Tukhachevsky, warned Stalin that this frightening information concerns only the first echelon of the enemy's armed forces. It is very likely that the armed forces of France and Great Britain may enter the war against the USSR. Tukhachevsky emphasised that in such a negative scenario, the Red Army would be guaranteed to be destroyed in a short time. However, despite his anxiety, Stalin generally took the warning of the Chief of Staff of the Red Army quite lightly. He soon came to regret such disregard for Tukhachevsky's information.

Surrounded by Enemies

By the beginning of the 1920s, the collapse of the popular Marxist concept of the World Revolution had become apparent to most Bolshevik leaders. However, they did not give up hope for the gradual spread of their utopian ideas in the world and made great efforts to speed up this process. After Lenin's death, Stalin continued his policy of covert communist expansion into neighbouring countries. One of the important goals of the Bolsheviks was a huge and densely populated China, which in the 1920s found itself in a permanent civil war. By supporting the Chinese Communists, Stalin actively intervened in the internal conflict. In early 1927, this position of the USSR provoked a protest from the British Empire, whose interests were hampered by the Chinese Communists' claims to power in the country. However, Stalin took the words of British Foreign Secretary Austen Chamberlain lightly. Not only did he not stop supporting the Chinese Communists, but he also organised an aggressive campaign of criticism of the British government in Soviet newspapers. However, Stalin's confidence in the security of the Bolshevik regime was soon shaken and he had serious reasons for alarm.

On 27 May 1927, the British government unexpectedly announced the severance of trade and diplomatic relations with the USSR. Such a demarche was perceived by Stalin as a threat of imminent war. The situation of military tension on the border of the USSR in 1927 was intensified by the belligerent position of Poland. After Marshal Jozef Pilsudski came to power, this country became the largest and most dangerous opponent of the Soviet Union. The Bolsheviks were well aware of the threat posed by this successful commander. In August 1920, Pilsudski defeated the Red Army troops led by Tukhachevsky in the Battle of Warsaw.[7] Thus, in 1927, Stalin had enough objective reasons to prepare for an imminent war. The outcome of the war completely depended on the balance of forces of potential participants in the conflict. In 1927, the Red Army had approximately 92 divisions with a total strength of 610,000 men, 5,640 field guns, 698 combat aircraft, 60 tanks, 99 armoured cars and 42 armoured trains. In the case of general mobilisation, the Red Army could double its strength, but even in this case, the ratio of the number of soldiers of the opposing armies was clearly not in favour of the USSR.

In this alarming situation, Tukhachevsky repeated to Stalin his verdict on the USSR's complete unpreparedness for war, which he had first proclaimed a year ago. According to the Chief of Staff of the Red Army, in 1927 the Soviet Union found itself surrounded by enemies that outnumbered and outgunned it. This information caused a real panic in Stalin, who well remembered the details of the report of 26 December 1926. Although Tukhachevsky and the Red Army intelligence department controlled by him significantly exaggerated the threats from potential opponents of the USSR, the paranoid Stalin fully believed in the high probability of defeat in the upcoming war. He was horrified at the prospect.

At the end of 1927, on the orders of the Bolshevik leader, emergency military measures were taken, resulting in real military hysteria. The hasty preparation of the USSR border areas for defence began. On Stalin's orders, the military mined bridges and railway stations, and laid caches of weapons and explosives for partisan activities in the event of an attack by numerous enemies. His meetings with the military continued almost continuously. Stalin's poor health could not withstand such a nervous strain. Against the background of permanent stress, his illnesses worsened and new ones appeared, namely, causeless and prolonged diarrhoea.

'War Communism'

Violence and voluntarism were the essence of the Bolshevik criminal sect created by Lenin. This trend culminated in the policy of 'War Communism' implemented by the leaders of the Soviet state in the context of the Russian Civil War of 1918–22. Private property and even money were abolished, and all industrial enterprises were nationalised. Special commissars appointed by Lenin were responsible for the centralised distribution of resources, including food for the population of the vast country and military ammunition for the Red Army.

The Bolsheviks explained their extreme approach to economics by the need to mobilise all resources to defeat external and internal enemies. However, the victory in the Russian Civil War did not lead the Red government to abandon the use of emergency economic management measures. 'War Leader of the Bolsheviks' Trotsky believed that the Labour Army could solve peacetime economic problems as effectively as the Red Army had succeeded in destroying the enemies of Bolshevism. His mortal enemy, Stalin, was also a proponent of the mobilisation principles of economic management. However, in the early 1920s, Lenin changed his mind about the extent of government interference in the lives of his citizens. The constant threat of famine, peasant rebellions, and finally, the armed uprising of the Baltic Fleet sailors in Kronstadt, which resulted from the incompetent management of the Bolsheviks, forced Lenin to abandon 'War Communism'.

On 15 March 1921, at the 10th Congress of the Russian Communist Party, the New Economic Policy was proclaimed by the leader of the Bolsheviks. These changes in the internal policy of the Bolsheviks meant the restoration of elements of a market economy while leaving all industry in state ownership. Another important sign of the elimination of 'War Communism' was the drastic decrease of the Red Army. By 1924, the size of the army had been reduced from five and a half million men to 500,000 or about ten times.

The partial restoration of the market economy and the demobilisation of the Red Army soldiers significantly improved the situation of the USSR population. After these measures, there was no famine in Russia for several years. However, this period of relative economic freedom did not last long. After Lenin's death, Stalin, who had established himself in power, began systematically curtailing the elements of a market economy. Already in the mid-1920s, Stalin was ready to return to the principles of 'War Communism'. Some of the foreign policy events of that time were perceived by him as threats to the existence of his government. Based on his fears, Stalin chose the path leading to the total militarisation of the Soviet Union. In his opinion, the internal and external security of the Bolshevik state could be ensured only in conditions of total control over the economy. He was waiting for concrete proposals from his servants and the top military leadership to increase the Red Army's military potential as soon as possible. From that moment on, Stalin's entourage felt that their position in the state and military hierarchy depended entirely on the effectiveness of their proposed plans to realise the main dream of their 'Master'.[8] Under these conditions, the competition for influence over Stalin grew every day.

'More royalist than the king'[9]

The most effective proposals to strengthen the military potential of the USSR were made by Chief of Staff of the Red Army Tukhachevsky. On 20 December 1927, he sent Voroshilov a memo 'On the radical rearmament of the Red Army'. In it, the Chief of Staff of the Red Army once again criticised the current state of the Red Army. Tukhachevsky wrote: 'Our army is lagging behind the European armies in terms of technical equipment. Its complete rearmament should be started immediately.'[10] Furthermore, he categorically defined the Red Army's rearmament strategy. The Chief of Staff of the Red Army wrote: 'It is necessary to take a completely new approach to the task of developing and reconstructing the Red Army. It is impossible to limit ourselves to amendments and allowances in certain areas of army construction'.[11] According to Tukhachevsky's plan, in order to counter the imminent threat of attack, it would be necessary to multiply both the quantitative and qualitative characteristics of the Red Army over several years. Further, he skilfully linked the grandiose plans to increase the military power of the USSR with Stalin's initiative to create a powerful military industry.

Tukhachevsky wrote:

> It is necessary to approach the structure of the Red Army reconstructively, in full accordance with our economic successes . . . The possibilities of increasing the number of aircraft and tanks can best be determined based on production capabilities, rather than formal plans to increase the existing aircraft and armoured vehicles of the Red Army by so many percent.[12]

To realise these grandiose plans, it was necessary to create a powerful military industry in a short time. Tukhachevsky pointed out that the implementation of the programme for the construction of dozens of large military plants would require record allocations from the state budget.

In conclusion, he proposed to reorganise the Staff of the Red Army, which actually provided for a significant increase in its powers. Tukhachevsky believed that the Staff should become a single planning and organising centre not only for the Red Army, but also for the entire military industry, which would make him a key figure in both.

Such indirect claims by Tukhachevsky to the role of the second person in the state after Stalin could not but irritate Voroshilov and many other high-ranking military officials. Influential competitors took advantage of what they considered to be 'Red Aristocrat's' mistake and launched a coordinated attack on him. After accompanying his rival's multi-page arguments with critical remarks, Voroshilov sent to Stalin Tukhachevsky's memo.

Such a radical approach by Tukhachevsky to multiply the power of the Red Army caused a very violent and ambiguous emotional response from the leader of the Bolsheviks. The main inspirer of Soviet militarism was amazed by the scale of Tukhachevsky's proposals. On the one hand, Stalin liked the ambitious development plans of the Red Army, but on the other hand, at that time he still did not believe in the possibility of implementing them in a poor agrarian country. Tukhachevsky's excessive ambitions for power in the Red Army and influence on the USSR economy, highlighted by Voroshilov's comments, also displeased Stalin. Eventually, he rejected Tukhachevsky's plan. To cool the militaristic ardour of the 'Red Aristocrat', he suggested that he prepare specific proposals to improve the technical level of the Red Army. Simultaneously with this decision, Stalin supported the more moderate option of building up the military power of the USSR, proposed by Voroshilov.

Instead of resenting the Bolshevik leader's refusal to implement his plan, the Red Aristocrat, on the contrary, showed frenzied activity in creating a new plan. In March 1928, the Staff of the Red Army, under the leadership of Tukhachevsky, developed and submitted for Stalin's approval a 'Plan for the technical improvement and development of weapons'. It emphasised the need for the rapid development, production and adoption of 2,520 tanks by the end of 1932 by the Red Army.[13] However, this document was rejected again. Despite Stalin's attention to Tukhachevsky's ambitious plans, he was not given any additional authority to implement them.

Voroshilov's constant intrigues forced the 'Red Aristocrat' to resign as Chief of Staff of the Red Army. Stalin accepted his resignation and in May 1928, Tukhachevsky was removed from office. Voroshilov's protege, former tsarist Colonel Boris Shaposhnikov,[14] was appointed Chief of Staff of the Red Army. Despite his openly hostile attitude towards Tukhachevsky, the new Chief of Staff of the Red Army fully shared his views on the need for technical modernisation of the Red Army. However, an important difference between Shaposhnikov and Tukhachevsky was his extreme caution and desire to please his superiors.

However, it was not possible for Voroshilov to completely remove Tukhachevsky from the Red Army. Stalin did not want to lose a capable military commander and appointed the 'Red Aristocrat' commander of the Leningrad Military District. Even being at a distance from Moscow, the troublemaker continued to periodically send his provocative notes and reports to Stalin. Meanwhile, things were going badly with the implementation of Voroshilov's alternative plan to saturate the Red Army with new military equipment, especially tanks. Just a year and a half later, Stalin had to change his critical attitude towards Tukhachevsky and return him to Moscow.

'It is necessary to increase the production of tanks by 15 times!'
On 2 January 1929, Stalin's Industrialisation programme was launched. In addition to a significant increase in the production of aircraft and artillery guns, the planned production rates of tanks have become the most fantastic. Thus, in accordance with the First Five-Year Plan, it was required to increase the annual production of tanks by 15 times by 1 October 1933! These fantastic figures were adopted by the USSR government under direct pressure from Stalin.

According to the Bolshevik leader, such an ambitious task should have significantly accelerated the implementation of organisational measures taken by that time to equip the Red Army with new tanks. For several years now, all efforts in this direction have been in vain. The three-year tank production programme agreed upon by the military and industry representatives on 2 June 1926, was chronically not implemented in the USSR. The main reason for this deplorable situation was the total inability of the Soviet industry to fulfil the requirements of the main customer of the tanks, the Staff of the Red Army, headed by Mikhail Tukhachevsky.

The military leadership advocated the creation of three types of armoured vehicles for the Red Army: tankettes with machine-gun armament, light infantry tanks and medium tanks, armed with guns.

The requirements for the three types of tanks were formulated by the military on the basis of foreign, primarily British, experience. Stalin's gigantomania required Soviet industry to immediately produce tanks in huge quantities. However, what the new tanks for the Red Army would actually be was determined by the very modest capabilities of the Soviet tank industry, which was in its infancy at the time.

The general management of all military factories was carried out by a special bureaucratic structure – the Main Directorate of War Industry (GUVP). It was established in 1921 during Lenin's lifetime and was located in Moscow. It was the GUVP managers who had to organise the design and production of tanks in accordance with the requirements of the military. In the conditions of weak industry that had developed in the USSR by 1926, this task was extremely difficult. First of all, GUVP specialists needed to create and carefully test prototypes of new types of tanks suitable for mass production in the improvised 'tank factories' of the USSR. In conditions of time constraints and a complete lack of tank design experience, the most logical solution to the problem could be to purchase ready-made examples of tanks abroad. This option made it possible to significantly accelerate the start of mass production of tanks in conditions of extreme urgency to solve the problem of rearmament of the Red Army. However, despite the efforts made in the mid-1920s, the Bolsheviks were unable to find tank firms abroad willing to sell tanks that met their requirements.[15] The only available solution to the problem was the independent design of tanks for the Red Army based on foreign experience.

In 1926, after agreeing on the requirements of the military, the GUVP leadership commissioned the design of new tanks by the special GUVP Technical Bureau (Tank Bureau). It was established on 6 May 1924. Senior engineer Sergey Shukalov was appointed Head of the Tank Bureau. It was he who in 1920–1 led a group of engineers who were engaged in the manufacture of copies of the FT-17 at the Krasnoye Sormovo Locomotive Factory in Nizhny Novgorod. Vladimir Zaslavsky became the chief designer of the new tanks. Like most Soviet engineers of the 1920s, the first Soviet tank designers were former tsarist specialists who agreed to cooperate with the Bolsheviks. They were talented professionals with extensive engineering experience.

The first Tank Bureau in the USSR received government funding and operated in Moscow under the full control of the GUVP. According to the Bolsheviks, such a managerial approach was supposed to reduce the high risks of disrupting the fulfilment of an important government task. However, from the first days of the Tank Bureau, it became clear that it was impossible to perform parallel design of three types of tanks. A small group of designers from the Tank Bureau was simply physically unable to perform such a large amount of engineering work. The way out of the difficult situation was the decision to focus on the priority development of one type – the light infantry tank. This tank was supposed to be designed based on the French FT-17. The experience of copying this tank in 1919–21 was supposed to make the work of Soviet designers easier. This approach to creating tanks seemed to the GUVP leaders to be the only possible one in this difficult situation.

Stalin's First Mass-Produced Tank

In early 1925, the designers of the first Tank Bureau in the USSR began developing a prototype light infantry tank. However, due to the constantly changing requirements of the military and the small number of designers, the design process was very slow. The main concern of the Red Army representatives was the weight of the future tank. This parameter was extremely important when determining the possibility of transporting the light infantry tank in the back of a truck or on a special wheeled trailer. The range of tanks on tracks was very limited at that time. The weight of the outdated French FT-17, based on the design of which Soviet engineers created a new tank, was more than seven tons. In the mid-1920s, the available Red Army foreign trucks had a lifting capacity of just over five tons. It was extremely difficult to find a truck capable of transporting a seven-ton tank or towing such a heavy wheeled trailer. For this reason, the combat capability of the fifteen copies of the FT-17, built by order of Lenin in 1920–1, was significantly limited. The problem of the trucks' limited payload capacity stimulated the Red Army management to pay special attention to the weight characteristics of the projected light infantry tank.

The initial idea of the military was to reduce the weight of the new tank to three tons. This made it possible to use the most affordable trucks in the USSR to transport the future light infantry tank. However, understanding the impossibility of mounting a gun with such a low weight of the tank forced the Red Army leadership to change its mind. The final decision of the military was to determine the mass of the future light infantry tank at five tons. The refinement of this important parameter allowed the designers to step up work on the creation of Stalin's first tank in the spring of 1925.

As noted above, when designing the new tank, Soviet designers took as a basis the general layout of the French FT-17. However, in order to meet the requirements of the military, they made significant changes to the design of the future light infantry tank.

First, the idea of installing a motor across the tank hull, borrowed from the Italian FIAT 3000 tank,[16] was implemented. This measure significantly reduced the length of the tank and, accordingly, reduced its weight by two tons compared to the FT-17.

Secondly, Soviet designers created a new suspension for the projected tank, which significantly increased the speed of movement. It was based on the suspension elements of the new French Renault NC27 tank, which is also a further development of the FT-17.

In March 1927, the Tank Bureau designers submitted the first prototype of the light infantry tank, designated T-16, for preliminary testing. The tank was assembled in Leningrad at Factory No. 232 'Bolshevik'.[17] Tests of the prototype showed that the designers generally managed to meet the requirements of the military. The design changes described above made it possible to double the speed of the first Soviet tank compared to the base FT-17. In addition, the engine installed on the tank from the Italian FIAT 15 Ter. military truck gave hope for accelerating the mass production of the tank. This engine was produced under licence in the USSR and was available for installation on a tank. However, the good news for Stalin ended there. During the tests of the first prototype of the light infantry tank, significant defects in the running gear design were revealed. It took several months of hard work for the Soviet designers to eliminate the identified shortcomings.

The construction of the second prototype of the light infantry tank, which was designated T-18, was completed only in May 1927. The tank was equipped with modified running gear, the number of road wheels on each side was increased by one. Despite the newly identified shortcomings, testing of the second prototype of the light infantry tank was considered successful. Stalin could not wait any longer! On 6 July 1927, in a great hurry, the modified prototype of the tank was adopted by the Red Army under the designation T-18 (MS-1 – 'light infantry tank No. 1'). However, subsequent events showed that the organisation of mass production of even such a primitive tank design as the T-18 proved to be a very difficult task in a poor agrarian country with an illiterate population.

Where to Find 'Tank Factories' in an Agrarian Country?

The desperate attempts of Stalin's managers to establish mass production of tanks faced enormous difficulties. First of all, they were faced by the problem of finding factories capable of performing such an extremely complex task as the production of armour, engines, transmissions and other high-tech parts. The idea of building special tank factories had to be immediately eliminated. In the mid-1920s, the

Bolsheviks did not have time for such a radical solution to the problem of tank production, and most importantly, they lacked financial resources.

Under these conditions, the former Tsarist state factories naturally became the basis of the Stalinist tank industry. Before the start of the Russian Civil War, they carried out orders for the production of sophisticated military equipment similar to tanks. However, even this standard path, used by many European countries at the end of the First World War, was fraught with great risk. During the years of chaos of the Russian Civil War, the primitive and low-tech heavy industry inherited by Stalin from the tsar fell into disrepair. An emergency audit of the military factories conducted by the Bolsheviks in 1927 clearly demonstrated the extreme weakness and smallness of the Soviet military industry.

The list of factories that could be involved in tank construction was very short and included two main groups. The first group included Sormovo Locomotive Factory (Nizhny Novgorod), Kharkov Locomotive Factory and Kolomna Locomotive Factory (a suburb of Moscow), whose main products were steam locomotives. The second consisted of Factory No. 232 'Bolshevik' and 'Krasny Putilovets' Factory,[18] located in Leningrad. These factories, which had a special state status in tsarist Russia, produced a range of military products, including artillery pieces and equipment for warships. To solve the problem of tank armour production, the Bolsheviks chose the Izhorsky steel mill[19] (Kolpino, Leningrad suburb). During the time of the Russian Empire, armour for warships was produced there.

Of the entire list of 'tank factories', only two had real tank creation experience, where fifteen copies of the Renault FT-17 were produced in the early 1920s. They were the Sormovo Locomotive Factory, where tanks were assembled, and the Izhorsky steel mill (a suburb of Leningrad), where armour was made for them. In addition, starting in the summer of 1921, Factory No. 232 'Bolshevik' began receiving orders for the repair and maintenance of Red Army armoured fighting vehicles. This was due to the poor quality of execution of orders for the Sormovo Locomotive Factory, which categorically did not suit the military. However, this experience, as well as the experience of producing copies of foreign tractors,[20] which were assembled in small quantities at future 'tank factories', could not be called successful.

In addition, many other small factories had to produce a number of parts and equipment for future tanks. These were such important components as engines, transmissions and guns. The preparation of tank production plans, the management of supplies of raw materials and equipment, as well as the organisation of interaction between numerous factories had to be carried out centrally from Moscow. Such a system of organisation of the military industry of the USSR seemed ideal to Stalin and his managers. However, in reality, the centralised administrative-command system of management turned out to be the main reason for the monstrous inefficiency of Soviet military industry. This problem was relevant from the moment the Bolsheviks came to power until the end of the Soviet Union.

Serial Production of Soviet Tanks using German Equipment

According to Stalin's decision, serial production of the T-18 (MS-1) light infantry tank was to begin on 1 February 1928 at Factory No. 232 'Bolshevik' in Leningrad. The choice of this factory was due to several reasons. It had the best technical equipment to fulfil such a complex order. In addition, Stalin attached great symbolic importance to the production of the first tanks in the 'cradle of Bolshevism'.

A special Tank Workshop was allocated for the manufacture of the new tank at Factory No. 232 'Bolshevik'. It was there that two light infantry tank prototypes (T-16 and T-18) were previously assembled. Stalin's managers arrogantly believed that the factory that produced the prototypes would be able to handle the mass production of the T-18 (MS-1). However, the miracle required by Stalin did not happen. In 1928, only twenty-three T-18 (MS-1) tanks were produced. The tank production plan in 1929 was also a complete failure. During the year, Factory No. 232 'Bolshevik' produced only 85 tanks. Such a small number of tanks did not correspond in any way to the ideas of mass production and meant a new delay in the start of the Red Army's rearmament.

For the archaic Stalinist industry, the production of the T-18 (MS-1) proved to be an extremely laborious process. The hull of the tank was assembled from armour plates attached with rivets and bolts to a frame made of metal corners (profiles). The manufacturing accuracy of the tank's parts was extremely low. The workers had to spend a lot of time individually fitting the parts to each other. The production of the T-18 (MS-1) was also complicated by the constant changes to the tank design. The designers were forced to take such risky steps due to the incessant complaints from the military, who were unhappy with the defects that appeared during the tests of tanks in the army. Thus, tanks from different production series could differ quite significantly from each other.

The real mass production of T-18 (MS-1) tanks became possible only in 1930, when Factory No. 232 'Bolshevik' managed to produce more than 300 tanks. The main reason for this belated 'success' was the purchase of a large number of machine tools and other important equipment in Germany, as well as the hiring of German engineers. However, the assembly of several hundred tanks per year, mastered with great difficulty, became the limit of the development of the production of T-18 (MS-1) tanks at Factory No. 232 'Bolshevik'. Such a small number could not satisfy Stalin's huge ambitions to equip the Red Army with tanks. To solve this problem, the Bolsheviks needed a new 'tank factory'. However, an attempt to organise the manufacture of T-18 (MS-1) tanks at the Motovilikha mechanical factory (Perm) ended in a crushing failure. For the entire period of the USSR's existence, this factory was never involved in the production of tanks again.

The Failed Ancestor of the T-34

After the 'success' of the development of the T-18 (MS-1), the GUVP leadership could focus on creating the previously planned medium tank. On 17 November 1927, the main characteristics of a new type of tank were agreed upon with the military. The Red Army leadership intended to use the medium tank to break through a well-fortified enemy defence line. To accomplish this task, the tank had to be armed with a 45mm gun and machine guns. Since the tank was supposed to be transported by rail, the maximum weight of 16 tons and the size of the tank were limited by the characteristics of a standard flat wagon of that time.

The Tank Bureau, which confirmed its qualifications when creating the T-18 (MS-1), became the sole contractor for GUVP's order for the design of the medium tank. The main role in the creation of the new tank was again played by the Head of the Tank Bureau, Sergei Shukalov, and the chief tank designer Vladimir Zaslavsky.

When creating the first Soviet medium tank, engineers followed a standard pattern of copying Western designs tested during the design of the T-18 (MS-1). This time, the American Medium Tank M1921 and its improved version Medium Tank M1922 were chosen as the base. In accordance with the chosen model, the location of the armament of the Soviet tank was arranged according to the American two-tiered scheme. A small turret with a machine gun was located on the roof of a large turret armed with a gun. This arrangement of weapons, widespread at the time, had its advantages and disadvantages. The ability to conduct all-round fire from two turrets seemed to the designers and the military to be a more important advantage than the disadvantages caused by the high profile of the tank.

However, as with the creation of the T-18 (MS-1), Soviet designers were critical of some obviously ineffective design elements of the copied samples. For example, they refused to copy the running gear of the Medium Tank M1921. This decision was dictated by the highly controversial merits of the original suspension of the American tank. For the new medium tank, Soviet engineers created a variant of the enlarged suspension tank T-18 (MS-1). The experience gained during the creation of the light infantry tank was also used in the design of the medium tank body. The tank body was assembled from armour plates on a frame of metal profiles according to a standard scheme borrowed from the West. The armour plates were attached to the frame using rivets and bolts.

The Kharkov Locomotive Factory (KhPZ) was selected to build a prototype and organise future serial production of the medium tank. As in the case of Factory No. 232 'Bolshevik', this decision was prompted by both objective reasons for the high industrial potential of KhPZ and Stalin's subjective desire to emphasise the complete control of the Bolsheviks over Ukraine. Until 1934, Kharkov was the capital of Soviet Ukraine. The production of the most powerful Soviet armoured vehicles at that time in this city was supposed to become a symbol of the inextricable link between all the heterogeneous parts of the Stalin's Empire.

On 2 April 1930, official tests of the prototype of the new medium tank began. To the surprise of the engineers and workers of KhPZ, they turned out to be record short in time. After 21 minutes, almost everything in the T-12 medium tank prototype failed, except for the armoured hull. During this time, the tank managed to travel only 2km. According to the test report preserved in the Russian archive, in addition to engine failure, the gearbox was found to be overheating, water boiling in the radiator, second gear malfunctioning and a breakdown of the right track when driving on soft ground. The repair and refinement of the prototype took a long time. The design defects of the tank turned out to be very serious. After a month of repairs, testing of the medium tank prototype continued. Although some publications claim that they were successful, according to the test results, the military recognised that the T-12 was very far from their requirements.

Unfulfilled Hopes

The Red Army leadership and Stalin personally had high hopes for the new medium tank and planned to produce it in huge quantities. The 11 July 1930 demonstration of the first prototype T-12 made a favourable impression on Voroshilov and his entourage. The results of the presentation were immediately reported to Stalin, and the production plan for new Kharkov tanks in 1932 was increased to a fantastic 1,600 units.

However, contrary to the expectations of the high authorities, the completion of the first and production of the second prototype of the medium tank, which received the T-24 index, was delayed for a year. Despite their enthusiasm, the young employees of the KhPZ Tank Bureau (T2K) were unable to fully solve the technical problems of the two medium tank prototypes (T-12 and T-24). The young Soviet engineers had no experience designing tanks, and the design of the medium tank turned out to be extremely complex. The elimination of technical deficiencies has turned into a vicious circle of endless improvements and changes. However, despite the fact that the tank did not pass the test range testing, it was recommended for mass production!

The KhPZ leadership also proved unable to implement Stalin's grandiose plans to rearm the Red Army. An attempt to produce medium tanks at KhPZ in 1931 ended in complete failure. Kharkov managed to produce only twenty-four T-24 medium tanks. However, the tank was not adopted for service by the Red Army, and the tanks produced with great effort by workers and engineers turned out to be useless to anyone. Thus, the excessive haste caused by Stalin's ambitions negatively affected the fate of the first Soviet medium tank. Among the factors that determined the failure were: the inexperience of the young designers, the factory's unwillingness to produce tanks, and the remoteness from Moscow, where key decisions were made.

A similar situation developed when designing a tankette ordered from GUVP by the Red Army leadership. Several Tank Bureau prototypes tankettes created by Tank Bureau designers in the late 1920s and early 1930s (T-17 and T-23) also failed. The tankettes produced, based on the lightweight design of the T-18 (MS-1) tank, turned out to be very complex and expensive. Prototype testing and endless refinement took so long that the tankette that Stalin expected was not allowed even to the stage of preparation for mass production.

'We tried to do everything ourselves, but we couldn't'

The disruption of Stalin's first Tank Programme naturally led to the search for those responsible. The Stalinist OGPU, citing the fact that GUVP employed too many former tsarist generals and colonels, accused managers and engineers of deliberate 'wrecking'. Meanwhile, there were many objective and subjective reasons for delays and problems in the design and production of military equipment. When designing tanks, Soviet designers had to combine the excessive requirements of the military and the technical capabilities for their mass production coming from military industry managers. These requirements from customers and manufacturers of military equipment often conflicted with each other.

The use of Western military equipment as the basis for the design made it possible to significantly reduce the time needed to design the first Soviet tanks. However, this engineering approach could not be fully implemented. The access of Soviet designers to the most advanced tank models from England was significantly limited. It was not possible to get the necessary assistance from foreign engineers at that time. Under these conditions, Soviet designers had to find a compromise between outdated French and Italian tanks from the First World War and the latest American experimental tanks, whose qualities had not yet been tested in combat. In addition, in order to meet the high requirements of the military, the first Soviet designers were forced to combine copying with the independent development of some important components and parts of the tank. All of these reasons created high risks of wasting time on prototype improvements and preparation for mass production. Instead of working methodically to create prototypes and thoroughly test them, the Tank Bureau designers were forced to carry out Stalin's orders in a frenzied hurry.

Another source of problems in the implementation of the Tank Programme was the very limited technical capabilities of the Soviet tank industry for mass production of tanks. The construction and equipping of special tank workshops at Factory No. 232 'Bolshevik' and the Kharkov Locomotive Factory (KhPZ) with imported equipment was completed only by 1932. In the mid-1920s, improvised 'tank factories' equipped with outdated equipment were completely unprepared even for the production of single tank prototypes. As a result, the structural elements borrowed from foreign tanks were subjected to forced simplification, which significantly reduced their effectiveness and reliability. In the manufacture of tank parts, less high-quality but affordable raw materials were used in the USSR. To speed up mass production, important parts of trucks, tractors, and even aircraft manufactured in the USSR under licence were widely used in the design of tanks. However, all these measures did not exclude the purchase abroad of many imported parts that could not be produced in the USSR. For example, all the electrical equipment of Soviet tanks of that period was manufactured by the German company Bosch. Ball bearings and a number of other important components were also manufactured in Germany.

All these weaknesses of the Soviet industry led to many risky compromises and improvisations in the design and production of future tanks. They had a negative impact on the combat performance and manufacturing quality of the first Soviet medium tanks. Stalin's stubborn disregard of these objective circumstances led to the logical failure of the implementation of the first Tank Programme. Thus, the Soviet designers and managers could not independently cope with the extremely difficult task of developing and producing the medium tank in such a short time.

Oblivion and Death of the First Soviet Tank Designers

While noting the lack of tank design experience, Soviet tank designers of the first generation cannot be blamed for a lack of talent and qualifications. In the face of feverish haste dictated by Stalin's desire to possess numerous tanks, Soviet engineers were able to do a lot. They sincerely tried to solve the extremely difficult task of simultaneously designing three types of tank equipment. However, only one of them, the T-18 (MS-1), proved to be relatively successful, becoming the first mass-produced Soviet tank.

The designers and managers of the tank factories became hostages to the unreasonable Stalinist policy based on an overestimation of strength and faith in Bolshevik enthusiasm. As subsequent events showed, with additional time, numerous defects of the first generation of Soviet tanks could be completely or partially eliminated. However, Stalin did not give Soviet engineers such an opportunity. In the totalitarian Bolshevik state, the conditions for the creation of a new type of military equipment were determined by the inconsistent and contradictory policy of the Bolshevik leader, which is a direct continuation of his pathological character.

The executors of Stalin's will had to pay dearly for his mistakes caused by his megalomania and total incompetence. The fate of the older generation of Tank Bureau designers and their leaders, Sergei Shukalov and Vladimir Zaslavsky, was tragic. In the 1930s, they were under constant suspicion of anti-Soviet activities. In the end, the former tsarist specialists were suspended from design work. Practically nothing is known about their professional activities during this dark period of their lives.

Having survived the period of struggle with the 'Wreckers' in the early 1930s, they remained in oblivion until the next, fatal wave of repression. Stalin's executioners remembered Shukalov and Zaslavsky during the preparations for the Great Terror of 1937. During this period, Stalin, enraged by another failure of his plans, demanded a lot of blood from the NKVD. The new wave of repression proved particularly deadly. Tank designer Vladimir Zaslavsky was arrested on 19 November 1936, accused of anti-Soviet activities and shot on 21 June 1937. His colleague Sergei Shukalov was arrested on 20 April 1938, convicted of the same charges, and died a few years later in the Gulag from starvation and overwork. The exact date of Shukalov's death and the place of burial in the collective grave for deceased prisoners are still unknown.

The fate of the first generation of Soviet tanks, created by Zaslavsky and Shukalov, also turned out to be very sad. Most of them had been rusting in Red Army warehouses for many years. The part was disassembled for spare parts or put into scrap metal. By the end of the 1930s, the Red Army leadership decided to use the surviving tanks as pillboxes to equip fortified regions on the border of the USSR.

Who Will be the First to Find a Way Out of the Tank Impasse?

In addition to the lack of experience of Soviet designers and the primitive 'tank industry', the main customer of military equipment, the leadership of the Red Army, was also not ready for the accelerated creation of tanks. Despite the awareness of the military significance of tanks, by the end of the 1920s the Red Army leadership had a very vague and often changing idea of their types and military specifications. Even after receiving the first prototypes of tanks, the military could not assess their combat qualities. Their comments on the design of experimental tanks were subjective and caused legitimate objections from Soviet tank designers. However, at that time, such difficulties with understanding the role of tanks and, accordingly, fundamental disputes between various military authorities about the types and designs of tanks were common to all technologically advanced Western countries.

By 1929, two influential groups with opposing views had formed in the Red Army during the discussion of the problem of using tanks. The first group, the 'Cavalrymen', which included Russian Civil War era commanders representing cavalry and artillery, was led by the official Head of the Red Army, Voroshilov. Most of them came from low-skilled workers or poor peasants. Their education was often limited to just two classes of the parochial school. The 'Cavalrymen' had gained their military experience during the Russian Civil War, where the use of tanks was sporadic, and the main battles took place between large masses of infantry and cavalry. As a direct consequence of these features, officers from the Voroshilov group had a sceptical attitude towards armoured vehicles. They considered a tall and fast horse and a well-honed sabre to be the best weapons of the future war. For this reason, the 'Cavalrymen' held extremely conservative views on the use of tanks. At best, they considered these expensive 'toys' to be a secondary means of supporting the attacking masses of infantry and cavalry. At the same time, the influence of this group on the key issues of Red Army rearmament was significant.

The 'Cavalrymen' group was distinguished by its complete loyalty to Stalin. Ever since the defence of Tsaritsyn, they have been ready to carry out any of his orders. Despite their negative attitude towards technical innovations, Voroshilov and his associates, seeing the interest of the 'Master' in tanks, actively tried to attract his attention with their stupid 'initiatives' in this area. The 'Cavalrymen' not only advertised their 'original' views on the use of tanks, but also actively offered their own versions of wonder tanks in the 1930s. Most of the prototypes of military 'equipment' presented by them were created by incompetent 'designers', most of whom were outright fraudsters.

The second group of military men, the 'Progressives', fully shared the views of the informal leader of the Red Army, Tukhachevsky. These mostly young Red commanders differed from the mature 'Cavalrymen' not only in their age and high intelligence, but also in their professional military education. Due to these features, they were distinguished by radically progressive views on the use of tanks and aircraft. Tukhachevsky and his supporters closely followed all the technical innovations in the field of armaments that appeared abroad. 'Progressives' carefully studied books and articles by Western developers of new strategies for using tanks and aircraft to wage future wars.

Based on the doctrine of a short-lived war, popular in the 1920s and 1930s, which was later embodied in the framework of the German Blitzkrieg, Tukhachevsky insisted on the mass use of armoured fighting vehicles in a new war. He stated the need to create numerous units in the Red Army, armed with thousands and even tens of thousands of aircraft and tanks. Since things were going very badly with the development and production of new tanks for the Red Army, Tukhachevsky offered his own way out of the tank impasse. His Concept of Mechanisation of the Red Army envisioned mass production of wheeled armoured cars and light tanks in automobile plants, and medium and heavy tanks in tractor plants. Tukhachevsky offered to buy these plants, as well as advanced samples of Western armoured fighting vehicles, for gold in America or the developed countries of Western Europe. As noted above, Stalin was initially sceptical of the radical ideas of the 'Red Aristocrat'. However, they gradually began to find new supporters in the ranks of the Red Army.

At military meetings on tank design and production in 1928–9, the numerous voices of young military specialists became particularly noticeable. Supporters of accelerated mechanisation of the Red Army offered to immediately purchase Western tank designs. They were supposed to be used as a backup option for mass production in case the efforts of domestic designers failed. Against the background of the permanent difficulties of implementing the Tank Programme in the 1920s, Stalin's negative attitude towards the radical proposals of Tukhachevsky and his associates gradually began to reverse.

In addition to the two groups that formed in the Red Army, another powerful force took part in the 'competition' for the saviours of Stalin's tank ambitions. The Soviet Secret Police, the OGPU, offered its own original way out of the tank impasse. This proposal was based on the specific capabilities of the Soviet punitive department. According to OGPU, the free labour of prisoners, many of whom were qualified engineers and workers, opened up fantastic opportunities to solve the problem of the Mechanisation of the Red Army. OGPU tank designs were developed in the strictest secrecy with the involvement of a group of German designers.

While not favouring any of the three influential groups, Stalin had long encouraged his subordinates to play hardball. He preferred to watch their fight from the sidelines, creating conditions for identifying the most effective fighter for his favour. Soon, as a result of fierce competition, the undisputed Technical Leader of the Red Army was determined. Enjoying Stalin's full confidence, he single-handedly defined the strategic path of technical development of the Red Army until 1937.

Chapter 2

VICKERS AND CHRISTIE

'I agree. J. Stalin'

November 23rd 1929. Moscow. Kremlin. Stalin's apartment.

Dead of night. Stalin is sitting alone at his desk sorting through the papers that were brought to him during the day. Most of the loyal messages did not arouse much interest in him. Finally, Stalin got to the reports of the Head of the Red Army's Mechanisation and Motorisation Directorate (UMM) Komkor (Colonel General) Innokenty Khalepsky. This new department in the Red Army management structure was recently created by his special order. Less than a month has passed since his appointment, and the energetic Khalepsky has already prepared an extensive report on the scale of Red Army's tank problems. Stalin appointed him to this high position precisely in order to find out the reasons for the failure of tank development and production.

Reading the papers made Stalin frown. The report reported on the extremely poor state of affairs in solving the problem of the mechanisation of the Red Army and the terrible quality of the few new tanks that entered the army. The pathologically suspicious leader of the Bolsheviks was convinced that the former tsarist specialists from the GUVP leadership were constantly deceiving him and deliberately designing and producing bad tanks. The information gathered in Khalepsky's report confirmed his concerns. Work on priority projects of the main types of armoured fighting vehicles, namely the improved version of the T-19 light infantry tank, the creation of prototypes of the T-12 medium tank and the T-17 tankette went very slowly. The experienced Khalepsky, preparing a report for Stalin, did not limit himself to stating the fact of serious difficulties in the implementation

34

of the first Soviet Tank Programme. The Head of the UMM offered an alternative way out of the tank impasse, which had long been discussed in the top leadership of the Red Army.

Khalepsky was good at guessing the wishes of the 'Master'. He promptly offered him indisputable evidence of the need to make the decision that Stalin himself had long been leaning towards. In turn, the 'Red Lord' did not hide his sympathies for this energetic young man. Stalin had good reasons for such a benevolent attitude towards Khalepsky. The Head of the UMM was a prominent representative of the Red Army group of young enthusiasts for technical re-equipment and became a useful expert for Stalin when making important decisions on tanks.

Tukhachevsky, released from Moscow to Leningrad, annoyed Stalin with his noble haughtiness and overwhelming military competence. Khalepsky came from the social bottom and was good at pleasing his superiors. His business qualities were also expressed at a high level. Khalepsky performed exceptionally well during a trip to the United States in October 1928. As a result of this important mission, a huge Ford automobile plant[1] was bought with money taken by Stalin from the starving population of the USSR. Thus, Khalepsky successfully passed the test and was rewarded by Stalin with a high position in the Red Army. However, in addition to his position and privileges, he received a difficult mission to rescue the grandiose plans of equipping the Red Army with tanks.

The super-complexity of this task was due to the fantastic tank dreams of the 'Red Lord'. In 1929, Stalin ordered the Supreme Soviet of the National Economy (VSNKh – Ministry of Industry of the Soviet Union) to produce 5,611 tanks and tankettes by the end of 1934! No technologically advanced Western country has ever had the experience of producing tanks in such fantastic quantities. This categorical order had to be carried out at makeshift tank factories in an agrarian country with a population teetering on the brink of starvation. Additionally, the situation was complicated by two important circumstances. The military did not have a clear understanding of exactly what requirements the new tanks were supposed to meet, and the Soviet designers did not have the relevant experience. Against this negative background, Khalepsky's proposed alternative path to break the tank impasse might seem quite reasonable and promising.

After reading report of the Head of the UMM one more time, Stalin took a red pencil and wrote on top of the sheet with a flourish: 'I agree. J. Stalin.'

Biography of the Main Organiser of the Technical Progress of the Red Army

Khalepsky's success in carrying out the difficult missions assigned by Stalin was due to a number of important qualities of his character. They allowed the son of a poor Jewish tailor to build a dizzying military and administrative career in the Bolshevik state.

Innokenty Khalepsky was born on 2 July 1893 in Siberia in the small town of Minusinsk. This town in the Russian Empire was a traditional place of exile for state criminals. Various representatives of the opposition to the tsarist regime, including the Bolsheviks, were sent to Minusinsk, isolated from the outside world. The extreme poverty of the family and the remoteness of Minusinsk from major cities limited the educational opportunities of the intellectually gifted Innokenty. He was able to get an incomplete secondary education at Minusinsk's secondary school. However, even such an extremely limited education in a remote Siberian town could only be expected by the most capable and motivated children. The prospects for further professional development for the young Innokenty were also limited. The best graduates of Minusinsk's secondary school who showed an interest in technology could join the local post and telegraph office. One of these lucky few was Innokenty Khalepsky.

At the age of 16, he began working as a lineman at the telegraph office in Minusinsk. Innokenty compensated for the lack of regular training with intensive self-education. Since childhood, his interest in technology and high activity allowed him to independently master the profession of telegraphist. Soon Khalepsky's diligence was noticed by his superiors and he was transferred to the post of telegraphist of the post and telegraph office in the large Siberian city of Krasnoyarsk. Since anti-Semitism was part of state policy in tsarist Russia, the position of telegraphist for Khalepsky, a Jew, was the limit of his professional development.

However, in 1917, under the pressure of external and internal problems, the rotten tsarist regime collapsed. After the Bolsheviks seized power, Khalepsky joined them with great enthusiasm. He, like most other Russian citizens suffering from restrictions on their rights, had genuine sympathy for communist ideas. In July 1918, Khalepsky voluntarily joined the Red Army at the age of 25 and soon became a member of the Bolshevik Party.

At the first stage of the Russian Civil War, the Red Army had enough infantry and cavalry, but the situation with the organisation of wired (telegraph and telephone) and wireless (radio) communications was catastrophic. In this situation, Khalepsky was able to prove himself to be a very valuable specialist and a talented organiser of military communications. His extraordinary abilities were noticed by the creator of Red Army, Trotsky. Khalepsky's further advancement in military service was extremely rapid. In 1919, he successively headed the division of military communications of the Southern, Southwestern and Caucasian Fronts.

In September 1920, Khalepsky was appointed the Head of the Directorate of Communications of the Red Army. After the end of the Russian Civil War, his career slowed down somewhat. However, Khalepsky finally found time to continue his education. In 1924, he graduated from Higher Academic Courses at the Red Army Military Academy. Shortly after, he was appointed to the position of the Head of the Directorate of Military Technical of the Red Army. And finally, on 3 November 1929, Khalepsky, by Stalin's will, became the Head of the Red Army's Mechanisation and Motorisation Directorate (UMM).

In addition to his high intelligence, broad technical competencies, hard work and organisational skills, the tailor's son had another extremely valuable character trait. Khalepsky was not only able to attract the attention of his patron, but was able to gain his full trust. For many years he faithfully served Trotsky, Tukhachevsky, and finally, the last master in his life, Stalin. Demonstrating complete loyalty to the previous boss, he was able to change his high patron to a more promising master in time. This quality of his character created excellent conditions for career growth. However, when choosing his main 'Master', he, like thousands of other high-ranking Bolsheviks, made a fatal mistake. The pathologically suspicious Stalin always shifted responsibility for his many mistakes to his closest favourites. In the terrible year of 1937, the brilliant career of the main enthusiast of the technical rearmament of the Red Army ended very sadly.

'We can't do this without foreign help'

In mid-1929, Stalin indirectly acknowledged the very likely failure of his ambitious plans to re-equip the Red Army with modern military equipment. The boundless ambitions of the incompetent 'Red Lord' faced the harsh reality of the economic and educational backwardness of the USSR. For a long time, Stalin did not want to recognise the severe shortage of educated people capable of designing complex military equipment and the lack of a developed industry capable of producing high-tech military equipment. Obsessed with absolute power over a country of millions, he believed in the possibility of accelerating the militarisation of industry several times with the help of extraordinary measures. Convinced of an imminent attack from the West, Stalin did not want to wait for the several decades necessary for the normal development of Soviet military industry and the training of qualified engineers. Disregarding objective circumstances, he drove the Soviet military industry into a tank impasse with his demands divorced from reality. However, Stalin did not consider himself at all to blame for the tank crisis, and moreover, he was not going to abandon his *idée fixe*, the accelerated militarisation of the USSR economy.

In a situation of crisis organised by himself, Stalin habitually performed a number of standard actions that he had worked out during the Russian Civil War. He created new organisational structures, often duplicating existing ones. He appointed new people to positions. And finally, he ordered those responsible for disrupting his plans to be found and punished. All these actions were accompanied by a typical propaganda campaign in newspapers and template messages at party or public meetings obligatory for all citizens of the USSR. The purpose of Stalin's propaganda was to create an acceptable public version of the reasons for the failures, to condemn the 'enemies' and to present the Soviet people with optimistic prospects for further development.

After Stalin recognised the possibility of the Tank Programme's failure, a vigorous campaign began at all levels of government to identify mistakes, punish those responsible, and implement urgent measures to correct the negative situation in the tank industry.

One of the first to join this company was Innokenty Khalepsky, who showed maniacal zeal in following the orders of his 'Master'. At the end of November 1929, he made a presentation at a meeting of the Board of the GUVP, in which he sharply criticised design bureaus and managers of the Soviet tank industry. Khalepsky accused Soviet tank designers of lacking the necessary experience and competencies. According to the Head of the UMM, design work was unnecessarily delayed, and the tank prototypes created were too complex or not finalised, and therefore not suitable for mass production.

Khalepsky further stated that the Soviet tank industry was unable to fulfil plans for the production of prototypes, and eventually organise mass production of tanks. The main reason for the impotence of the industry was the poor organisation of production and the shortage of imported machine tools and equipment. Although the chief technical officer of Red Army did not directly name those responsible for the failure of the tank production programme, he hinted at some 'wreckers' and 'saboteurs' who had allegedly infiltrated the ranks of Soviet engineers and managers.

At the end of his report, Khalepsky announced an alternative option approved by Stalin to remedy the difficult situation with the equipment of the Red Army. It consisted of the need to urgently purchase samples of Western tanks and attract foreign engineers to organise their mass production. This step was supposed to be a kind of insurance in case of possible failures that could befall promising tank projects implemented by Soviet designers.

Who Will Replace Tukhachevsky?

To solve the problem of exposing and punishing those 'responsible' for disrupting tank production, Stalin had a well-established system of party control and a large punitive OGPU structure. However, the problem of technical re-equipment of the Red Army could not be solved without a competent expert who was a member of the supreme military leadership of the USSR. The removal of Tukhachevsky from the post of Chief of Staff of the Red Army in 1928 deprived the group of Soviet military personnel advocating the technical re-equipment of the Red Army of an ambitious leader. The confusion and uncertainty that prevailed in the top leadership of the Red Army on this crucial issue forced Stalin to urgently seek a replacement for Tukhachevsky. He needed someone willing to take personal responsibility for breaking the tank impasse. At that time, Stalin was not yet ready to independently determine the specifications of the tanks needed for the Red Army. He won't take on such a role until the end of the 1930s.

Stalin's search for a candidate for the role of Technical Leader of the Red Army proved to be a difficult task, since a potential candidate had to possess at least four very rare qualities. Firstly, this high-ranking officer had to be part of a narrow group of people who proved their loyalty to the Bolsheviks in the battles of the Russian Civil War and personally to Stalin after he came to power.

Secondly, it should be a person who was as technically competent as possible and who was able to determine the specifications, testing procedures, and acceptance procedures for adopted for service by the Red Army military equipment, including those purchased abroad.

Thirdly, he had to be able to predict the features of a future war, develop a strategy for the development of the Soviet armed forces, taking into account new weapons, and therefore determine the future of the Red Army for many years to come.

Fourthly, it had to be a determined and courageous person who is ready to take personal responsibility for fundamental decisions related to the results of future wars and the expenditure of huge resources in a very poor country.

The range of candidates for this role was extremely narrow. The first person Stalin had to exclude from the list of possible candidates was the People's Commissar for Military and Naval Affairs Kliment Voroshilov. The uneducated and intellectually limited leader of the 'Cavalrymen' was initially unsuited to the role of leader of the Red Army rearmament company. The formal Head of the Red Army was able to effectively perform only representative functions. Sitting in the saddle on a tall horse, Voroshilov commanded military parades perfectly. He regularly gave speeches in front of Red Army troops, and signed important orders and reports. In the 1930s Voroshilov was depicted next to Stalin on numerous propaganda posters. Despite Voroshilov's promotion of several tank projects, most of them ended in unfortunate failure. In the end, his role in solving the most important issue of technical re-equipment of the Red Army was reduced to the fact that he obediently sent the 'Master' all reports on the development and production of tanks and waited for his orders.

Stalin pinned more reasonable hopes on Boris Shaposhnikov, Chief of Staff of the Red Army, to solve the problem of equipping the army with tanks. The former tsarist Colonel was a capable staff officer who was well versed in all matters of armament and technical equipment of the Red Army. Shaposhnikov's complete loyalty to the Bolsheviks was proven by his effective service during the Russian Civil War. Stalin also had no doubts about his personal loyalty. However, Shaposhnikov was the exact opposite of the bright and ambitious Tukhachevsky. He completely lacked the qualities of character that allowed Tukhachevsky to become the undisputed leader of the Red Army mechanisation.

Well aware of the vindictive nature of his 'Master', Shaposhnikov preferred to avoid the risky responsibility of carrying out fantastic plans to equip the Red Army with tanks. From Stalin's numerous attacks, he preferred to hide in the depths of his headquarters behind a 'defensive line' of numerous official papers. Shaposhnikov wrote long reports for the 'Master' with competent and reasonable calculations of the use of tanks. However, he did not show any enthusiasm or energy in solving the problem of mechanisation of the Red Army.

The real salvation for Stalin was the young and energetic Innokenty Khalepsky, who headed the UMM. However, despite his enthusiasm and technical competence, he lacked the solidity and thoroughness of Tukhachevsky. Khalepsky was not a member of the circle of senior officers and did not have sufficient authority in the Red Army. Despite his obvious sympathy for the young enthusiast for his precision and efficiency, Stalin did not respect him for his weakness of character and excessive obsequiousness. The peace-loving Khalepsky often had to endure the dirty insults of his 'Master', which he lavished on him for minor, and most often imaginary mistakes.

It seemed that there was no worthy alternative to Tukhachevsky among the top management of the Red Army. However, on 20 November 1929, Stalin appointed a worthy, in his opinion, candidate to the new position of Head of Armaments of the Red Army. The Technical Leader of the Red Army has become a young but highly respected high-ranking officer in the Red Army, Ieronim Uborevich. Stalin was convinced that the new Technical Leader would successfully cope with the problem of rearmament of the Red Army. He also hoped that being under his complete control, Uborevich would become an obedient puppet in his hands. Time would show how deeply Stalin was mistaken in his choice.

The Most Underrated Red General

In 1929, Ieronim Uborevich was 35 years old. He was the youngest of the Red Army's top officers. His biography provides an answer to the question of why Stalin chose him to be the person who should be responsible for the future of the Red Army.

Uborevich was born on 24 December 1896, into a large peasant family in the village of Antandraja (now the Republic of Lithuania) on the northern outskirts of the European part of the Russian Empire. His low social status did not allow the intellectually gifted Ieronim to receive a prestigious gymnasium education. However, the peasant's son was able to enrol in a Realschule (a type of secondary school) in the city of Dvinsk (now Daugavpils in Latvia), from which he graduated in 1914 with a gold medal. His excellent academic results and interest in technology allowed Uborevich to become a student at the Faculty of Mechanics of the Saint Petersburg Polytechnic Institute in September 1915. However, he was soon subjected to repression for his participation in activities opposed to the tsarist regime. To avoid prison, Uborevich was forced to join the Russian Imperial Army as a 'volunteer' in November 1915.

The backward Russian army, which suffered constant defeats in the First World War, was in great need of educated people with technical competencies. In the spring of 1916, Ieronim Uborevich graduated with honours from the accelerated courses for junior officers at the Constantine Artillery School. With the rank of Praporshchik,[2] he was assigned to serve in the 15th Heavy Artillery Battalion, which held the defence on one of the sectors of the Eastern Front. Uborevich was soon promoted to Podporuchik (second lieutenant) for his bravery.

Meanwhile, the rotten Russian Empire was living out its last year of existence. Ever since the incompetent and intellectually limited Tsar Nicholas II took over the post of commander-in-chief in the autumn of 1915, the Russian Empire was doomed. After the abdication of the last Russian emperor from the throne, the promising career of the young officer was temporarily interrupted. In March 1917, shortly after the February Revolution of 1917, Uborevich became a member of the RSDLP(b). He reacted with great enthusiasm to the armed seizure of power in November 1917 by Lenin and Trotsky. By abolishing the power of the tsarist officers, the Bolsheviks wreaked havoc in the huge army that continued to hold the long Eastern Front by inertia.

In November 1917, the Bolsheviks concluded an armistice with the Triple Alliance countries, and a temporary lull ensued on the Eastern Front. Soon, in the front-line town of Brest-Litovsk, Lenin's emissaries began negotiations with the Germans for peace, which ended in failure. Hostilities resumed, and German troops began to rapidly advance deep into the territory of Red Russia. The newly formed Bolshevik units were forced to retreat under pressure from the enemy, only occasionally engaging in a hopeless battle with the Germans.

In January 1918, the Bolshevik Uborevich became the commander of the Red Army detachment in Bessarabia. This event launched his brilliant career in Red Army. In February 1918, in a battle with the Germans, Uborevich was wounded and captured.[3]

On 3 March 1918, the Treaty of Brest-Litovsk was signed by representatives of Soviet Russia and representatives of the Central Powers. Peace was achieved at the cost of huge territorial losses, but Red Russia's withdrawal from the war allowed the Bolsheviks to focus on their internal enemies.

Taking advantage of the situation caused by the revolutionary unrest in Germany, Uborevich escaped from captivity, which lasted a long four months. In August 1918, he returned to the Red Army and took part in the Russian Civil War. In 1919, the military talent of the 23-year-old Red commander was noticed by Trotsky. From that moment on, Uborevich began to move rapidly up the military hierarchy. Judging by the reviews of the top management of the Red Army, Uborevich, successively commanding the 14th, 9th and 13th Armies, achieved significant success in battles with the troops of the White army.[4]

Over the years of the bloody Russian Civil War, he began to play the role of the 'Firefighter of the Bolsheviks'. Uborevich was sent to command troops in the most critical areas of the huge front. And he almost always managed to turn the tide in favour of the Bolsheviks. In addition to his military skills, other traits of his character appeared in battles with the regular troops of the White Army. As Tukhachevsky's deputy, Uborevich displayed Bolshevik fanaticism and extreme cruelty. He actively participated in the bloody suppression of peasant uprisings in Russia, Ukraine and Belarus. Like Tukhachevsky, Uborevich oversaw mass shootings of peasants, hostage-taking, and the creation of concentration camps. His ruthlessness towards the enemies of communism and fanatical devotion to Bolshevism was personally highly appreciated by the creator of the Red Army Trotsky.

For outstanding services, in June 1922, Ieronim Uborevich was inducted into the Staff of the Red Army. Prior to that, Mikhail Tukhachevsky (May 1920), Alexander Yegorov[5] and Mikhail Frunze (December 1920) were awarded such a high honour. None of these red commanders had a tertiary military education. At Trotsky's insistence, the formal requirement for Staff of the Red Army officers to have tertiary military education was ignored. Among Trotsky's favourites, who made up the elite of the Red Army, Uborevich was the youngest, and therefore the most underrated. Being in the shadow of the bright and ambitious Tukhachevsky, the young and modest Uborevich constantly felt bitter resentment for the lack of appointments to high positions. Due to his extraordinary abilities, he was undoubtedly worthy of more.

The new supreme patron of the Soviet military, Stalin, also noticed the talents of the youngest commander of the Red Army. He was impressed by Uborevich's fanatical willingness to carry out any orders from the top leadership of the USSR. Stalin, sensitive to the weaknesses of his subordinates, took advantage of Uborevich's frustration to recruit him as one of his personal agents embedded in the top leadership of the Red Army.

Stalin soon had the opportunity to reassess his protege's loyalty. In the autumn of 1927, at the height of the military panic caused by the alleged threat of an attack on the USSR by Poland, the top officers of the Red Army were sent to study in Germany. Germany, being at that time a rogue country that had been defeated in the First World War, was the only place where Soviet officers could receive the much-needed tertiary military education. Before he left, on 4 November 1927, Stalin personally instructed Uborevich at the Kremlin. On the instructions of the Bolshevik leader, the young commander of the Red Army carried out a special mission in Germany as a personal agent-informant of the 'Red Lord'. His secret duties were to monitor the loyalty of former officers of the Tsarist army to the Bolsheviks, who found themselves studying in a friendly but not a Bolshevik country.

In addition to fulfilling Stalin's assignment, Uborevich sought to maximise the opportunity to improve his military skills. During his one-year stay in Germany, he completed his third year of War Academy (Kriegsakademie), and also participated in Reichswehr field manoeuvres. While studying in Germany, Uborevich became an ardent advocate of the need to borrow the technical achievements and the military strategy and tactics of the Germans. Just like Tukhachevsky, he understood that tanks and aircraft would be the key success factors in the new war.

After studying in Germany, Stalin's young favourite quickly rose through the Soviet military hierarchy. In 1928, Uborevich was appointed to the responsible position of commander of the Moscow Military District. Finally, in 1929, Stalin appointed him to the high post of Head of Armaments of the Red Army. He believed that Uborevich could easily replace Tukhachevsky. At the same time, Stalin's plans were not limited to this. He did not rule out the possibility that Uborevich would take over the position of Head of the Red Army in the near future. However, fortunately for the devoted but incompetent Voroshilov, the position of Head of Armaments of the Red Army and Deputy People's Commissar for Military and Naval Affairs became the limit of Uborevich's career.

Head of Armaments and Technical Staff of the Red Army

In November 1929, a new administrative structure appeared in the Red Army – the Technical Staff of the Red Army (Technical Staff). This structure was managed by the Head of Armaments of the Red Army, Ieronim Uborevich. The idea of creating and the set of functions of this military structure were proposed to Stalin by Tukhachevsky. The main purpose of the Technical Staff was to accelerate the technical re-equipment of the Red Army. Employees of this department, under the leadership of the Head of Armaments, were supposed to develop the Armament System, formulate requirements, test and adopt new armaments samples for service by the Red Army, and monitor the work of the military industry and design bureaus.

Formally, the new senior leader of the Red Army had extensive powers to carry out his tasks. The Head of Armaments of the Red Army was subordinated to the Artillery Directorate, Military Technical Directorate, Military Chemical Directorate and Red Army's Mechanisation and Motorisation Directorate (UMM). However, in fact, the Head of Armaments and its Technical Staff duplicated many functions of the People's Commissar for Military and Naval Affairs, Staff of the Red Army, Revolutionary Military Council (RVS) and Defence Commission at the Council of People's Commissars of the Soviet Union. And in matters of Red Army mechanisation, they also duplicated the functions of the UMM.

Stalin was completely satisfied that all these numerous administrative structures had to compete with each other for the main role in equipping the Red Army with new military equipment, and most importantly, to control each other. Moreover, many senior officers were members of several management structures of the Red Army and the Soviet government. However, in reality, such a multiplicity of governing structures created bureaucratic and managerial chaos. Endless coördination and multi-volume paper correspondence between numerous commissions, headquarters and councils took up a huge amount of time. Meetings of one or another structure were held almost daily. However, all this 'activity' had virtually no effect on the pace of implementation of the Tank Programme for the First Five-Year Plan.

Uborevich's first mission as Head of Armaments was to refine the System of Tank-Tractor-Automotive Vehicles of the Red Army (Armament System). This problem had been long overdue. More than three years had passed since the approval of the first version of the Armament System and the tank building programme implemented in accordance with it. For the stage of rapid development that Soviet Mechanised Troops was going through, it was a very long period. Many concepts that were relevant in the mid-1920s were outdated and required immediate updating. However, due to disagreements between the military, the decision to make changes was constantly postponed. In anticipation of the fulfilment of fantastic plans to multiply tanks in the Red Army, design bureaus and the tank industry needed updated specifications for the development of new models of armoured fighting vehicles. Finally, the Special Tank Purchasing Commission, which was being formed, was waiting for a decision on which tanks the Red Army needed. The new Armament System was supposed to define specifications for purchased samples of foreign armoured fighting vehicles. The specialists of the Technical Staff, led by Uborevich, had to fulfil Stalin's task as soon as possible.

Stalin Begins to Get Angry

At the end of 1929, amid endless setbacks and delays, the 'Red Lord' felt that his dreams of quickly saturating the Red Army with thousands of Soviet tanks, planes, and artillery pieces were under threat. His appeals and threatening warnings were broken down by the unavailability of the military industry and the lack of experience of Soviet designers. The tank production plan, approved and repeatedly agreed upon at the highest level, was drowning in the production chaos of primitive industrial enterprises. The appalling shortage of skilled workers and engineers compounded the problem. Unskilled and almost illiterate workers tried to work on foreign machines bought for gold. Constant breakdowns of expensive equipment devalued all efforts to purchase them abroad. The invited German engineers and technologists have not yet had time to significantly influence the improvement of the production culture of tanks and other complex equipment. On Stalin's orders, OGPU investigators constantly identified and arrested numerous 'wreckers' who allegedly staged sabotage and damaged expensive German machine tools. However, no emergency measures could significantly affect the current crisis situation in the factories tank industry. Under these conditions, Stalin's concern about the fate of his plans for the technical modernisation of the Red Army was constantly growing.

In early December 1929, numerous Soviet bureaucratic structures began documenting the failure of the Tank Programme and suggesting possible ways out of the tank impasse. On 5 December 1929, the resolution of the Political Bureau of the Central Committee of the Communist Party of the Soviet Union 'On the Implementation of the Tank Programme' stated:

1. To date, only the light infantry tank T-18 (MS-1) has been adopted for service by the Red Army (speed 12km per hour, armed with a 37mm gun and 2 machine guns and protected by 16mm armour), which is manufactured at Factory No. 232 'Bolshevik'.
2. The T-18 does not meet modern requirements for this type of tank sufficiently.
3. Apart from the T-18, there are no developed medium, heavy tank and tankettes designs.
4. The five-year Tractor Programme and Engine Programme are not linked to the Tank Programme and the need to meet the army's needs for powerful tractors. The provision of the Tank Programme with armour and engines has not been worked out, there are not enough tank designers to ensure the implementation of the Tank Programme, and there is no approximate development plan for military factories to implement the Political Bureau programme of 15 July 1929.
5. Ensuring the implementation of the established Political Bureau Programme requires:
   a) accelerated resolution of all issues related to the production of tanks and tractors (armour, engines, steel, etc.);
   b) prompt receipt of tank samples that meet modern specifications;
6. Due to the insufficient number of tank designers and their low qualifications, as well as the lack of ready-made tank designs, no later than 20 December 1929, send abroad a Purchasing Commission from

representatives of VSNKh and the People's Commissariat for Military and Navy Affairs and assign it the task of:

a) selecting and purchasing types and samples of tanks, especially medium and heavy tanks;
b) finding out the possibilities of obtaining technical assistance and inviting foreign designers.

The Purchasing Commission is required to complete its work no later than 1.04.1930.[6]

This resolution of the Political Bureau reflected Stalin's anger directed at his subordinates, who, as it seemed to him, stubbornly ignored all his orders. At the same time, in addition to emotions, there were signs of recognition of problems and identification of ways out of the tank impasse. In particular, the degree of failure of the Tank Programme was determined and the main solutions aimed at an early exit from the tank crisis were outlined. In addition, specific dates and the number of types and samples of tanks planned for production were specified. However, all the deadlines set by Stalin in the resolution of the Political Bureau were again missed!

Who Will Become 'Stalin's Firefighter'?

Against the background of the titanic efforts of the GUVP and VSNKh managers trying to cope with the production chaos at the military factories, the organisation of the Purchasing Commission seemed like a very simple mission. Trips abroad by Soviet Purchasing Commissions became regular by 1929. Buying foreign engines and many other complex technical components, and later buying automobile and tractor plants with a production licence, became a common practice in solving complex technical problems in the USSR. The novelty of the new mission was only in the specifics of the equipment being purchased and the scale of the planned purchases. For the first time, it was planned to directly purchase many samples of sophisticated military equipment, rather than purchasing individual parts or dual-use technical facilities.

The issue of the management and composition of the Special Tank Purchasing Commission was resolved fairly quickly. Khalepsky's candidacy for the position of chief negotiator did not raise objections from anyone from the top leadership of the USSR and the Red Army. Several competent engineers accompanying him had to ensure the efficiency of the Special Tank Purchasing Commission. Covert support for the mission was again to be provided by the Soviet special services, which had extensive networks of foreign agents.

The more difficult aspect turned out to be determining which specific samples of armoured fighting vehicles needed to be purchased and which specifications the purchased tanks had to meet. This issue, which required great personal responsibility, had to be resolved by the military. The cautious Voroshilov, in order to avoid the possible wrath of Stalin in case of failure, entrusted the Chief of Staff of the Red Army with solving this problem. Shaposhnikov could not directly evade his superior's orders.

On 13 December 1929, the Chief of Staff prepared his recommendations on the types and specifications of foreign tanks most desirable for purchase.[7] However, Shaposhnikov, no less cautious than Voroshilov, formulated the most generalised specifications for the types of tanks purchased abroad, avoiding risky details. Moreover, he evaded personal responsibility for the fulfilment of this important Stalinist mission. He clearly declared that the Head of Armaments of the Red Army Ieronim Uborevich, the Head of the UMM Innokenty Khalepsky, and the Head of the Red Army's Fourth Bureau (GRU – military intelligence) Yan Berzin,[8] were responsible for solving the problem.

The Head of Armaments of the Red Army should have said the last word in determining the specific specifications of the types and designs of foreign tanks.

Thus, Ieronim Uborevich once again confirmed his status as the 'Firefighter of the Bolsheviks'. Once again, he was single-handedly solving an acute problem at a time when all other top commanders preferred to evade responsibility. Under the leadership of Uborevich, the necessary refinement of the System of Tank-Tractor-Automotive vehicles of the Red Army (Armament System) was carried out in record time.

Anglo-German Tank Armament System

On 18 December 1929, the Revolutionary Military Council (RVS) hastily approved the updated System of Tank-Tractor-Automotive vehicles of the Red Army. The new Armament System included the following types of tanks:

a) **tankette (wheel-and-track).** The purpose is reconnaissance, surprise attack. Weight – no more than 3.3 tons. It is desirable to reduce the weight to 2.5 and 2 tons. Speed – at least 60km/h on wheeled drive and 40km/h on caterpillar drive. The armour must ensure that armour-piercing bullets are not penetrated from a distance of 300m. Armament – 1 machine gun with 360° horizontal firing or two machine guns that do not simultaneously operate with 360° horizontal firing. Ammunition is not less than 2.5 thousand cartridges. The tankette crew consists of 2 people. The range is 300km on caterpillar drive, 450km on wheeled drive. The width of the obstacle to be overcome is at least 1.25m, height – 0.5m, ford depth – 0.75m (buoyancy is desirable). The diameter of the felled trees is 10cm. The transfer from wheeled drive to caterpillar drive should take no more than 0.5 minutes, without the crew exiting the tankette. The height of the tankette is no more than 1.5m. In addition, to design a tankette with the same specifications, but armed with a single 37mm gun with the task of anti–tank warfare;

b) **light tank.** The purpose is the Mechanised Troops strike weapon, which carries out a breakthrough in conditions of manoeuvrable combat. Weight – no more than 7–7.5 tons. The speed is 25–30km/h. The thickness of the armour should guarantee against penetration of 37mm shell at an initial velocity of 700m/s from 1,000m. Armament – one 37mm gun and 2 machine guns, of which one is a separate machine gun. Ammunition – at least 75 shells and 3,500 cartridges. The tank's crew consists of three men. The range is 200km. The width of the horizontal obstacle to be overcome is at least 2m, the height of the obstacle is 0.6–0.8m. The depth of the ford is at least 1.3m (preferably the tank is to be buoyant). The diameter of the felled trees is 20cm. Experimentally, it is also desirable to design a wheel-and-track light tank with the same data, but with a weight tolerance of no more than 8 tons, a speed of 45km/h on a wheeled drive and a range of 300km on a wheeled drive. Leave the T-18 (MS-1) tank in service with the Red Army units until the design of the new light tank is ready. Artillery Directorate of the Red Army (AU) to take all measures to increase the speed of the T-18 (MS-1) to 24–25km per hour;

c) **medium tank.** The purpose is to break through fortified positions in conditions of both manoeuvrable and positional warfare. Weight – no more than 15–16 tons. The speed is 25–30km per hour. The thickness of the armour should guarantee against penetration of 37mm shell (at an initial speed of 700m/s) at a distance of 750m. Armament – one 45mm gun and three simultaneously-operating machine guns. Ammunition – at least 100 shells and 5,000 cartridges. The crew of the tank is 4–5 men. The range is 200km. The width of the obstacle to be overcome is at least 2.5m, the height is 1m. The depth of the ford to be overcome is at least 1.3m. The diameter of the trees to be felled is 30cm;

d) with regard to the creation of the **heavy tank**, limit ourselves for the time being to the theoretical development of the tank design, inviting the Military-Industrial Directorate VSNKh[9] to submit a draft design by 1 October 1930, and then decide whether to include it in the Armament System . . .[10]

The System of Tank-Tractor-Automotive Vehicles of the Red Army (Armament System), approved on 18 December 1929, as in the previous version, adopted in 1926, clearly reflected foreign and primarily English and German influences. As noted above, Uborevich, like many other senior Red Army officers, believed that the modernisation of the USSR armed forces should be carried out according to the German model.

Compared to previous versions, a new trend in the Armament System had become the requirement to create wheel-and-track tankettes and the recommendation to create a wheel-and-track light tank. These requirements reflect the latest innovations in the field of foreign armoured fighting vehicles. Uborevich, like most Soviet senior officers, closely followed the latest developments in the field of Western tank construction. At the end of the 1920s, numerous examples of such innovations in tank design began to appear actively in Europe and the United States.

Chief of Staff of the Red Army Tukhachevsky was the first to draw the attention of the top leadership of the USSR to the intensive work of foreign designers to create wheel-and-track armoured cars. In his special report, he logically justified the need to create armoured fighting vehicles with 'convertible drive' for the Red Army: 'Due to the extreme off-road conditions in the USSR, the Staff of the Red Army considers it necessary to gradually transition from wheeled armoured cars to wheel-and-track armoured cars'.[11] While revealing the topic of technical innovations in tank construction in his report, he also paid great attention to Christie's 'convertible tanks'.

After Tukhachevsky's resignation as Chief of Staff in the spring of 1928, the discussion of the advantages of armoured fighting vehicles with a 'convertible drive' continued to be a popular topic among the top Red Army commanders. However, at the end of 1929, the idea of using wheel-and-track running gear was no longer related to armoured cars, but to tankettes and light tanks. In Boris Shaposhnikov's recommendations for the Special Tank Purchasing Commission mentioned above, he explicitly stated that of the four types of light and medium tanks planned for purchase, three were to have wheel-and-track running gear.[12]

Stalin shared the opinion about these prospects, and, consequently, the need to create hybrid tanks. Later, under the influence of Tukhachevsky and Uborevich, he became the main proponent of this unusual design. This stubborn position of a technically incompetent tyrant, implemented with fanatical tenacity, led to another severe tank crisis in the end of the 1930s. The subsequent painful overcoming of the tank impasse paradoxically led Soviet designers to create the T-34 tank.

Along with the progressive innovation orientation, the new Armament System Red Army had one important drawback. The requirements of the Soviet military for tank types were formulated under the influence of the German doctrine of technical rearmament of the army, which relied on the advanced capabilities of German industry. However, as it soon became clear, in the USSR it was impossible to follow such an extremely high guideline in the conditions of a backward tank industry. If the Soviet designers and managers coped with the creation and production of light tanks with great difficulty, then they could not create their own type of medium tank.

Khalepsky's Fantastic Success in England

On 30 December 1929, the Special Tank Purchasing Commission embarked on a long voyage to Western Europe.[13] Unfortunately for Khalepsky, his fears were confirmed, and the beginning of the trip turned out to be a complete failure.[14]

The cold reception given by the French and Czechs and the tendency for limited cooperation hidden under the mask of German friendliness severely undermined Khalepsky's confidence. He was well aware of the sad consequences of the failure of his mission in continental Europe. The last hope for the success of an important mission was the trip of the Tank Purchasing Commission to Britain and the USA.

The main object of interest of the Special Tank Purchasing Commission in Britain was Vickers Armstrongs Ltd. At the end of the 1920s, it was the undisputed world leader in the design and manufacture of tanks. However, the previous experience of relations with this company did not give the Bolsheviks reasons for optimism. Since September 1925, representatives of the USSR have repeatedly made persistent attempts to buy several tank prototypes from Vickers. However, all the efforts of the Bolsheviks to get their hands on the latest British tank technology ended in vain.

Fortunately for Khalepsky, at the end of 1929, objective prerequisites appeared for the potential success of the Special Tank Purchasing Commission's mission. After the Labour government came to power, the previously openly hostile relations between Britain and the USSR improved significantly. In addition, the outbreak of the Great Depression led to the fact that a significant number of large Western companies that produced military equipment were on the verge of bankruptcy. One of the ways out of the difficult financial situation was the sale of armoured fighting vehicles to technologically backward countries in the East. Under the circumstances, the British, who had previously been extremely picky, were ready to sell their tanks even to such an openly hostile regime to the West as the USSR. Thus, Stalin's agents got a great chance to take advantage of the positive experience of their tsarist predecessors, who were very pleased with the purchase of high-quality British armoured fighting vehicles.

For foreign buyers, Vickers Armstrongs Ltd. has kindly prepared a whole range of various armoured fighting vehicles: from tankettes to heavy tanks. The British tank 'supermarket' had everything Stalin dreamed of and even more. The members of the Special Tank Purchasing Commission had a hard time hiding their delight at the variety of Vickers products. The Russians wanted to buy literally everything from the British: the Carden-Loyd Mk VI tankette, the Vickers 6-ton light tank, the Vickers 12-ton Medium Mark II and the five-turret Independent A1E1 heavy tank.

Having convinced themselves that their interests coincided, the partners began preliminary negotiations on the sale of armoured fighting vehicles samples. Behind the external mask of excessive demands for foreign technology, Khalepsky also tried to hide his deep insecurity, which was the result of Russia's total technical backwardness. Flattered by the friendly attitude of the British, Khalepsky tried to minimize the cost of the future deal. Knowing about the difficult financial situation of Vickers, he offered to conclude an agreement on the purchase of one copy of each type of tank with the provision of complete technical documentation. Such an obviously unfavourable offer did not suit the British. They were ready to sell small batches of 15–20 tanks of each type to the Russians, and at fairly high prices for each tank. Given the Russians' interest in the three types of tanks, it was a deal worth more than £200,000, or 20 million rubles.

After agreeing on the terms of the deal with Moscow, the second round of negotiations between the Special Tank Purchasing Commission and the management of Vickers Armstrongs Ltd. was held in a constructive atmosphere. In addition to selling tanks, the British expressed their willingness to provide a complete set of drawings, as well as to provide technical assistance for the organisation of mass production of tanks in the USSR under licence. Thus, the parties met each other's demands, and the deal was generally agreed upon.

In the future, both sides gained significant benefits from signing the contract. The payment of the Soviet order significantly supplemented the income of the British company from contracts for the supply of tanks to other countries, in particular Poland. This money helped solve many of the economic problems of Vickers Armstrongs Ltd. The benefits of the Soviet side from the contract were even more significant. As subsequent events showed, the Carden-Loyd Mk VI tankette and especially the Vickers 6-ton light infantry tank became the backbone of the Red Army tank forces until 1941. However, the Bolsheviks were not able to apply all the innovations transferred by the British to their tank industry. It will not be possible to maximise the benefits of cooperation with Vickers Armstrongs Ltd due to the shortage of qualified personnel and the erroneous decisions of Stalin and his servants.

'Tank Christie surpasses all tanks in the world in its speed...'[15]

On 7 April 1930,[16] Khalepsky and the famous inventor Walter Christie met for the first time in the New York office of the intermediary company Amtorg.[17] The reason for the Special Tank Purchasing Commission's special interest was the hybrid Christie M.1928 'wonder tank'. It embodied in its revolutionary design all the innovations created by the American inventor over many years of technical experiments.

For several years, the US military leadership stubbornly refused to recognise Christie's achievements in the development of armoured fighting vehicles and did not want to buy his tanks. Offended by the American military bureaucracy, Christie decided to find new buyers overseas. The aggressive international advertising of the Christie M.1928 tank has achieved its goals. There were more than enough people in the East who wanted to buy Christie's invention. Tukhachevsky soon found out about the American 'wonder tank', who informed Joseph Stalin, the main lover of military innovations in the USSR, about it.

The main feature of Christie's invention was the original suspension system, which allowed the tank to move both on wheels and on tracks. This suspension system, combined with an unusually powerful 400 horsepower engine with a relatively low weight, allowed the Christie tank to demonstrate outstanding capabilities. At the first presentation in October 1928, the Christie M.1928 showed amazing speed. On tracked tracks, the maximum speed of the tank was 68km/h, and on wheels the speed was an amazing 112km/h. Against the background of the modest results achieved by the Soviet design bureaus, which were generously funded by the state, such characteristics of a tank created by an American lone designer seemed fantastic to Khalepsky.

Khalepsky's negotiations with Christie took place in an extremely businesslike atmosphere. Both sides needed each other badly. The American inventor proposed to the Special Tank Purchasing Commission three types of armoured fighting vehicles: Christie M.1928, amphibious tank and self-propelled gun with a 76.2mm (3in) gun. During the conversation, Christie warned Khalepsky that he had already sold the rights to manufacture the M.1928 to Poland and Japan. This information significantly fuelled Khalepsky's interest in the Christie tank.

The Stalinist agent offered Christie to buy two copies of the tank on condition of handing over the drawings and providing technical assistance to Soviet engineers. Such an offer from Khalepsky, which is usually completely unacceptable for reputable Western companies, was quite acceptable to Christie. His technical experiments were very expensive, and he chronically experienced significant financial difficulties. At the next meeting between Christie and Khalepsky,[18] dedicated to the presentation of the tank, all the details of the upcoming contract in the amount of $100,000 were agreed.[19]

German Tank Designers from OGPU

While Khalepsky was looking abroad for backup options for tank designs develop by Soviet designers, the situation with the Tank Programme remained extremely alarming. As noted above, in 1930, the Red Army received only 300 T-18 (MS-1) light infantry tanks. Despite the effort and resources spent, they were only capable of fulfilling the role of training tanks. Against this bleak background, Stalin's approved plans for the production of more than 5,000 tanks by the end of 1932 seemed an absolute fantasy. During the tank crisis, Stalin's servants made great efforts to find the means to accomplish an impossible task. Huge human and financial resources were devoted to accelerating the design and manufacture of prototypes of the T-19 light infantry tank, tankettes (T-17 and T-23) and medium tanks (T-12 and T-24). However, despite the cheerful reports of Soviet designers and managers of military enterprises, the prospects for these projects looked very doubtful. Hostile groups competing for Stalin's attention in the highest civilian and military administrative structures of the USSR were feverishly looking for a way out of the tank impasse.

At the end of 1929, when Stalin became convinced of the impossibility of Soviet designers to create acceptable tank designs, the immediate environment had at least two alternative solutions to this problem. One of them was the direct purchase of tank samples abroad and licences for their production in the USSR. This project was implemented by a powerful group of supporters of the radical technical transformation of the Red Army, conventionally called the 'Progressives'. They actively advocated the rearmament of the Red Army on the German model. After Tukhachevsky's resignation, Ieronim Uborevich became the new leader of this group. The implementation of this project through the Khalepsky Tank Purchasing Commission is described above.

The initiator of the second way out of the tank impasse was the leader of the 'Cavalrymen' People's Commissar for Military and Naval Affairs (Minister of War) Voroshilov. Motivated by the decline of his influence in the armed forces of the Soviet Union, he feverishly searched for ways to satisfy Stalin's tank ambitions. Soon such an option was found.

The heads of the special Soviet secret service – EKU OGPU[20] – offered Voroshilov an original solution to the problem. It consisted in the realisation of the idea of creating a prototype of a new tank with the help of prisoners' labour. During the formation of the monstrous Gulag labour camp system, the practice of using slave labour seemed to the Bolsheviks to be a universal way to solve all problems. Against the background of a shortage of trained specialists from the tertiary technical education, the executions of tsarist engineers seemed to many prudent Bolsheviks to be a senseless waste of valuable resources. After the mass arrests of 1928–30, OGPU had a large number of engineers and other highly qualified specialists in its hands.

However, Voroshilov could not directly commission the design of the medium tank from 'enemies of the people'. The way out of this impasse was the OGPU officers' proposal to implement the project with the involvement of foreign technical assistance. According to the 'cunning' plan of the partners, the project will be headed by a German engineer, and all the 'menial' work on the design and construction of the prototype tank will be performed by the arrested 'wreckers'. The pragmatic Bolsheviks from the OGPU believed that the collaboration of a small group of foreign designers paid in gold and the free labour of numerous 'enemies of the people' promised them not only quick results, but also great savings in money. Voroshilov was completely satisfied with OGPU's proposal, but a new problem appeared on the way to its implementation.

Grote Design Bureau

The problem of starting the development of an alternative medium tank project was to find suitable foreign specialists. OGPU officers, together with Voroshilov, considered several German designers. Germany suffered more than other European countries from the Great Depression, and many German specialists were out of work. According to the personal choice of the People's Commissar Voroshilov, Edward Grote was invited to the USSR. In making this decision, an important role was played by the fact that Grote requested less money for the work of his Design Bureau team than other German engineers. In addition to favourable financial conditions, the choice of the incompetent

Voroshilov was also determined by the Bolshevik ideology. One of the Grote Design Bureau engineers was a member of the German Communist Party, and Edward Grote himself was very sympathetic to the Bolsheviks. Voroshilov and his OGPU partners believed that people with such views would be sympathetic to working with prisoners and would not ask unnecessary questions.

At the end of 1929, several German engineers led by Grote arrived in the USSR. The place of work of the German specialists was Factory No. 232 'Bolshevik' in Leningrad. There, a special room was allocated for them, carefully guarded by OGPU agents. In addition to generous pay, the Soviets provided the Germans with good working conditions. Before receiving the order, they even had several months to develop the concept of a new medium tank.

In April 1930, the Grote Design Bureau received a technical specification from the Khalepsky department for designing a tank weighing 18–20 tons, armour 20mm and a speed of 35–40km/h. The tank was supposed to be armed with 76.2mm and 37mm guns and 4–5 machine guns. The UMM left all other parameters of the medium tank to the discretion of the German engineers.

In official documents, the alternative medium tank project was named TG (Tank Grote). Thanks to Voroshilov's patronage, the implementation of the project received the highest priority. The German designers had no shortage of resources and people. All work on the tank was carried out in conditions of deep secrecy. About 130 Soviet prisoners worked on the production of a prototype tank in a special workshop, fenced off from the main areas of Factory No. 232 'Bolshevik' by a high fence with barbed wire. Apart from the OGPU leadership, only a few people knew about the existence of the TG tank project, including Stalin, Voroshilov, Uborevich and Khalepsky.

The Collapse of the Voroshilov 'Wonder Tank'

Despite the supervision of People's Commissar Voroshilov and the efforts of OGPU officers, the TG tank project was implemented extremely slowly. Apparently, one of the main reasons for this was the unexpected freedom of creativity granted to the Germans by the Bolsheviks. Unlike the inexperienced Soviet tank designers, who chose the cautious path of copying Western models, Grote acted very boldly. In his medium tank project, almost all the elements were innovative: from the fully welded tank hull to a specially designed tank engine. This risky design strategy proved fatal for Voroshilov's 'wonder tank'.

The promising medium tank Grote was so innovative that even making a prototype turned into an almost impossible task. In addition,

Grote's unwillingness to work in the feverish haste usual for Soviet designers had a major impact on the progress of the project. For reasons completely incomprehensible to the Germans, the Russians, after several months of relative inactivity, suddenly demanded immediate results from Grote. Physical and psychological overstrain negatively affected the health of the German designer. In the autumn of 1930, Grote became so seriously ill that he could not continue working on the project of a promising medium tank. The production schedule of the prototype was completely disrupted. Soon, information about the serious problems of the TG tank reached Stalin. Against the background of the inevitable failure of the medium tank T-24 project, this unpleasant news caused the 'Master' disappointment and concern.

On 17–18 November 1930, Voroshilov, the curator of the project, arrived from Moscow at Factory No. 232 'Bolshevik'. The formal reason for visiting the factory was to check the state of work on the serial production of T-18 (MS-1) light infantry tanks. However, the main focus of People's Commissar's attention was in fact the prototype of the TG tank, which was being assembled at that moment in a separate secret workshop. Following the trip, Voroshilov promised Stalin that, despite the objective difficulties, the prototype of the 'wonder tank' would be completed by the end of December 1930.

The failure of the T-24 medium tank project forced Stalin to switch his attention to the TG. He considered the implementation of the TG project to be the most important task in the field of manufacturing prototype tanks for 1931. In accordance with Stalin's directive, on 20 February 1931, in the resolution of the Central Committee of the Communist Party of the Soviet Union 'About the Tank Programme', it was decided to recognise the TG tank as the main type of medium tank and cancel the task of organising mass production of T-24 medium tanks at the Kharkov Locomotive Factory (KhPZ).

The first series of TG tanks in the amount of 50–75 units was planned to be produced in 1931. In 1932, it was planned to manufacture and send up to 2,000 new TG medium tanks to the Red Army.[21] Despite the objective facts that indicated major problems in the manufacture of the prototype, KhPZ, on Stalin's orders, began preparing equipment for the mass production of TG tanks.

Meanwhile, the problems with the production of the prototype TG tank had worsened. Due to Grote's illness, 'enemies of the people' had to finish the prototype of Voroshilov's 'wonder tank' on their own. The rush was so great that the prisoners were transferred to a 24-hour work schedule. However, even such extraordinary measures did not save the project from failure. There were too many problems with TG, and their solution turned into a vicious circle of endless improvisations and improvements.

Many of the most important components of the 'wonder tank' simply did not exist. For example, a working version of the innovative engine, specially designed by Grote for his tank, could not be produced. In a mad rush, the water-cooled M-6 V8 aircraft engine was installed on the tank, which completely did not fit into the dimensions of the engine compartment of the innovative tank. In addition to the engine, it was urgently necessary to find a suitable replacement for many important components of the prototype tank.

A mock-up 76mm gun was installed in the turret of the TG prototype. They could not produce a real tank gun of this calibre. Due to the lack of turret traversing mechanisms, it was simply welded to the tank hull. Having installed a temporary replacement for non-existent components and various kinds of models of other important parts on the tank, enemies of the people nevertheless completed the construction of a prototype of the TG tank. In such a strange way, on 27 June 1931, this 'Frankenstein' tank was sent for testing, which naturally ended in a complete collapse.

More than three million rubles were pointlessly spent on the TG project. Contrary to the expectations of Voroshilov and Stalin, unlimited resources, combined with the use of free labour by a huge number of prisoners (workers and engineers), led to a negative result. In August 1931, the 'wonder tank' project was finally shut down. The hard-made prototype of the TG medium tank went to rust senselessly in the Red Army warehouse.

Thus, Voroshilov's attempt to please Stalin in the implementation of the Tank Programme for the First Five-Year Plan ended in complete failure. However, this was far from Voroshilov's last unsuccessful attempt to patronise the creation of 'wonder tanks'. There was only annoyance and disappointment waiting for him along the way. Success came to the stubborn and intellectually limited Voroshilov many years later in the form of the newest heavy tank named after him.

Dyrenkov 'Tanks'

In addition to the medium tank projects discussed above, which were worked on by inexperienced, but still professional designers, there was another very strange project. It was proposed by locksmith and impostor designer Nikolai Dyrenkov. This native of the social strata of Russian society gained fame during the chaos of the Bolshevik coup and the subsequent Russian Civil War. There is no exact data on what he was doing in the early 1920s. However, due to the pathological features of his character, the adventurer Dyrenkov was ready to do anything. The main goal of his 'activity' was not the result, but universal attention and money. If a 'brilliant' project could not be implemented, Dyrenkov swiftly abandoned it and with the same maniacal energy set about implementing the next promising idea.

In the second half of the 1920s, the manufacture of armoured fighting vehicles became a popular and famous occupation in the USSR. For this reason, Dyrenkov left the unpromising city of Rybinsk for the Leningrad suburb, where he was able to get an engineering position at the Izhorsky steel mill. In conditions of a shortage of qualified personnel, no one asked him for a diploma of tertiary technical education or other proof of qualifications. The total Stalinist militarisation led to the fact that there was an abundance of work at military factories and people with even minimal technical skills were in great demand. Due to his accidental success, Dyrenkov gained some notoriety in the progressive military circles concerned about the problem of the technical equipment of the Red Army. According to his project, an armoured railcar with petrol engine was manufactured.

In addition to his mania for strange technical inventions, this outspoken adventurer was distinguished by his amazing ability to promote his very original but useless projects. Dyrenkov had no doubts about his genius, and he drew his 'original' technical ideas from foreign technical literature. Due to the fact that the Soviet military read the same foreign sources as Dyrenkov, his technical proposals were always strikingly relevant.

Sociability and manic energy allowed Dyrenkov to break through with his 'projects' to the highest level of the Red Army command. On 5 October 1929, the design of the original wheel-and-track tank[22] designed by him was sent for consideration to the Revolutionary Military Council (RVS). Despite the lack of serious evidence of competence in tank design, Dyrenkov easily gained Voroshilov's trust. This devoted servant of Stalin, because of his low level of mental development, easily believed in miracles. However, the attention to his projects by Khalepsky, Uborevich and, later, even Tukhachevsky, is genuinely surprising. Soon Khalepsky, concerned about problems with the development of the medium tank, took the promising 'tank designer' Dyrenkov under his care.

On 18 November 1929, at a meeting of the Tank Commission of the Revolutionary Military Council (RVS), Dyrenkov's report on the 'technical requirements and combat specifications of the developed medium tank project' was heard. The presentation of the speaker, who combined the solid appearance of a university professor and peasant origin, was very much liked by the Soviet military. Based on the results of the report, they unanimously made the following decision: 'It is advisable to put the Dyrenkov tank to the test. To do this, give an urgent order to Izhorsky steel mill for the manufacture of six tank prototypes with the deadline for delivery of the first tank no later than 1 April 1930.'[23]

In December 1929, by order of Khalepsky, the Design and Testing Bureau of the Red Army's Mechanisation and Motorisation Directorate (UMM) was created at the Izhorsky steel mill specifically for the implementation of the Dyrenkov medium tank project. The tank project was designated D-4 by the name of its creator. The number '4' in the index hinted that this model of armoured fighting vehicles was far from the first creation of the 'brilliant' Soviet designer.

Such attention from the top management of the Red Army to his person further increased Dyrenkov's pathologically inflated conceit. With even greater contempt, he ignored all the reasonable advice from competent colleagues about the need to receive a tertiary technical education.

Dyrenkov was passionate about the simultaneous implementation of many 'brilliant' ideas. His Design Bureau carried out work on several dozen multidirectional technical projects. In addition to creating the medium tank, he designed armoured cars, armoured tow tractors and armoured railcars. Moreover, Dyrenkov tried to develop new technologies for the production of fully welded and fully stamped tank hulls, invented a new armour composition, and designed tank transmissions! Thus, his pathological nature did not give any chance for the implementation of the medium 'wonder tank' project, which was so anticipated by the Soviet military.

Despite the fact that the Dyrenkov Design Bureau was literally in full swing, the deadlines for the presentation of the prototype medium 'tank' D-4 were naturally missed. In response to Khalepsky's alarming requests, Dyrenkov sent lengthy reports blaming 'incompetent' engineers and workers at the Izhorsky steel mill for the delays. In addition, he resentfully rejected any professional help that was persistently offered to him by engineers from the Red Army's Mechanisation and Motorisation Directorate (UMM). For some time, this tactic of shifting responsibility for one's failures onto others has been successful for Dyrenkov. The 'brilliant engineer' continued to fool the Red Army leadership, promising to soon present a prototype of his 'unique' medium tank.

In early 1931, the Dyrenkov Design Bureau was transferred to Moscow and located at the Locomotive Repair Factory (Moscow).

The final assembly of the prototype D-4 medium 'tank' was carried out there. In March 1931, the trials of the ridiculous Dyrenkov's technical freak naturally ended in complete failure. The Convertible 'wonder tank' could not move independently on both road wheels and caterpillar tracks.

More than one million rubles were spent on fruitless attempts to create the Dyrenkov 'wonder tank'. Such unproductive spending of money in a country where the population was dying of hunger fit well into the Stalinist term 'Wrecking'. However, neither Dyrenkov nor his high patrons at that time suffered any punishment for their at least unprofessional actions.

On 1 December 1932, the Dyrenkov Design Bureau was disbanded, and all its numerous projects were curtailed. For several more years, he tried to offer his 'brilliant ideas' to the Red Army command. Sometimes he even managed to get financing for the production of a prototype. However, the D-4 wonder tank became the pinnacle of his 'engineering' career.

Dyrenkov was arrested by the NKVD on 13 October 1937. On 9 December 1937, he was sentenced to death on charges of 'participating in the activities of a Sabotage and Terrorist Organization'. On the same day, Dyrenkov was executed at the NKVD Kommunarka shooting range (Moscow region). His body was buried in an unmarked collective grave along with other executed 'wreckers' and 'spies'.

'English Workman' or a Tank for Suppressing Uprisings in the Colonies

The creation of a medium tank suitable for mass production in the time frame desired by Stalin turned out to be a completely unsolvable problem for the Soviet Design Bureaus. Despite a number of attempts, the testing of the manufactured prototypes ended in a logical failure. To achieve at least some result, Stalin's servants showed amazing ingenuity. They organised work on several parallel projects to create medium tanks in the hope that at least one of them would bring success. However, copying foreign designs, inviting German designers, using the slave labour of 'enemies of the people', using foreign components and materials, and so on, did not give the desired result. The lack of experience of the few Soviet tank designers could not be compensated for by Bolshevik's enthusiasm or threats of arrests and executions from the OGPU.

The only hope of salvation in this situation could be the 12-ton Vickers Medium Mark II, purchased in England by the Special Tank Purchasing Commission. According to Khalepsky's original plan, this British tank was intended as insurance in case of failure of the Soviet-designed medium tank projects (T-12 and T-24). Serial production of the foreign tank was supposed to be carried out at the Kharkov Locomotive Factory (KhPZ).[24] However, a few months later, the production plans for the Medium Mark II were unexpectedly cancelled. On 11 November 1930, Khalepsky reported to Uborevich that the British tank did not satisfy the Soviet military due to the weakness of the engine and thin armour.[25] For this reason, instead of mass-producing the Medium Mark II, he suggested using its individual units in the design of Soviet tanks. Considering that by this time the British tanks had not yet been delivered to the USSR, much less tested, this decision looked very strange.

Meanwhile, in England, the production of tanks ordered by the Bolsheviks was behind schedule. Vickers employees who sympathised with the USSR informally referred to the specially commissioned Medium Mark II as the 'English Workman'. Deceived by Bolshevik propaganda, British workers and engineers did not know all the circumstances of life in the USSR and relied on beautiful fairy tales spread by Stalin. It would be a big surprise for them to learn that in order to pay for the production of tanks, Stalin's servants took away the last food grain from Soviet peasants for sale abroad. For fifteen units of these tanks, the Soviet government paid Vickers the huge sum of £125,500, or 125 million rubles. Meanwhile, in 1931, several million Soviet citizens died of starvation caused by Stalin's inhumane policies.

Due to production delays, the first two Medium Mark IIs arrived in the USSR only on 1 February 1931. Soon they were sent for testing to an improvised Test Range in the vicinity of Moscow in the Nakhabino district work settlement.

On 13 February 1931, at a meeting of the Revolutionary Military Council (RVS), Khalepsky made a presentation 'On the progress of the implementation of the System of Tank-Tractor-Automotive vehicles of the Red Army' and mentioned that the Medium Mark II was under testing.[26] It is known that in the summer of 1931, one Medium Mark II was demonstrated to the highest command staff of the Red Army. It even participated in the Red Square parade.[27] However, the Medium Mark II, specially purchased to insure against the failure of all medium tank type projects, was not adopted for service by the Red Army and mass-produced. Moreover, judging by the production experience of other Vickers tanks, it was relatively easy to mass-produce the Medium Mark II at Soviet tank factories. Due to the increased attention to another Vickers product, this English tank did not find any supporters among the leadership of the Red Army.

The tank's design was unreasonably considered outdated, and it had no lobbyists. Moreover, in official documents, the Medium Mark II was contemptuously referred to as a tank designed to suppress uprisings in the British colonies.

The main reason for the refusal to use this tank turned out to be the opinion of Tukhachevsky. He was able to convince all the top commanders, and above all Stalin, of the complete uselessness of the Medium Mark II for the Red Army. The fact is that the former Chief of Staff of the Red Army was a staunch supporter of another tank produced by Vickers. After Tukhachevsky returned to Moscow in 1931 and regained his influence over Stalin, his opinion on the issue proved decisive. None of the top management of the Red Army, including the Head of the Red Army Ieronim Uborevich and the Head of the UMM Innokenty Khalepsky, not only objected to Tukhachevsky's opinion, but on the contrary, fully supported it. As a result of this decision, the Vickers Medium Mark II tanks purchased for gold were practically not used in the Red Army.

Most of the fifteen tanks that arrived from Britain were soon sent to the Red Army warehouses. The fate of the other tanks was also unenviable. Several Medium Mark II tanks were used in tank schools as visual aids. As it turned out much later, Tukhachevsky's decision could not be called indisputable, but soon everyone forgot about the existence of the Medium Mark II.

'. . . When you're in a hurry, you make mistakes more often'

On 11 June 1931, Stalin made an unexpected and seemingly illogical decision. Ieronim Uborevich was removed from the posts of Deputy People's Commissar for Military and Navy Affairs, Head of Armaments of the Red Army and Deputy Chairman of the Revolutionary Military Council. He was appointed Commander of the Byelorussian Military District, and this was a clear demotion. At the same time, Stalin appointed Mikhail Tukhachevsky to the vacant positions of Head of Armaments and Deputy Chairman of the Revolutionary Military Council.

This decision by the Bolshevik leader is usually explained as a reaction to the failure of the grandiose plans to rearm the Red Army. There is a lot of evidence to confirm this version, which is widespread among historians. With a production plan of 340 tanks, only 170 were produced in 1929–30. According to the aircraft production plan, only 899 aircraft were produced instead of the planned 1,231.[28] The Soviet military industry chronically failed to fulfil ammunition manufacturing assignments, especially artillery shells.

Uborevich was not the ideal Head of Armaments. Formally, he can be blamed for serious errors in determining the specifications of the necessary Red Army tanks. Uborevich was also responsible for the frequent change of models intended for the organisation of mass production of armoured fighting vehicles samples. This problem was especially pronounced during the development of the medium tank. However, it should be noted that at that time none of the Soviet senior military had an accurate idea of the combat qualities and specifications required for each type of tank.

Red Army tank tactics were based on the experience of the First World War and the Russian Civil War. It was very difficult to determine the degree of combat capability of the prototypes presented by the designers. At that time, there were no reliable methods for testing new tank models. If we add to these objective problems the constant harsh interference of Stalin, then we must admit that in these difficult conditions Uborevich brilliantly coped with the task assigned to him. The level of military production achieved by Soviet industry by the middle of 1931 was worthy of reward, not punishment. The Head of Armaments of the Red Army cannot be blamed for being extremely diligent in fulfilling Stalin's demands.

In a letter to Gregory (Sergo) Ordzhonikidze, Uborevich explained his professional failure in this way:

> I worked like never before in my life, seven days off, at night, clearing up the incredible chaos and neglect. I know . . . that a lot has been done, a lot of mistakes. One thing serves as an excuse for me – I was damn afraid of the war in 1930 and 1931, seeing our unpreparedness. I was in a hurry. When you're in a hurry, you make mistakes more often.[29]

In his letter, Uborevich acknowledged his responsibility for the failure of the Red Army rearmament programme, but at the same time he subtly hinted at the main creator of the chaos. Uborevich took full responsibility for Stalin's mistakes, and thus rendered him an invaluable service. After this act of the former Head of Armaments, nothing cast a shadow on the indisputable authority of the 'Great Leader' and 'Father of Nations'.

By 1934, Stalin and his servants preferred to forget about the failure of the first generation of Soviet tanks. In the summer of 1937, the Bolshevik leader remembered his former favourite and used him for the last time to solve his problems. On 12 June 1937, after terrible torture, Ieronim Uborevich was shot on Stalin's orders.

Chapter 3

THE AMERICAN ANCESTOR
OF THE T-34

The New Technical Leader of the Red Army

January 9th 1931. Moscow. Kremlin. Stalin's reception room.

On Friday, Stalin, who received many people on other weekdays, invited only one person to his Kremlin residence. At exactly 2:40 p.m., a tall, broad-shouldered man in a handsome military uniform entered the office. His proud bearing and confident movements made it unmistakably clear that he was a former officer of the Russian Imperial Guard. It was Mikhail Tukhachevsky. Stalin, usually restrained in showing emotion, greeted his guest very warmly. On 9 January, there were serious reasons for the smile on the face of the owner of the office and polite treatment.

A year ago, Stalin harshly criticised Tukhachevsky, contemptuously called him a 'Red Militarist' and even accused him of counter-revolutionary views. However, at the beginning of 1931, the Bolshevik leader felt that the problems of producing the latest tanks and aircraft that worried him were gradually being solved. Over the past two years, the threat of an attack on the USSR by external enemies had decreased significantly. The emergency plan for the transformation of the army according to the German model, implemented by Uborevich, was no longer so relevant in the prevailing realities. The boring, always busy Head of Armaments of the Red Army began to seem to Stalin insufficiently ambitious in his views on the development of the Red Army. The 'Master of the USSR' wanted a lot more. Against this background, Stalin began to like Tukhachevsky's fantastic plans, and the author of these plans himself, to a much greater extent than a year ago. Letters with proposals for the total militarisation of the economy, which Tukhachevsky sent to him during 1930, were met by Stalin with much less scepticism than the earlier proposals of 1928. In two years, Stalin's confidence in the military capabilities of the USSR increased significantly. He began to think no longer about defence, but about other, more active actions in relation to numerous external enemies. To realise these optimistic plans, Stalin needed just such an uncompromising fanatical militarist as Tukhachevsky.

However, he was slow to decide on the return of 'Red Aristocrat' to his inner circle. Stalin was troubled by doubts about Tukhachevsky's loyalty. He remembered whose favourite he had been for a long time. The ghost of his worst enemy, hiding abroad and continuing to annoy Stalin with his malicious articles, haunted the 'Red Lord'. Trotsky, who had elevated Tukhachevsky to senior positions in the Red Army, was alive, which means that his people posed a danger to Stalin. Only he could challenge Stalin's right to the Bolshevik state inherited from Lenin. Has Tukhachevsky completely disowned Trotsky? This issue bothered the 'Master of the USSR'.

For several years, OGPU officials had been bringing Stalin numerous denunciations of Tukhachevsky. In these multi-page 'documents', the secret services accused the 'Red Aristocrat' of having dangerous ties with former tsarist generals and criticising the top military leadership. OGPU officers carefully recorded harsh remarks by Tukhachevsky about Voroshilov and other top Red Army commanders. However, Tukhachevsky never gave serious reasons to doubt his personal loyalty to the 'Master of the USSR'. Stalin felt that as long as Tukhachevsky claimed absolute power only in the Red Army, he was not dangerous to him. For this reason, the Bolshevik leader always crossed out the name Tukhachevsky in the long lists of persons subject to OGPU arrest. On 9 January 1931, the 'Red Lord' decided to make sure once again that the 'Red Aristocrat' posed no danger to him.

Tukhachevsky, who entered the office, unlike most of Stalin's visitors, did not feel any awe before the 'Master of the USSR'. He saluted Stalin with a familiar gesture and confidently sat down at the proffered seat at the long table in the middle of the giant office. Next, the 'Red Aristocrat' began to read out to Stalin a multi-page report on the state of affairs in the Leningrad Military District. It was this boring information that was the formal reason for the meeting with Stalin. Predictably, Tukhachevsky focused on the story of possibilities for the interaction of new technical types of weapons: aircraft and tanks.

Using the example of the exercises conducted in the Leningrad Military District, he once again proved to Stalin the need to transform tanks and aircraft from infantry support into the main means of warfare. Contrary to his habit, the 'Master of the USSR' did not interrupt the speaker or ask questions that baffled the timid visitors to his office. He listened attentively to Tukhachevsky's arguments, occasionally nodding approvingly. Stalin liked the idea of the Red Army's transition from the concept of defence to the concept of an active offensive against external enemies, which the 'Red Aristocrat' was advocating. However, listening to Tukhachevsky's arguments was not the main purpose of this meeting. It was important for Stalin to perceive not the content of the 'Red Aristocrat's' speech, but the non-verbal manifestations accompanying the speech. The 'Red Lord's' attention was focused on the slightest signs of disloyalty or pretensions to power on the part of Trotsky's former favourite.

Fascinated by his ideas, Tukhachevsky did not suspect that during this routine report, his future fate depended on his intonation and facial expression. This time, the 'Red Aristocrat' was lucky. The pathologically suspicious Bolshevik leader was pleased with how his guest passed the test prepared for him. Finding nothing alarming in Tukhachevsky's behaviour, Stalin offered tea and fruit to the visitor, indicating that the official part of the conversation was over. After the check, the 'Master' was in a good mood, laughing and joking a lot. From that moment on, the hidden psychological tension between the two bloody Bolsheviks disappeared. Tea was accompanied by a casual, almost friendly conversation. Smiling, Stalin ended the conversation with Tukhachevsky with the promise of an early transfer from Leningrad to Moscow to a new high position. But he explained that this process would take some time and Tukhachevsky would have to stay in Leningrad for now. Stalin explained the delay by saying that he needed to settle some important bureaucratic issues related to the new position for Tukhachevsky in the Red Army.

There was another important nuance in this meeting between Stalin and Tukhachevsky that needs to be explained. On the day when the issue of the future of the Red Army was being decided, there was no official Head of the Red Army in Stalin's office. The explanation for this strange fact was very simple. Stalin did not care at all about the opinion of Voroshilov, who for many years had been trying to get rid of his main competitor for leadership in the Red Army. Moreover, he believed that the permanent conflict between Tukhachevsky and Voroshilov would be a good incentive for their mutual control over each other. Thus, Voroshilov's plan to discredit Tukhachevsky, which was initially so successfully implemented, eventually failed. Tukhachevsky's long-time enemy had to accept his defeat. Another six months would pass after the events described, and the 'Red Aristocrat' would receive from Stalin the official position of Deputy People's Commissar of Defence of the Soviet Union. This appointment officially cemented his status as the second person in the Red Army. However, Voroshilov, who harboured a grudge, would not give up his feud with Tukhachevsky. The results of this deadly struggle for power in the Red Army would be summed up only in the summer of 1937.

At 3.30 p.m., Tukhachevsky left Stalin's office in a new, though not yet official, status of Technical Leader and second in command in the Red Army. From that moment until his execution in 1937, he was the only one who determined what type of new military equipment the Red Army needed. Thus, an important event took place in the history of the development of the Soviet tank forces. It was Tukhachevsky's opinion that indirectly determined the appearance of the T-34 with those specifications that became the main attributes of the myth of this tank.

The Chieftain of Soviet Military Industry

If the Technical Leader of the Red Army was definitively determined by Stalin only in 1931, then Stalin found a candidate for the position of leader of Soviet military industry back in 1926. Unlike Tukhachevsky, who was a compromise and temporary figure in the top leadership of the Red Army, Gregory (Sergo) Ordzhonikidze was a member of Stalin's inner circle. Moreover, it can be assumed that the 'Red Lord' considered him as his successor and personally promoted Ordzhonikidze to the highest level of the Soviet leadership. The reasons why Stalin treated him as a 'younger brother' are revealed in his biography.

Gregory Ordzhonikidze, the son of an impoverished Georgian nobleman orphaned at an early age, had a typical life path for a Bolshevik fanatic. He was born in October 1886 in the village of Ghoresha Kutaisi Governorate on the far outskirts of the Russian Empire. Gregory received a standard secondary education for his social status. He then entered the medical assistant school in Tbilisi, graduating in 1905. In 1903, on the recommendation of his older brother, he joined one of the branches of the Russian Social Democratic Labour Party (RSDLP), whose supporters later became known as the Bolsheviks. In 1907 Ordzhonikidze was accused by the tsarist authorities of banditry, arrested and placed in Bayil prison in Baku. In a prison cell, he met Joseph Dzhugashvili, who was then better known by his nickname Koba. Stalin was Ordzhonikidze's senior by almost eight years and took his compatriot and colleague in the revolutionary struggle under his protection. Since then, a warm friendship had been established between them, close to the relationship between an older and a younger brother.

Until 1917, Ordzhonikidze continued to lead a dangerous life as a professional revolutionary, consisting of frequent arrests, incarceration, and exile to Siberia. Stalin's maniacally active 'younger brother' was a diligent student in the theory and practice of Bolshevism. Ordzhonikidze enthusiastically took a course of theoretical training in revolutionary struggle from Lenin in the Paris suburb of Longjumeau and a practical course in bank robbery in a gang from Stalin. The young revolutionary, who was emotional and obsessed with activity, liked such a turbulent life.

The Bolshevik coup of October 1917, in which Ordzhonikidze took an active part, allowed him to choose the position of political commissar in the Red Army corresponding to his explosive temperament. During the bloody Russian Civil War Ordzhonikidze showed all facets of his character. Unlike his 'older brother', who was very concerned about his own safety, he was always at the centre of the most dangerous events. Distinguished by boundless courage, he personally led the Red Army regiments in bayonet attacks. When managing the troops, the 'younger brother' acted much more professionally than Stalin. In contrast, Ordzhonikidze paid great attention to the opinions of former tsarist officers who joined the Red Army.[1]

After the end of the Russian Civil War, Lenin, who highly valued Ordzhonikidze's ability to solve the most difficult problems, sent him to manage the Soviet Caucasus, a very troubled province of Soviet Russia. There, Stalin's 'younger brother' showed not only his efficiency in management, but also extreme emotional intemperance. Sometimes, with his own fists, he 'convinced' comrades in the revolutionary struggle who did not agree with him. Ordzhonikidze's straightforwardness and extreme quick temper contrasted especially against the background of his 'older brother's' restraint and penchant for intrigue. However, these opposing character traits did not prevent Ordzhonikidze from always demonstrating complete loyalty to his 'older brother'. After Lenin's death, the new Bolshevik leader was in great need of loyal people. Soon, the energy and abilities of the 'younger brother' were in demand by Stalin, who consistently surrounded himself with loyal people on his way to absolute power.

'Yes, Koba! I'll do it immediately!'

In the midst of the deadly confrontation with Trotsky, Stalin transferred his 'younger brother' from the position of Head of the

Soviet Caucasus to Moscow. On 5 November 1926, he appointed Ordzhonikidze People's Commissar of the Workers' and Peasants' Inspectorate. This administrative structure played the role of the Bolshevik 'inquisition'. According to the idea of its creator Lenin, the employees of the inspectorate had to keep a close eye on all Soviet officials. Simultaneously with this appointment Ordzhonikidze received the high position of Deputy Chairman of the Council of People's Commissars of the Soviet Union (deputy prime minister). Among other duties, Stalin personally instructed him to monitor the activities of the conditionally loyal Chairman of the Council of People's Commissars of the Soviet Union (head of government) Aleksey Rykov.

The rude and determined Ordzhonikidze quickly silenced and got out of Stalin's way the last Bolshevik intellectuals remaining from Lenin's government. On 19 December 1930, Aleksey Rykov was removed from the post of Head of Government, and Vyacheslav Molotov, a close servant of the head of the Bolsheviks, was appointed in his place. Stalin was very pleased with such effective help from his 'younger brother'. After this event, all the top positions in the Red Empire were filled by people who were personally loyal to Stalin. Any, even the most sluggish opposition in the top leadership of the USSR was eliminated. The power of the 'Master of the USSR' over all aspects of the life of the 'Red Empire' has become total.

In addition to the large-scale problems of seizing power in the USSR, Ordzhonikidze successfully coped with smaller-scale tasks. In December 1929, Stalin instructed a special commission led by his 'younger brother' to study the reasons for the failure of the development of the prototype medium tank and outline specific measures to break the tank impasse. As described above, Ordzhonikidze's vigorous investigation resulted in the discovery of the inability of Soviet engineers to create acceptable tank designs and the dispatch of a Special Tank Purchasing Commission led by Khalepsky abroad to purchase foreign armoured fighting vehicles.

However, Stalin's main concern in 1929 was Industrialisation. This meant that Ordzhonikidze had a new job. The impatient 'Master' demanded fantastic growth rates from the primitive Soviet economy, which it could not give him. Stalin's gross interference in the economy jeopardized the implementation of the ambitious First Five-Year Plan. Emergency measures were taken Ordzhonikidze jointly with Uborevich to save the Stalinist authority. As noted above, the problem of chronic non-fulfilment of the plan was solved with the help of fantastic volumes of purchases of equipment, machine tools and raw materials abroad. The old management structures of the military industry, where, according to Stalin, all positions were occupied by former tsarist officers, were hastily reorganised. To eliminate the industrial chaos caused by the wave of repression against tsarist specialists, OGPU agents were appointed to many high positions in the industrial management structures. Stalin's executioners did not have the necessary managerial competencies, but they were ready to carry out the orders of their 'Master' at any cost. However, these emergency measures had only a short-term effect.

To realise the fantastic plans of Industrialisation, a total reorganisation of the USSR economy was required. Stalin literally needed to create a new Soviet military industry and, consequently, a new management system for it. Ordzhonikidze and his team were tasked with solving this huge problem. Stalin's 'younger brother' eagerly took up this super-difficult job. Thus, Ordzhonikidze, a Georgian by nationality, a nobleman by birth, and a medical assistant by profession, became the chief manager of Soviet military industry and the 'Father of Industrialisation'.

When carrying out a difficult mission, Stalin's 'younger brother' relied on his military experience. He transformed the industrial management system along the lines of the Red Army command used in the Russian Civil War. Instead of the former tsarist officers, young Soviet 'managers', personally selected by Ordzhonikidze, were appointed to high positions. In their factories, the young directors had almost unlimited powers. However, these powers were given to them only for strict and precise execution of orders from Moscow. Using Trotsky's experience, Ordzhonikidze appointed former tsarist specialists who had survived the wave of repression to the positions of technical advisers to inexperienced young managers. Thus, contrary to Stalin's opinion, Ordzhonikidze retained experienced managers and engineers in the Soviet military industry.

Simultaneously with the transformation of the management system, Ordzhonikidze oversaw the construction of new military factories. In 1929, the Soviet military industry consisted of either primitive handicraft workshops inherited by the Bolsheviks from the tsar, or giant excavation pits excavated to lay the foundations of future military factories. The giant industrial flagships of Stalin's Industrialisation, created by American industrial architects, had yet to be built. Western equipment and Western technologies purchased abroad still travelled across the ocean or were delivered to the USSR by rail. A new generation of young Soviet managers needed to learn how to manage military factories that did not yet exist in reality.

In the 1930s, with the help of foreign engineers, Ordzhonikidze managed to radically reconstruct the tsarist military factories and establish new giants of Soviet military industry. The management problems of the military industry exacerbated the fact that the construction of new and reconstruction of old factories had to be combined with the implementation of the production plan. There were not enough resources to implement Stalin's fantastic plans. The construction time was often interrupted. The commissioning of new military factories and individual workshops was delayed for many years. Thus, the production of military products in workshops and factories under construction and reconstruction became the norm for the Soviet military industry for a long time in the 1930s.

Ordzhonikidze's American Factories

On 10 November 1930, Ordzhonikidze was appointed chairman of the Supreme Soviet of the National Economy (VSNKh) (Minister of Industry) by Stalin. By that time, the Soviet military and civilian industry had lost the last signs of economic independence. It had become a fully centralised structure, controlled from Moscow. It seemed to the Bolsheviks that they had discovered the main 'secret' of industry management, which was not available in the West. Having gained full control over the entire industry, Ordzhonikidze acted as a 'battering ram'. He resolutely pushed through any obstacles in the way of Stalinist Industrialisation. He used his military experience, leading his people to victory despite any difficulties and obstacles. There turned out to be an extremely large number of such insurmountable obstacles on the way to the realisation of Stalin's fantastic plans. Most often, the reasons for their occurrence were in the head of the 'Master of the USSR', who was trapped in his own megalomania.

At the beginning of the 1930s, the USSR turned into a huge construction site, where American engineers played a major role. It was under their leadership and direct participation that Ford automobile plants were built in Moscow and Nizhny Novgorod. For example, tractor plants in Stalingrad and Chelyabinsk were built according to the design of Albert Kahn Associates. The giant steel mill in Magnitogorsk was built according to the plans of the American Arthur McKee & Company. Similar steel mills using foreign intellectual and technological potential were built in the cities of Lipetsk and Novokuznetsk. Industrial equipment and technologies were purchased aboard on a large scale for new factories. For example, in 1931, the USSR purchased about a third, and in 1932, about half of the world's exports of all machine tools and equipment. As mentioned above, the result of such fantastic expenses in a country with an extremely poor population was a catastrophic famine that claimed the lives of millions of Soviet citizens.

These gigantic projects were implemented in great haste with a total lack of qualified specialists. Ordzhonikidze paid great attention to solving this problem. In 1931, using his influence on Stalin, he secured an end to the arrests of tsarist specialists and forbade OGPU commissions of investigators to enter military factories without his permission. On Ordzhonikidze's initiative, special tertiary technical education institutes were created, where accelerated training of young Soviet engineers was conducted. The problem of the shortage of specialists was also solved by inviting in foreign, primarily German and American, technical specialists.

Despite the ostentatious successes, accelerated Industrialisation had a downside, not so presentable. Combined with an extremely inefficient bureaucratic management system, haste often led to industrial chaos on construction sites. The energetic Ordzhonikidze tried to react quickly to such problems. He did not sit in an office like Stalin, but was on constant business trips. He regularly personally travelled to inspect the sites where new industrial enterprises were being built, appearing especially often where there were serious problems.

Eyewitnesses recall that upon arriving at an industrial facility, Ordzhonikidze literally started running around the construction site. Impatience and overwhelming emotions made him wave his arms vigorously and he often shouted when talking to workers and engineers. He didn't need instructions and explanations, he easily acted on his own. With the help of rude personal intervention, he sometimes literally kicked the irresponsible manager in the ass to solve the most difficult problems. However, as a rule, after the departure of the formidable Ministry of Industry, the former seemingly solved problems came back.

The impatient Ordzhonikidze, following Stalin's instructions, constantly accelerated the deadlines for the commissioning of foreign equipment. Ordzhonikidze and his team were more concerned about the performance of the plan than compliance with the technology that affected product quality. Compliance with safety standards, on which the health and even the preservation of workers' lives depended, was also ignored by him.

For example, the first blast furnace of the Magnitogorsk steel mill was installed by Soviet workers under the guidance of American specialists in 2.5 months. It took them only 25 days to install the second blast furnace. The third blast furnace was already installed by Soviet workers in just 20 days without foreign help. After receiving information about such a success, Ordzhonikidze literally screamed with joy! The downside of disrupting technology in order to speed up construction was the frequent accidents and deaths of workers. However, as a rule, the Soviet investigative authorities did not indicate a violation of safety rules as the cause of such accidents, but 'wrecking' organised by numerous 'enemies of the people'.

At the cost of incredible efforts, human sacrifices, and temporary compromises, Ordzhonikidze was able to fulfil the basic quantitative indicators of Stalin's plan to militarise the Soviet economy by the mid-1930s. However, as noted above, in the pursuit of quantitative indicators, the quality of military equipment produced was completely ignored. The consequences of such machinations and total self-deception manifested themselves quickly enough. After just a few years of operation in the military, equipment produced with a violation of technology in a feverish hurry will be absolutely not combat capable. Thousands of tanks and planes, which recently formed the pride of Stalin's parades, will turn into piles of useless rusty scrap metal cluttering military warehouses and airfields. At the beginning of the terrible year 1937, categorically disagreeing with Stalin's assessment of the results of his work, the 'Father of Soviet Industrialisation' was driven to commit suicide.

The Hard Road to Failure

Thanks to Khalepsky's efforts, at the end of November 1930, the issue of the Christie tank was considered at a meeting of the Revolutionary Military Council (RVS). In his speech, Khalepsky said: 'Since the Christie tank does not meet the requirements of the System of Tank-Tractor-Automotive vehicles of the Red Army and is not in service, in order to avoid confusion, the army designation (index 'T') should not be assigned to it. It seems more reasonable to assign it the two-letter designation "ST" – high-speed tank, or "BT" – high-speed tank.'[2]

By the decision of RVS, the existence of the Christie tank was legalised, and the official designation BT was assigned to it. However, no steps were taken to organise the production of the tank again. Heated discussions between the Soviet military about which types of tanks were needed for the upgraded Red Army continued. Even in the group of radical 'Progressives', headed by Tukhachevsky, there was no consensus on this topical issue. The leader of the 'Cavalrymen', Voroshilov, also tried to express his opinion. The innovative design of the Christie tank caused particular controversy among the military. In the end, everyone involved in the discussion recognised that the American tank had no less weaknesses than advantages.

It is important to note that similar discussions about the types of tanks and tactics of their use were conducted not only in the USSR. The

Christie 'convertible tank' design had been widely discussed by tank engineers and militaries around the world. After the initial admiration, the effectiveness of the innovations applied by the American designer began to cause great doubts among experts from different countries.

In November 1930, the Red Army's military intelligence created a new reason for heated discussions about the Christie tank. At one of the meetings, the Head of the Red Army's Fourth Bureau (GRU – Military Intelligence), Jan Berzin, presented high-ranking Soviet military officials with classified information about the results of the Christie tank study by German tank engineers and the military. The Head of military intelligence reported:

> German engineers, having studied the data of the Christie tank and comparing them with the data of the tank they were designing, came to very unfavourable conclusions regarding the Christie design: a) the Christie tank has an engine of 400–420hp and gives a road speed of 100km/h, the German model with an engine of 150hp gives a speed of 80km/h; b) With four pairs of road wheels, the Christie tank has only one-axle drive – this, according to the Germans, is a design flaw; c) The Germans also consider the disadvantage of the Christie tank to be the need to remove and put on caterpillar track chains. It takes at least 30 minutes, which can play a bad role in a combat situation; d) The Germans consider the weight of the Christie tank (with armour, obviously, 12 tons) to be excessive.[3]

Similar unflattering information about the Christie tank's shortcomings were also received by Soviet military intelligence from England. British experts expressed doubts about the need to create a tank with such a technically complex and time-consuming 'convertible' drive. The only person who never doubted the need for an American tank for the Red Army was Innokenty Khalepsky. The Head of the UMM ignored doubts about the value of the Christie tank and stubbornly continued his hard struggle for the decision to start mass production of the American tank in the USSR. He never missed an opportunity to advertise and promote the Christie tank he bought.

The decision on BT production could be accelerated by the arrival of two tanks specially built by Christie for the USSR. However, financial problems and the next extravagant actions of Walter Christie led to the fact that the production dates of the two tanks purchased by the Soviets shifted by several months. As a result, instead of September, the tanks were ready only by mid-December 1930. However, their readiness was conditional, since the tanks did not have turrets and weapons. Finally, in early 1931, armoured hulls of two tanks arrived in the USSR.

Khalepsky hoped that the results of their tests, and most importantly the demonstration to the top leadership of the USSR, would help to speed up the solution of the problem of the production of American tanks. In addition, as a result of Stalin's decision to appoint a new Head of Armaments of the Red Army, Khalepsky gained an influential ally in the difficult work of promoting the Christie Convertible M1940 Medium Tank.

A Performance for Voroshilov

At the beginning of 1931, the issue of the production of the Christie tank was still awaiting a decision. Several months of heated discussions between the Soviet military about its advantages and disadvantages led to nothing. The American tanks that had arrived in the USSR stood motionless in the warehouse. The drawings of the American tank were also in a reliable German safe in the Tank Bureau. It turned out that the Christie tank had too many opponents. Most of the high-ranking Soviet military doubted its necessity and lobbied for other types of tanks. Soviet tank industry designers and managers did their best to prevent the organisation of the production of foreign tanks. They focused their efforts on refining and launching their tank projects into mass production. Supporters of the Soviet tank industry hoped that the hopeless situation would magically improve and then the Khalepsky foreign tanks could be forgotten. However, time passed, and the hopes of Soviet tank designers for the success of their projects did not come true.

In the end, everyone had to agree that something had to be done with the samples of foreign tanks bought for gold. The most reasonable solution was to test foreign tanks. Three Vickers 6-ton light tanks (Type A, armed with two .303in [7.71mm] water-cooled Vickers machine guns), commissioned by the Soviets in England were the first to be tested. The tests took place from 24 December 1930 to 5 January 1931 in a suburb of Moscow. Although the British tanks performed well in harsh winter conditions, the report for the military leadership focused on their shortcomings. Such biased reports by Soviet engineers could not help solve the problem of organising the production of foreign tanks.

At that moment, Khalepsky realised that the situation had reached an impasse again. It is impossible to solve the protracted problem of adopting foreign tanks during endless meetings of numerous commissions in stuffy offices. For success, new progressive methods are needed, like those used by the American Christie, who advertised his tank in the publications of the world yellow press. While travelling to America and communicating with Christie and his staff,

Khalepsky realised the importance of a high-quality presentation. The effectiveness of advertising techniques developed on the basis of American behavioural psychology (behaviourism) impressed the Stalinist agent. The Head of the UMM decided to use this experience to demonstrate the capabilities of the tanks he bought abroad. Of course, Khalepsky could not demonstrate secret tanks in the Soviet press, as Walter Christie did. However, he could well have organised a secret demonstration of the capabilities of foreign tanks to the military leadership of the Red Army. This is exactly the path he chose.

On the frosty morning of 8 January 1931, two British tanks were demonstrated to a high-ranking commission headed by the formal head of the armed forces of the Soviet Union, Kliment Voroshilov. Among the retinue of the People's Commissar were the ardent supporters of the technical re-equipment of the Red Army Mikhail Tukhachevsky and Ieronim Uborevich. The performance organised by Khalepsky caused great delight among the Soviet military leadership. The military were surprised by the modern appearance and mobility of the British tanks. Their previous negative experience of tank presentations was to watch the grotesquely clumsy T-18 (MS-1) light infantry tanks slowly creeping along or the T-12 medium tank constantly breaking down shrouded in blue smoke. Compact, high-speed British tanks confidently climbed small hills and crossed infantry trenches. Their progressive and at the same time simple design was a clear embodiment of modern tank technology. When the tanks came close to the commission after passing through all the obstacles, the Red Army command was delighted and surrounded the tanks like small children. Some of them even climbed on them and questioned the crew about the specifics of controlling British tanks. The result of the first presentation of Khalepsky's foreign tanks was stunning.

The next day, 9 January, after a short report to Stalin, Kliment Voroshilov issued an order: '. . . to finally resolve the issue of the expediency of organising the production of T-26 in the USSR!'[4] On 23 January 1931, at a meeting of the Revolutionary Military Council (RVS), it was decided to adopt the Vickers 6-ton Red Army light tank for service as soon as possible.[5]

Delighted with this effect, Khalepsky realised that it was necessary to hold a similar presentation of the American tank as soon as possible. However, in the case of the controversial Christie tank, getting the maximum effect from this event depended on the support of influential military men. Fortunately, when it came to the need to produce an American tank for the Red Army, the most influential Soviet soldier was on Khalepsky's side.

The Main Thing for a Tank's Success is Good Advertising!
March 14th 1931. Test Range in the near Moscow region.

In the early morning, luxury foreign limousines delivered all members of the Revolutionary Military Council (RVS) to the Test Range. The purpose of their visit was a new tank show, prepared by the dedicated Khalepsky. At the head of the delegation of high-ranking Soviet military was the Chairman of the RVS and the formal Head of the Red Army Kliment Voroshilov. The presentation of the new tank was attended by Yan Gamarnik,[6] Ieronim Uborevich, Mikhail Tukhachevsky, Innokenty Khalepsky, Robert Eideman, Iona Yakir,[7] Romuald Muklevich,[8] Pyotr Baranov,[9] Alexander Yegorov and Semyon Budyonny.[10]

The distinguished guests were greeted by Khalepsky, along with Head of the UMM Gromov and Engineer of the Tank Station Lavrentyev. After saluting and giving a brief report to Voroshilov, the Head of the UMM led the guests to the Christie tank. The main character of the presentation stood on a special platform, shining in the sun with fresh paint. A group of top Red Army commanders surrounded the tank and began to examine it with great interest.

It was really an unusual sight. A tank without a turret impressed high-ranking Soviet military with its unusual streamlined shape, inherited from a racing car. The photos of the American tank faintly reflected what they saw in front of them. The management of the Red Army saw the real Christie tank for the first time.

After a brief report by Khalepsky on the features of the Christie tank, the guests were seated on benches on a high wooden platform prepared for them. From it, it was possible to comfortably observe the movement of the tank. Khalepsky gave his men a hand signal, and the American tank began to perform a carefully rehearsed presentation programme. The performance for high-ranking military personnel was distinguished by a carefully developed script and professional direction. After demonstrating the phenomenal speed capabilities, the tank headed to a special area with anti-tank obstacles. There he had to demonstrate to the RVS members his abilities to overcome natural and artificial obstacles.

These capabilities were also quite impressive. The Christie tank easily climbed fairly steep ascents and smartly climbed out of small ravines. At high speed, it easily overcame six rows of wire obstacles and jumped over the 2m-wide anti-tank ditch by inertia. The presentation programme also included a separate presentation demonstrating the removal of tracks from the tank and the transition to a wheeled drive. The two men who made up the tank's crew completed this simple operation in just 30 minutes. After the end of the performance, the tank effectively stopped in front of a wooden platform with high-ranking guests. Senior military officers jumped up from their seats, approached the tank and began asking questions to the driver and tank commander. Then there was a heated discussion about the details of what he saw at the presentation. Judging by the vivid emotions on their faces, the tank made a very favourable impression on the RVS members. Before leaving, Voroshilov, pleased with the performance, personally shook hands with Khalepsky and his staff and warmly thanked them for their excellent work.

Further Christie tank screenings for high-ranking guests, represented by the military and members of the government of the USSR, continued for several days. The interest in the American tank was so great that there was a real stir when it was demonstrated at a secret training ground. Khalepsky's 'Tank Circus' gave one 'performance' after another with great success, almost without rest.

Where Will We Produce the Christie Tank?

Although the issue of the need for the production of the Christie tank was resolved, there were many organisational, bureaucratic, technical and production obstacles on the way to its practical implementation. Rightly considering that choosing a factory to produce an American tank is the most important aspect, Khalepsky has devoted all his efforts to solving this problem. Along the way, he expected to encounter strong resistance from the management of military factories. All the directors to whom he planned to assign the task of mass production of the Christie tank categorically refused. The reasons for this resistance were hidden in the new management structure of the Soviet military industry.

As noted above, fundamental changes in the structure and management of the Soviet military industry were initiated by Stalin in the end of the 1920s. This move by the 'Master' was a reaction to the failure in the design and production of tanks and other military equipment. By order of the VSNKh, at the end of 1929, a design bureau was created at each military factory.[11]

According to the Ordzhonikidze team's plan, new models of military equipment were to be developed in these design bureaus based on military factories. It was assumed that the designers would carry out their work in accordance with the requirements of the military and taking into account the production capabilities of a particular military factory. By taking such emergency measures, senior managers of the Soviet industry tried to copy the work of Western military firms, most of which worked according to this scheme. However, in the realities of the Soviet planned economy, copying Western management experience, as well as copying models of military equipment, led to completely unexpected results.

Design bureaus were part of the factory structure, which means that their work completely depended on the decisions of the factory management. The all-powerful directors of military factories, in collusion with the heads of design bureaus, began to actively defend their local interests. They actively lobbied at the level of the government of the USSR and VSNKh for the production of military equipment designs for the Red Army that were only beneficial to them. The motives of their actions were obvious. The models developed in the factory design bureau, taking into account local specifics, could be produced in large quantities on existing equipment using very low-skilled workers. Thus, the military factory could successfully execute the plan. For the successful implementation of the plan, the workers and engineers of military factories received large bonuses, and the directors received awards and privileges.

Since Stalin demanded that military factories perform only quantitative indicators, the quality and combat characteristics of the products produced did not matter to the directors of the factories. However, the main and only customer of military equipment in the USSR, the leadership of the Red Army, could not agree with the complete or partial disregard of their requirements in favour of the convenience of manufacturing a particular model of military equipment at a particular military factory. The military, outraged by this abnormal state of affairs, tried to actively interfere in the activities of the military industry. But, as a rule, they received an organised rebuff in response, both from the leadership of the military industry and from specific directors of military factories. It was expressed either in open conflicts between the military and managers, or in hidden intrigues and ignoring each other's demands.

The only instrument of direct influence of the Red Army leadership on the work of military factories was the Military Quality Control System for Weapons. Specially-trained Red Army officers (Military Representatives) officers had to test and accept each unit of military products from the manufacturer. It was only after going through this rigorous procedure that the factory received money from the state budget for its work. However, it was only in rare cases that Military Representatives managed to maintain their independence from the factory where they carried out quality control. Most often, factory directors simply corrupted Military Representatives.

Despite the negative test results, the bribed Military Representatives agreed to send low-quality or simply defective tanks and planes to the Red Army. Thus, at the beginning of the 1930s, in the Soviet military factories, fully funded from the state budget, began to form a semblance of mafia structures. Their influence increased so much that they tried to dictate their will to the government and even to the 'Master of the USSR' himself.

Stalin, who felt that the situation was getting out of his control, gave a direct order to NKVD to carry out large-scale purges in the leadership of the military industry. However, even with the help of the most brutal repressions of 1937–8, Stalin could not completely cope with the arbitrariness of the directors of military factories. In place of the murdered factory management, new people appeared, appointed personally by Stalin, with exactly the same motives as their predecessors. After some time, in pursuit of meeting the quantitative indicators of the plan, the new directors again began to supply defective military equipment to the Red Army. Thus, a kind of vicious circle formed in the Soviet military industry. Being a part of this vicious circle, Stalin used bloody repression for many years to struggle unsuccessfully with the consequences of his own orders.

Even more tension between the military and the directors of military factories was caused by Khalepsky's desire to impose the production of foreign tanks on them instead of implementing their own projects. At the first attempt to place an order for the production of the Christie tank, the director of the Yaroslavl Automobile Plant managed to avoid the production of an American tank. He convinced the leadership of VSNKh (Ministry of Industry of the Soviet Union) that the factory did not have the necessary equipment and skilled workers to produce such a technically complex vehicle. Factory No. 232 'Bolshevik' (Leningrad) became the next candidate for the role of the manufacturer of the American tank. T-18 (MS-1) light infantry tanks were already being produced there and they were preparing to produce the British Vickers 6-ton tank (T-26). The management of Red Army considered that the experience and available foreign equipment at this factory were sufficient for the production of the Christie tank. The factory director was categorically against this decision.

The last solution to the problem was to transfer the order for the production of tanks Christie to the Kharkov Locomotive Factory (KhPZ). KhPZ director Leonid Vladimirov[12] turned out to be less influential than his colleague from Leningrad. He was forced to submit to military pressure and began preparing the factory for the production of an American tank. However, he still had hope that the military would reconsider their decision again. During 1931, the state task for the production of tanks was changed three times to KhPZ. As noted above, the factory first planned to produce the TG tank, then the T-24, and finally, in May 1931, decided to mass-produce the Christie tank. Such a change of tasks caused serious dissatisfaction among the management, engineers of the design bureau and workers of the tank factory. This negative emotional background has increased the already big problems of organising the production of the BT tank at KhPZ.

Tanks for Tukhachevsky's 'Blitzkrieg'

On 11 June 1931, Tukhachevsky finally received the official status of the second man in the Red Army. Stalin simultaneously appointed him Deputy People's Commissar for Military and Navy Affairs, Deputy Chairman of the Revolutionary Military Council and Head of Armaments of the Red Army. Thus, the radical Tukhachevsky emerged as the absolute winner in a long-term struggle with cautious and moderate rivals for power in the Red Army. This happened because of the nature of absolute power in the USSR. The rise or fall of the highest officials of the state depended only on the degree of their usefulness to the cause of the realisation of the *idée fixe* of one person. By the early 1930s, Stalin had finally abandoned the defensive strategy and planned to use the future power of the growing Red Army to actively solve the problem of numerous external enemies in Europe. The ambitious proposals of the 'Red Aristocrat' for the total militarisation of the USSR and the transformation of the Red Army into the most powerful offensive military force surprisingly precisely coincided with the secret plans of the 'Master of the USSR'.

Tukhachevsky's defeated opponents were forced to accept the loss of high positions and some of their influence in the Red Army. Boris Shaposhnikov was removed from the post of Chief of Staff of the Red Army and, with a significant reduction in status, was moved to the position of Commander of the Volga Military District. Ieronim Uborevich, although he was not an opponent of Tukhachevsky, also lost all his high positions in the Red Army. He was appointed Commander of the Byelorussian Military District. In this remote province of the USSR, Uborevich was once again forced to deeply experience his under-valuation.

Only Voroshilov did not lose anything. He retained his positions and continued to be the official leader of the Red Army. However, the 'Cavalrymen' led by him were forced to take a back seat, resigned to the complete loss of their positions under the pressure of the Concept of Mechanisation of the Red Army.

The rise of the 'Red Militarist' and the departure of competitors resulted in a total revision of approaches to the rearmament of the Red Army. In particular, the System of Tank-Tractor-Automotive Vehicles of the Red Army (Armament System) and the Tank Programme underwent significant changes. Under the direct influence of Tukhachevsky, Stalin made important decisions that determined the development of the tank industry and Mechanised Troops Red Army until the end of the 1930s.

During the summer and autumn of 1931, all the medium tanks (TG, T-24 (T-12), light tanks (T-19, T-20) and tankettes (T-17 and T-23) projects lobbied for by former Tukhachevsky competitors were closed. Compromise projects based on combining parts of foreign tanks and experimental Soviet tanks (TMM-1 and TMM-2) were also cancelled. As a last resort, they were actively promoted by Soviet designers, offended by the total domination of foreign tanks. Thus, it was officially recognised that the period of long-term experiments on the creation of Soviet-designed tanks had ended in complete failure. From the summer of 1931, the Soviet tank industry had to produce only copies of American and British tanks. Moreover, making any significant changes to their design was strictly prohibited. Stalin demanded from the Soviet military industry the rapid organisation of mass production of cheap and reliable tanks of foreign design.

The quantitative indicators of the plans for the production of new military equipment were amazing! To implement the militaristic concept of the Tukhachevsky Soviet tank industry, it was necessary to produce tens of thousands of tanks in a few years! On 3 September 1931, at a meeting of the Revolutionary Military Council (RVS), it was planned to hastily create the most powerful Mechanised Troops[13] in the world. Based on this, only in 1932 it was planned to produce 10,000 tanks of all types at once![14]

However, Stalin had to wait much longer than he expected for the results of his ambitious plans. Even the plans that were later reduced several times could not be fulfilled. All hopes for the mass production of simple, technologically advanced and cheap foreign tanks using the existing equipment of Soviet automobile and tractor plants turned out to be a beautiful illusion.

The First Problems with BT Production

As noted above, Leonid Vladimirov, director of the Kharkov Locomotive Factory (KhPZ), had been trying for several months to get rid of the order for the production of the Christie tank. However, all his efforts were in vain. On 1 June 1931, the director of KhPZ received a state assignment from Khalepsky to prepare for mass production of the BT tank. According to this assignment, the Christie tank was to be produced without any design changes or improvements.

According to Khalepsky, if the tank produced was an exact replica of the American model, it would greatly simplify production and save endless improvements. But the most important reason for the ban on making changes was Khalepsky's desire to eliminate the very possibility of justifying production delays by design errors. The Head of the UMM really did not want a repeat of the situation with the failed plans for the release of the T-24 tank. Despite the seemingly complete dependence of the KhPZ leadership on Moscow, resistance to the implementation of the decision to produce the BT tank continued.

The degree of discontent can be judged by the fact that KhPZ Chief Engineer Ivan Bondarenko[15] openly called the Christie tank the brainchild of the 'wreckers'. In order to avoid sabotage by the factory management and somehow speed up the process of preparing for mass production of the tank, Khalepsky's deputies had to stay in Kharkov all the time. They personally controlled all the work at the factory. In fact, the external management of the military was introduced at KhPZ. However, as subsequent events showed, even this emergency measure proved ineffective.

In June 1931, Moscow planned to start manufacturing the first six examples of BT tanks. However, the start dates were constantly postponed for various reasons. Finally, on 20 September, Khalepsky issued state order No. 70900311 to the director of KhPZ Vladimirov. According to the requirements of the military, the factory was ordered to urgently produce six BT tank prototypes by 1 November 1931. The rush was due to the desire to demonstrate to the Soviet people and foreign journalists a clear proof of the growth of the Red Army's military power. Despite all the efforts of the factory's management and pressure from Moscow, by this time KhPZ had managed to produce only three tanks. Moreover, due to problems with the production of armour steel parts, the tanks had hulls and turrets made of ordinary steel. Two of the three tanks produced at KhPZ participated in the military parade on 7 November 1931 in Moscow. The third BT-2 could not reach the Stalin's parade on Red Square due to an engine fire. Later, engine fires, which caused BT tanks to burn out in just a few minutes, became a chronic problem for all tanks of this type.

Meanwhile, the problems with the production of the American tank at KhPZ were increasing every day. By November 1931, all the factory employees, from the director to the very last worker, were exhausted by fruitless attempts to establish mass production of the Christie tank.

The factory management tearfully asked Moscow again to rid them of the damned American tank. However, Ordzhonikidze and Khalepsky, striving to fulfil Stalin's orders, did not compromise on this issue.

On 6 December 1931, Afanasii Firsov, convicted of participating in the activities of the 'Wrecking Group', was appointed Head of the KhPZ Tank Bureau (T2K). His five-year imprisonment in a Gulag labour camp was 'mercifully' replaced by a new 'voluntary' job. This extraordinary man appeared in Kharkov in handcuffs under the escort of OGPU employees. The designer's wife and three children remained in Leningrad as hostages. Firsov was placed under the supervision of the OGPU in the KhPZ dormitory. Before his arrest during the wave of Stalinist repression in 1930, 'enemy of the people' Firsov worked as chief designer of the 'Russian Diesel' plant (Leningrad). This plant produced diesel engines for submarines. His entire guilt before the Bolsheviks was that he received his brilliant education abroad at the Hochschule (the University of Applied Sciences) in Mittweida (Germany) and the Eidgenössische Technische Hochschule (federal polytechnic school) in Zurich (Switzerland). Prior to his arrest, Firsov's main design activity was diesel engines. His high engineering qualifications allowed him to solve other complex tasks, in particular, to provide engineering support for the production and modernisation of the Christie tank.

Ordzhonikidze personally made the decision to appoint Firsov to the senior position of Head of the Tank Bureau KhPZ (T2K). He was well aware of the catastrophic situation with qualified engineers that arose after the wave of repression in 1928–30. Unlike Stalin, Ordzhonikidze treated former tsarist engineers calmly and made extensive use of their abilities and qualifications to develop the military industry. Time has shown that Stalin's 'younger brother' was not mistaken in his choice. Despite the constant haste caused by Stalin's fantastic plans, Firsov managed for a long time to find a risky compromise between the quantity and quality of BT tanks produced. However, Moscow's harsh dictates prevented him from implementing many experimental solutions that later became part of the T-34 design. In addition, all the activities of this talented designer took place against the background of permanent mental depression and even doom.

Being in prison for a year after his arrest in 1930, under constant threat of execution, had a detrimental effect on Firsov's character. His 'acquaintance' with Stalin's OGPU executioners left a dark mark on his later life. Fear and constant expectation of imminent arrest became an integral part of his life. The label 'enemy of the people' put on him by Stalin's executioners, and the corresponding aloof attitude on the part of his colleagues, broke Firsov's will. The precarious balance between the threat of punishment for incorrect design decisions and punishment for failure to fulfil the plan paralyzed his creative activity. Unfortunately, the gloomy forebodings that tormented Firsov for several years during his work at KhPZ were realised in 1937 in the most terrible way.

BT-2 to BT-5 Conversion

The unofficial status of a 'temporary tank' suggested the gradual transformation of the BT from a training tank into a combat tank. One of the ways to achieve this goal was to equip the tank with a new, more powerful gun. When defining the parameters of a fantastically ambitious Tank Programme for 1932, Stalin demanded that the military industry create and mass produce the 45mm tank gun. Guns of this calibre was supposed to arm a new type of Tanks to Destroy Tanks (TIT). The creation of such a tank was suggested by Tukhachevsky's Concept of Mechanisation of the Red Army.

According to the 1932 plans, 350 BT-2s produced at the beginning of the year were to be armed with individually-mounted 37mm B-3 guns and 7.62mm DT machine guns. Next, it was supposed to arm 1,650 45mm gun tanks produced during 1932. However, as already described above, all of Stalin's ambitious tank production plans in 1932 and subsequent years were completely defeated. Plans to create a prototype 45mm gun also did not escape failure.[16] As a result of these sad circumstances for Stalin, the dates of mass production of this gun and, accordingly, the armament of the BT with this gun were postponed to 1933.

In January 1932, the Tank Bureau KhPZ (T2K) began work on upgrading the BT-2 tank. The new version of the Christie tank was designed by Afanasii Firsov and his team of young designers. The first draft of the BT tank with a 45mm gun was prepared in the summer of 1932. To install the new enlarged turret, it was planned to extend the tank hull by 225mm in the fighting compartment area. This solution solved the problem of lack of space for the tank crew, which arose when installing a new turret with a 45mm gun. However, Khalepsky categorically rejected this option of upgrading the tank. He was terrified that the lengthening of the tank hull would lead to new delays in mass production and another failure of the Tank Programme next year. Admittedly, Khalepsky's concerns were well-founded.

Failures of planned production dates were a common occurrence in the Stalinist military industry. For example, in 1932, in addition to disrupting the production of the 45mm gun, attempts to develop composite armour and a diesel engine for the BT tank also ended in complete failure. Thus, due to these circumstances, Khalepsky decided to abandon risky experiments and adhere to a conservative approach when choosing options for upgrading the BT tank.

In the end, the new version of the BT tank, which was named BT-5, differed from the BT-2 only in the larger turret with a 45mm gun and minor tank hull modifications. On 1 January 1933, at a meeting in Moscow, Head of the Tank Bureau KhPZ (T2K) Afanasii Firsov assured the leadership of the UMM that 'these alterations do not cause technical difficulties and do not require special equipment'. This decision gave hope for the transition to the release of a new modification without stopping production, starting with the 601st BT tank. However, these hopes were not destined to come true.

At the meeting, it was also decided to switch to a new elliptical turret, designed to house a 45mm gun. In his optimistic report, Firsov did not foresee the serious problems that the armour manufacturer would have with the new enlarged turret. Contrary to expectations, the production of the new turret at Mariupol steel mill caused enormous difficulties. Again, as in the case of the BT-2, several tank hulls of the first tanks and fifty turrets for the BT-5 had to be made of ordinary steel. Thus, despite the optimistic plans, the first BT-5 tanks began to be produced only in March 1933. The decision to start production was made again under unprecedented pressure from Moscow. The director of the KhPZ begged to postpone the production of the BT-5 for a few more months, but Khalepsky and Ordzhonikidze were adamant.

The new tanks were planned to be shown to Stalin at the May 1933 parade. As a result of this 'political' decision, Military Representatives had to carefully select several dozen of the least defective tanks to be sent to Stalin for display. In the parade on 1 May 1933, fifty BT-5s demonstrated to the Soviet leadership and foreign guests the growing firepower of Soviet tanks. Fortunately for the KhPZ leadership, none of the tanks caught fire while passing in front of Lenin's Mausoleum. After the parade, the BT-5s were returned to the factory for repairs and the elimination of many identified defects.

After successfully showing the new modification of the BT tank to Stalin, Ordzhonikidze focused all the efforts of the military industry on fulfilling the tank production plan in 1933. In order to implement this Moscow directive, KhPZ's management once again had to completely neglect the quality of its products. However, exactly the same tendency to ignore quality was observed in all Soviet military factories producing tanks, aircraft and other sophisticated military equipment. This chronic problem of the military industry was no secret to the top military and government leadership of the USSR. On 16 July 1933, Voroshilov, in a report prepared for Stalin 'About the System of Tank-Tractor-Automotive vehicles of the Red Army for the Second Five-Year Plan', wrote:

> The product quality also lags behind specifications: a) armour has a large defect in production (45–50%, and hence its shortcomings and poor quality); b) there is a defects in individual parts and individual assemblies of tank mechanisms for reasons of poor production. Sloppy assembly of armoured fighting vehicles, especially the engine and gearbox; c) heavy dependence on imported ball bearings and electrical equipment of the tanks.[17]

In 1933, the Kharkov Locomotive Factory (KhPZ) produced 1,005 BT tanks, including 784 BT-5s. Thus, for the first time, the factory fulfilled the annual production plan! However, these productivity miracles were the result of a significant reduction in the quantitative indicators of the plan. Compared to the insane plan of 1932, the annual production of tanks was halved.[18] As a result, 1,884 BT-5 tanks were produced in two years of mass production.

However, the quality of the BT-5 tanks produced in an incredible hurry differed little from the BT-2. Once again, the combat effectiveness of the tank was sacrificed to the quantitative performance of the production plan. Moreover, contrary to the reassuring statements of Soviet and Russian historians, there was no further improvement in quality during the production of the BT tank during the 1930s. For example, in early 1934, Khalepsky's deputy Gustav Bokis reported to Voroshilov the results of an assessment of the quality of tanks produced in 1933:

> . . . According to an analysis of the production of BT tanks, despite the implementation of the programme, the quality of tanks cannot be considered good. . . . Rejected in the test run of tanks: March – 5%, April – 5%, May – 8%, June – 6%, July – 5%, August – 10%, September – 11%, October – 9%, November – 33%, December – 41%.[19] This indicates a decrease in attention to quality, especially in assembly.[20]

Plants which supplied BT production parts to KhPZ followed the same vicious pattern. Rubber idler tyres and road wheels, manufactured at the Red Triangle Plant, were of extremely low quality. Steel for the production of caterpillar tracks from the Kramatorsk steel mill did not meet the stated specifications. The armour produced by the Mariupol steel mill had a permanent defect in the form of through-thickness cracks. The only exceptions in this series of defective parts were the electrical equipment of the tank and ball bearings purchased in Germany. There had never been any problems with the quality of German components. However, their excellent quality did not play a big role in the total amount of endless defects. It was the quality problem, which had been unsuccessfully tried to solve for many years, that eventually led to a series of tragic events at KhPZ.

'Shock Wheel-and-Track Long-Range Tank (TDD)'

The history of the new BT modification began with Stalin's desire to equip this tank with a 76mm gun. This idea came from the 'Master of the USSR' in 1931, influenced by the new Head of Armaments of the Red Army. Tukhachevsky initially proposed installing a gun of exactly this calibre on the Christie tank. However, it was not possible to immediately implement Stalin's will.

On 28 January 1933, a contract was signed between UMM and KhPZ for the design and manufacture of a BT tank with a 76.2mm gun and a new hull nose design. According to the adjusted plans, the first 100 BT tanks with 76mm gun were to appear at the end of 1933. However, due to the busy work of Tank Bureau KhPZ (T2K) engineers correcting the shortcomings of the BT-5 and other projects, work on a new modification of the tank was very slow. It was not until early December 1933 that Firsov submitted to the UMM a draft BT tank with a 76mm gun. The project was generally approved by the military. The only objection was the idea of installing a separate machine gun next to the tank driver. However, further work on the new tank project slowed down again.

In late 1933 and early 1934, the main part of Firsov's designers were busy painfully trying to install the BD-2 diesel engine and the Mikulin M-17 aircraft engine in the BT tank. These works had the highest priority. After Stalin forbade the purchase of American engines, and its Soviet counterpart, the M-5 engine, was discontinued, the BT tank turned out to be not only without a 76mm gun, but also without an engine. The problem with the diesel engine was 'solved' very quickly. Contrary to the optimistic attitude of the engineers, the prototype suffered from flaws, which required several more years of hard work to eliminate. Since there were no prospects for mass production of the diesel engine, it was soon necessary to abandon its installation on the tank. All the forces of Firsov Design Bureau were thrown to work with an upgraded version of the Mikulin M-17 aircraft engine (a licensed copy of the German BMW IV engine). However, the implementation of this option also did not go according to plan. Aircraft Engine Plant No. 26 (Rybinsk, Yaroslavl region) disrupted the delivery of the first sample of the modified Mikulin M-17 engine to KhPZ. As a result of this delay, work on the creation of a new modification of the tank had to be stopped for several months. Only on 27 November 1933 did the long-awaited engine enter Experimental Workshop T20. Work on installing the engine in the tank, as usual, dragged on for a long time.

Ultimately, due to all these reasons, a set of drawings for the manufacture of a prototype wheel-and-track tank, named BT-7, was ready only in March 1934. In early April, Moscow approved specifications for the BT tank with a new engine. The cautious Khalepsky again emphasised that the installation of the M-17 engine should have been carried out without changing the basic dimensions of the engine compartment of the tank. Problems with the development of the 76mm gun forced Khalepsky to approve a backup version of the BT-7 tank with the installation of a 45mm gun. Moscow set August 1934 as the production date for the prototype.

By 1 May 1934, the first prototype of the BT-7 tank with the Mikulin M-17T engine was manufactured at Experimental Workshop T20. A 76.2mm KT-28 gun[21] and a ball-mounted 7.62mm DT machine gun were installed on the tank in an elliptical turret with a sloping roof. Due to problems with the supply of armour, the hull and turret were made of ordinary steel. The second prototype of the BT-7 tank with a 45mm gun was manufactured by 7 November 1934. During factory testing of BT-7 prototypes, an increased engine coolant temperature (105°C) was noted. To fix the problem, KhPZ engineers had to make significant changes to the engine's cooling system.

Since all the production dates were missed, work on the refinement and testing of prototypes took place in a great hurry. Repeated factory testing of the modified prototype BT-7 tank took place on 13 June 1934. They were recognised as successful. However, an investigation by the NKVD commission conducted two years after the 'successful' testing showed the opposite results. It turned out that special testing of the long-term effect of the Mikulin M-17T engine with a larger torque than the previous engine on gearbox, taken unchanged from the previous BT-5 modification, was not carried out at all.[22]

Meanwhile, in 1934, problems with the development of the 76mm M1933 PS-3 gun were still unresolved. In May 1933, this tank gun was adopted and even tried to be mass-produced at the gun factory in Leningrad. But all the 'serial' 76mm M1933 PS-3 tank guns turned out to be unusable and invariably returned to the gun factory to eliminate endless defects. Refinement and improvement of this gun continued until 1938, but no satisfactory result was achieved.[23] Thus, the plans to install the M1933 PS-3 gun on the BT-7 had to be abandoned.

As a temporary option, they decided to install the standard turret and armament of the BT-5 tank on the BT-7. In November 1934, KhPZ was given an order to manufacture 300 tanks with the 45mm gun in 1935. In December of the same year, the order was increased to 650 tanks. Production of the BT-7 with a 45mm gun was planned to begin on 1 January 1935. However, these optimistic plans could not be realised again. Almost all suppliers of components did not fulfil their obligations on time. Mariupol steel mill was unable to produce the armour parts on time. Aircraft Engine Plant No. 26 was also unable to upgrade the M-17T engines in time. In addition, it turned out that the production drawings of the tank needed significant improvements. For these reasons, the actual production of the BT-7 tank at KhPZ was started only in the autumn of 1935. In 1935, the factory naturally failed to meet the production plan and instead of the planned 650 BT-7s produced only 500.

In the midst of these attempts to speed up BT production, Stalin's close servants persuaded him to adjust the fantastic plans adopted in 1932. As a result of this decision, on 19 June 1935, an important document was adopted in Moscow, which stated: 'To leave the BT tank in service. Refuse to replace it with the PT-1 tank.[24] It is necessary to produce a BT tanks with an M-17T engine installed on it in 1935. Since 1936, a diesel engine manufactured at the Kharkov Locomotive Factory has been installed on the BT tank.'[25]

Stalin's decision saved the KhPZ management from enormous problems with the proposed development of the production of the new wheel-and-track PT-1 amphibious tank. In these favourable conditions, there was a reasonable hope for a gradual increase in the production of the BT-7. Despite the missing of planned targets in 1935, the KhPZ leadership sent an optimistic report to Moscow on the steady growth of tank production. In response to the good news, Stalin showered the factory's management with awards and prizes. Even 'enemy of the people' Afanasii Firsov was awarded the Order of the Red Banner in 1935!

The production of BT-7 tanks continued successfully until June 1936. In the first half of 1936, KhPZ was even able to fulfil its tank production plan. However, this idyll soon ended. At the beginning of the summer, a terrible scandal broke out, which turned into a real disaster for KhPZ! The reason for the loud complaints of the military were the discovered defects of the new wheel-and-track tank. By this time, 687 ill-fated BT-7 tanks had been transferred to the Red Army. For many of the creators of this tank, it was the last project in their lives.

The BT-7 Becomes the 'Wreckers' Tank'

Over several years of operation, Red Army tank units became accustomed to the BT's defects. The constant repair and maintenance of these tanks became routine for the military. However, against this very unfavourable background, the BT-7 tank performed much worse than its predecessors. When used in the military, it managed to surpass all records for the rate of loss of combat capability. In addition to the usual defects for all tanks of this type, the BT-7 had a new problem, which appeared after the installation of the new M-17T engine.

Despite the similar engine power to the M-5 engine, the higher (by 58 per cent!) torque of the M-17T engine turned out to be a real disaster. The new engine quickly disabled the gearbox of the tank, designed for the much smaller torque of the M-5 engine. As a result of this fatal defect, the BT-7 tank could only travel 500km or less before the gearbox was completely destroyed. Outraged by this result, the military made reasonable claims about the design of the new tank to the leadership of KhPZ. The engineers at Tank Bureau KhPZ (T2K) were aware of the significantly higher torque of the M-17T engine compared to the M-5. Possible problems with the gearbox when using the new engine and possible engineering solutions to these problems were discussed by the designers. As a result, they decided that some strengthening of the gearwheels in the gearbox would be enough to ensure its reliable operation in conjunction with the M-17T engine. However, even this dubious gearbox upgrade was not implemented in reality.

As noted above, the BT-7 prototype was created and tested under acute time constraints. All the attention of the designers was focused on solving the problem of engine overheating. Factory tests of the BT-7 prototype did not reveal the destruction of gearbox parts after running over 2,300km. Thus, this significant defect was not detected during the tests of the prototype tank.

In the report of the Investigative Commission of the NKVD dated 14 July 1936, it was noted: 'during the design of the BT-7 gearbox, as well as other mechanisms, no changes were made, no strength calculations were performed, but the old drawings of the BT-5 tank were redrawn, and serial production was started according to these drawings'.[26] Such irresponsibility on the part of KhPZ's managers and designers, who were aware of the problem and initiated mass production of defective tanks, is surprising. However, in the 1930s this was a common practice in all military factories of the USSR.

After sending the reports of the Investigative Commission of the NKVD to Stalin, a terrible scandal broke out! If the problem with the BT-7 tank had manifested itself in the middle of the calm 1935, this situation would not have caused such disastrous consequences for KhPZ. Everyone had already become accustomed to Stalin's rather mild reaction when various serious defects were found in the design of the BT tank. For example, the chronic problem of destroying rubber tyres of the road wheels existed without any special consequences until the end of BT production. At the same time, the destruction of the rubber tyres also caused the tank to lose its ability to move after 500km, and therefore its combat capability. Most likely, in 1935, the reaction to the destruction of gearbox parts would have been limited to another batch of curses from tank mechanics and volumes of angry bureaucratic correspondence between KhPZ and Red Army military units. However, unfortunately for the factory management, the defect was discovered in the middle of 1936. By this time, Stalin's blissful mood, and the correspondingly calm attitude of NKVD investigators towards such incidents, had changed to the exact opposite. On Stalin's instructions, another wave of hunting for 'wreckers' and 'spies' began in the USSR.

The first reaction of the KhPZ leadership to the huge flow of complaints from the military was complete disregard. Everyone at the factory had long been accustomed to constant complaints about the quality of tanks. KhPZ managers and designers considered these military complaints to be petty quibbles. Moreover, they tried, not without success, to shift responsibility for the occurrence of fatal breakdowns onto the tankmen themselves, referring to the improper operation of tanks in the army.

When the BT-7 scandal broke out with renewed vigour, KhPZ representatives decided that the best defence was an offensive. They began to accuse the military of hooliganism, hinting at the popular jumping with BT tanks. The designers of KhPZ argued that it was precisely such massive cases of hooliganism that disabled gearboxes, which, of course, was not designed for such an extreme load. In particular, for example, they cited Captain Evgeny Kulchicky's jump in a BT-7 tank captured on film in 1936. Accelerating to a top speed of 72km per hour and using a specially built springboard, the tank flew 42m in free flight and landed safely in the lake. Kulchicky believed that in this way it was possible to overcome trenches, anti-tank ditches, and small ravines. The calculations showed that the BT-7 tank, without modifications, could, under certain conditions, 'jump' a distance of 37m. This 'the ability to fly' of the tank was quite enough to overcome small but deep rivers.

However, this time the arguments of KhPZ managers and engineers were not accepted by Moscow. Even the factory's subsequent admission of guilt over the gearbox's defects did not change Stalin's position. Contrary to usual practice, Moscow unexpectedly took extraordinary measures. In the spring of 1936, the Military Quality Control System for Weapons stopped accepting ready-made tanks into Red Army units. As a result, the production of BT-7 tanks at KhPZ was completely halted for several months. In the USSR, only one person could stop the operation of a strategic tank factory for such a long time! The search for those responsible for the fatal gearbox defect had begun.

In July 1936, by order of Stalin, a special Investigative Commission of the NKVD was sent to KhPZ. It did not take long for the members of the Investigative Commission to determine the causes of the problems with the combat capability of the BT-7 tanks. The Head of the Commission, a high-ranking officer of the NKVD special department, stated in his report: 'The materials available to us indicate that the situation at the factory is not accidental, but is the result of criminal negligence committed during the design of the BT-7 tank. No less criminal negligence was committed when testing the tank before launching into mass production.'[27]

The conclusion of the Investigative Commission left no doubt about the guilt of the management and engineers of KhPZ. After such a document was sent to Stalin, their fate was sealed. The management and engineers of KhPZ could only wait for their arrest and execution. However, the plant's director Ivan Bondarenko, his deputies and the Head of the Tank Bureau KhPZ (T2K) Afanasii Firsov hoped that they would be able to avoid the worst. They remembered well that they had previously been given the opportunity to fix the problem to one degree or another. This has already happened many times in a critical situation that developed with the combat capability of the first hundreds of BT-2 and BT-5 production tanks. They had reason to hope for Stalin's forgiveness and the usual censure for serious defects in the BT-7 design.

Without waiting for Moscow's response, the KhPZ management habitually tried to hastily fix the BT-7's gearbox problems. The T2K designers quickly presented a draft of an upgraded and even new gearbox for the BT-7 tank. However, after the appearance of damning articles in Soviet newspapers, in which BT-7 began to be called the 'Wreckers' Tank', it became clear to the leadership of KhPZ that disaster could not be avoided. NKVD investigators initiated thorough inspections of Tank Bureau KhPZ (T2K) engineers. According to the results of the inspections, the 'terrible' truth was discovered! It turned out that the vast majority of KhPZ designers at the Design Bureau were not members of the Communist Party, including all heads of the departments. In the run-up to the bloody 1937, this blatant 'violation' meant truly terrible consequences.

Thus, by the end of the autumn of 1936, an extremely tense psychological situation had developed at KhPZ. The first victim of the BT-7 scandal was naturally 'enemy of the people' Afanasii Firsov. He was suspended from work, arrested after a while, and shot in mid-1937.

Stalin's Main Fear Returns

The period of relative remission of Stalin's severe emotional disorder lasted less than two years, namely from the beginning of 1934 to the end of 1935. The good mood that dominated during this short period was soon replaced by gloomy anxiety and fear for his own life. The culmination of Stalin's euphoria caused by the imaginary successes of Industrialisation was the pompous 'Parade of Steel and Motors' on 9 February 1934. However, these relatively quiet two years turned out to be the period of the real heyday of the activities of Soviet military equipment designers. This was largely due to the fact that many talented designers and managers were released from prison. Aircraft designer Dmitry Grigorovich and 'King of Fighters' Nikolai Polikarpov,[28] Afanasii Firsov, creator of the BT-5 and BT-7 and Nikolai Astrov, creator of the amphibious tank, were released. Their receipt of almost unlimited resources for the implementation of their projects resulted in a rapid increase in the number of models of new military equipment.

Thanks to Stalin's favour, the advanced ideas of the 'Red Militarist' for the rearmament of the Red Army were implemented at a rapid pace. The 'golden age' in the technical re-equipment of the Red Army began. In a short time, all the main types of tanks and aircraft were created. It was the models of this period that determined the technical level of the Red Army until the beginning of the 1940s. Massive purchases of Western equipment and machine tools allowed the directors of military factories to organise mass production of new tanks and aircraft. In pursuit of fulfilling the quantitative indicators of the plan, they simply turned a blind eye to design defects and monstrous defects in the production of military equipment. The huge number of tanks and aircraft supplied to the Red Army created a beautiful illusion of the success of the Soviet industry and the growth of the military power of the USSR. Against this positive background, the repression subsided. For a short period, the OGPU executioners stopped searching for 'wreckers' in military factories.

Pleased with these achievements, Stalin lavished rewards and privileges on his servants. In February 1933, Tukhachevsky was awarded the Order of Lenin. A year later, in February 1934, the 'Red Aristocrat' received the status of a high-ranking Bolshevik functionary (candidate for membership of the Central Committee of the Communist Party of the Soviet Union).

The first significant blow to Stalin's relative emotional stability and, as a result, to the tendency to weaken repression was dealt on 1 December 1934. On this day, as a result of a domestic conflict, the formal head of the Leningrad Bolshevik party organisation, and in fact Stalin's viceroy in Leningrad, Sergei Kirov, was killed. This man was part of the 'Red Lord's' closest circle, with the unofficial status of a 'younger brother'. However, unlike the rude and straightforward Ordzhonikidze, whom the 'Master of the USSR' respected for his energy and desperate courage, the sociable and charming Kirov was Stalin's beloved 'younger brother'. He oversaw Leningrad, one of the main centres of the military industry of the USSR. To control the important centres of the huge 'Red Empire' Stalin needed super-loyal people like Sergei Kirov.

The murder of Kirov caused a serious emotional shock to Stalin. He urgently left for Leningrad to personally lead the investigation of the crime. However, due to the banal motives of the murder, no investigation was necessary. Kirov's killer did not try to escape. After a failed suicide attempt, he was detained by NKVD officers. However, Stalin stubbornly refused to believe that his closest servant had been killed by a pathologically jealous husband who suspected Kirov of having an affair with his wife. He immediately rejected the NKVD leadership's version of a domestic homicide. Stalin demanded that his servants look for the perpetrators of this crime among the mythical opposition in the Bolshevik Party. In the end, under pressure from Stalin, the Kirov murder trial was completely fabricated. The banal domestic dispute was presented to the Soviet public as the assassination of a top-level party functionary organised by a group of oppositionists, committed solely for reasons of political struggle. During the short trial, several suspects were sentenced to death. Just an hour after the verdict was announced, they were shot. Except for the real killer of Kirov, none of the executed people had anything to do with the crime.

The main role in the fabrication of the materials of the court case was played by party functionary Nikolai Yezhov. Before Kirov's murder, he served as a high-ranking controller and 'cleaner' of the Bolshevik Party. He arrived in Leningrad with the 'Master' to monitor the progress of the investigation. At Stalin's behest, Yezhov effectively suspended the NKVD investigators and conducted his own 'investigation' in parallel with the official one. The evidence fabricated under his leadership was later handed over to the court. It was this false information that became the basis for the court's conviction. Stalin was completely satisfied with Yezhov's 'work'. Soon, the new servant became his closest favourite, endowed with virtually unlimited power.

After the 'investigation' of Kirov's murder, the devoted servant continued his sinister work of exposing the mythical enemies of the 'Master of the USSR'. In early 1935, Yezhov fabricated a new political case. This time, the 'criminals' were accused of creating the Anti-Soviet Organization and planning an attempt on Stalin's life. The unofficial status of Stalin's saviour obtained by Yezhov as a result of this 'investigation' finally strengthened the close relationship between the two dangerous psychopaths. Yezhov captivated the leader of the 'Red Empire' with complete immorality and boundless fanaticism in an effort to fulfil the will of the 'Master'. In turn, Stalin, after each successful 'investigation', gave Yezhov new powers to search for internal enemies. Two years later, this man played a sinister role in a new wave of unprecedented bloody repression unleashed on Stalin's orders.

'Provide active military assistance to Republican Spain!'
The second significant event that significantly affected the deterioration of Stalin's emotional state was the Spanish Civil War. It started unexpectedly in the summer of 1936. The high-ranking military mutiny that preceded the war emotionally shook the 'Master of the USSR' no less than the murder of Kirov. The pro-communist government of Spain turned out to be completely unprepared for the mutiny of its own military and reacted rather sluggishly and ineffectively to rapidly developing events.

Stalin not only closely followed the events of the Spanish Civil War, but also tried to actively interfere in its bloody events. He did not limit himself to bloodthirsty advice, which amounted to the immediate execution of all the 'enemies' of the Spanish people, who, in his opinion, made up a significant part of the Spanish population. Stalin decided to send military aid to the left republican government.

On 29 September 1936, at a meeting of the Political Bureau of the Central Committee of the Communist Party of the Soviet Union, Stalin decided to conduct the so-called Special Operation 'X', – 'Provide active military assistance to Republican Spain'.[29] The essence of the Special Operation was to send military advisers and specialists to help create a regular army. They were supposed to help the Republicans in training their military and developing operational war plans. Among the candidates proposed by Voroshilov, Stalin personally selected several young junior and middle-level commanders: pilots, tankmen, artillerymen and sailors.

With complete secrecy, planes[30] and tanks were sent to Spain, which were accompanied by Soviet military specialists. Military equipment, weapons, ammunition and other military materials were supplied with generous payment from the Republican government. Stalin deliberately sent mostly new models of military equipment to Spain. In addition to material benefits, the Bolshevik leader hoped to conduct combat tests of new equipment. For this reason, Soviet specialists returning to the USSR wrote detailed reports on how the new military equipment proved itself. Based on these reports, production tanks and aircraft were being upgraded, and new models were being developed.

In addition to wanting to test new models of military equipment in combat conditions, Stalin wanted to use new tanks and aircraft to propagandise the military might of the USSR. He wanted to show the whole world that Soviet weapons were superior to the samples of German and Italian armoured fighting vehicles and aircraft supplied to General Francisco Franco. These propaganda demonstrations brought Stalin mixed results. For example, during the first stage of the war, the advantage of the latest Soviet military vehicles was undeniable. Soviet tanks and aircraft looked especially contrasting against the background of outdated models of military equipment supplied by Germany and Italy. However, when the first versions of the Bf 109 fighter appeared in the skies of Spain, and there were a sufficient number of anti-tank guns on the ground, the situation changed to the exact opposite.

On 12 October 1936, the first fifty T-26 tanks arrived on the ship *Komsomol*. The low technical reliability of Soviet military equipment forced the Soviets to send a large number of spare parts to Spain after the planes and tanks. Engines, gearboxes, starters, and other parts and mechanisms were delivered on ships along with tanks. Soviet repairmen and a mobile repair shops were sent to Spain for operational repairs.

The T-26 tanks performed quite poorly in Spain. The weak armour and insufficient mobility of the tank due to the low engine power and the weakness of the suspension significantly limited its combat effectiveness. The only significant advantage of the T-26 was the 45mm gun, which effectively proved itself against Italian and German tankettes armed with machine guns. The failure of the T-26 tanks forced Stalin to decide to send to Spain the most combat-ready, in the opinion of the Soviet military, the BT-5 tank. However, the advantages of the BT-5 over the T-26 were only in the wheel-and-track running gear. Both tanks were protected by thin armour, unable to withstand heavy machine-gun fire. The design of their turrets was unified, and the main armament was a 45mm gun.

On 24 July 1937, the Spanish transport ship *Kabo San Augustin* sailed from Sevastopol with fifty BT-5 tanks on board. However, the first experience of combat use of these Stalin's 'wonder tanks' dispelled the propaganda myth about their extraordinary combat capability. In total, between 1936 and 1938, Stalin sent 281 T-26s and 50 BT-5s to participate in the Spanish Civil War.

'Comrade Ordzhonikidze, what's the matter here? J. Stalin'

In the second half of 1936, Yezhov, on Stalin's instructions, fabricated a new case against the 'Opposition'. This time, seventeen high-ranking government officials were arrested. As a result of the 'investigation', the arrested were presented with another set of absurd accusations, which were a bizarre mixture of Stalin's pathological fears. However, this time Georgy Pyatakov, Ordzhonikidze's deputy and main favourite, was among the main defendants. Stalin's closest servants interpreted the arrest of the Deputy People's Commissar of Heavy Industry as a blow to Ordzhonikidze's authority and an expression of the 'Master's' dissatisfaction with his methods of managing military industry.

Before Pyatakov's arrest, Ordzhonikidze managed to restrain Stalin's attempts to explain the problems in the military industry by mass 'wrecking' in the People's Commissariat of Heavy Industry (Ministry). However, the desire of the 'younger brother' to protect his subordinates led to numerous quarrels with the 'Master'. Increasingly, Ordzhonikidze's conversations with Stalin turned into verbal altercations. In these situations, they switched from Russian to their native Georgian under the influence of emotion. Moreover, both 'brothers' did not even restrain themselves from using obscene language against each other. As 1937 approached, the conflict between the 'brothers' deepened, and the situation for military industry managers became increasingly tense. On 8 December 1936, by order of Stalin, the management structures of the military industry were reorganised. From the People's Commissariat of Heavy Industry (Ministry), the People's Commissariat of the Defence Industry was singled out. As a result of Stalin's decisions, Ordzhonikidze was stripped of most of his power over the military factories.

In January 1937, at a public trial, Pyatakov, who had been specially 'trained' in the torture basements of the NKVD, spoke in detail about numerous cases of 'wrecking' allegedly organised by him and his 'accomplices' at military industry enterprises. All the facts he pointed out about the disruption of plans for the construction of military factories and the production of military products, major accidents with human casualties, and the stoppage of mass production of military equipment due to monstrous defects actually took place throughout the 1930s. However, the real culprit of all these incidents was not the mythical members of the Trotskyist Anti-Soviet Organization, but Stalin himself, who demanded that the People's Commissariat of Heavy Industry (Ministry) immediately carry out his fantastic plans for the militarisation of the USSR.

The Yezhov-directed 'court' handed down the death sentence expected by all to high-ranking government officials accused of disloyalty to Stalin. In addition to Pyatakov, twelve other people were found guilty and sentenced to death. After the trial, Stalin, who had long been dissatisfied with the work of his 'younger brother', publicly accused Ordzhonikidze of political 'blindness'. He demanded that he hand over to the NKVD all the 'wreckers' who had infiltrated high positions in the military industry. Pyatakov's 'confessions' published in all Soviet newspapers broke Ordzhonikidze's resistance. Under the combined pressure of Stalin and Yezhov, the recklessly brave 'younger brother' showed weakness unusual to him before and admitted his 'mistakes'.

Immediately after that, endless inspections, searches, and arrests began at the People's Commissariat of Heavy Industry. Ordzhonikidze's favourites, suspected of disloyalty by Stalin, were killed. Ordzhonikidze's henchmen in the Caucasus also came under the close attention of NKVD executioners. The situation escalated Ordzhonikidze's conflict with Stalin's new favourite Lavrentiy Beria. The psychologically crushed 'younger brother' tearfully complained to Stalin about the attacks from Beria and hinted at suicide. In February 1937, Stalin, sensing Ordzhonikidze's weakness, gave his 'brother' one last chance to 'correct himself'. He suggested that he prepare a report on 'wrecking' at military factories.[31]

On 18 February 1937, Gregory Ordzhonikidze, exhausted by the choice between loyalty to his 'elder brother' and the inevitable betrayal of his favourites, shot himself. Stalin ordered the concealment of the true cause of death and gave his 'younger brother' a lavish state funeral. From that day on, managers and designers of military enterprises lost their last protection from the executioners of Yezhov. The massacre carried out by NKVD employees in the People's Commissariat of Heavy Industry and in the leadership of military enterprises lasted from mid-1937 to the end of 1938. Very few experienced managers survived the extermination carried out by Stalin and Yezhov.

The 'Bloody Dwarf' Goes Wild

On 26 September 1936, Stalin appointed Nikolai Yezhov to the post of People's Commissar for Internal Affairs (Minister, Head of NKVD). On the eve of a new war, the 'Master' decided to finally resolve the issue of 'wreckers' and 'enemies of the people'. Sensing the smell of a lot of blood, Yezhov spent more than ten months preparing NKVD structures subordinate to him for unprecedented arrests and shootings.

In 1937, the darkest years of Stalin's bloody rule began. The initiator and main leader of the repressions was Stalin, and Yezhov was a faithful executor of his will. The cynicism and ruthlessness of the new leader of Stalin's Great Terror machine exceeded all possible limits. At the initiative of the new Head of NKVD, a real pipeline of arrests and murders was created. Stalin's approved execution plans for 'enemies of the people' were sent to every region of the USSR. The flywheel of repression was spinning at a terrifying rate. NKVD agents worked almost without interruption. The specially created shooting grounds system, which were designed for the mass destruction of 'enemies of the people', was overcrowded. The country was completely paralyzed by fear.

Not a single Soviet citizen was immune from arrest, torture, and execution. Many residents of large cities waited in horror for nightfall and listened anxiously. They expected a loud knock on the door and the invasion of NKVD officers with revolvers in their hands. Those who fell into the bloody hands of Stalin's executioners disappeared without a trace, and virtually none of them returned to their homes. It was only after the collapse of the USSR that many Russian citizens learned the details of the tragic fate of their disappeared relatives. In 1937 and the first half of 1938, more than a million people were arrested, and 681,692 people were shot! According to Russian historians, during Yezhov's time in power, NKVD executioners shot one 'enemy of the people' every minute. This terrible period in the history of the USSR lasted almost until the end of 1938. In the West, it was called the Great Terror, and in the USSR, by the name of Stalin's terrible executioner, the Yezhovschina ('period of Yezhov').

Yezhov quickly earned a reputation for ruthlessly destroying the 'enemies' of the Stalinist regime, and became one of the most powerful Soviet leaders. In addition to his pronounced sadistic tendencies and alcoholism, Yezhov stood out in the circle of Stalin's closest servants with a very small stature, only 151cm (4ftt 11½in). Against the background of the new NKVD head, even the short Stalin seemed like a giant. Due to the combination of short stature and monstrous bloodlust, Yezhov received the nickname 'The Bloody Dwarf'. During the Great Terror, launched on Stalin's orders in 1937, he fully confirmed his terrible nickname. Yezhov spared no one, making no exceptions even for the employees of the punitive department headed by him.

There is no doubt that these two psychopaths were reinforcing each other's bloodthirsty symptoms. In 1937–8, Nikolai Yezhov visited Stalin's Kremlin office almost 290 times and spent a total of more than 850 hours with him. It was a kind of record for the duration of communication between two bloody murderers. At that time, only the formal head of the Soviet government, Vyacheslav Molotov, spent more time in Stalin's cabinet.

Chapter 4

THE T-34 IS A BY-PRODUCT OF STALIN'S REPRESSIONS

Stalin's Last Meeting with Tukhachevsky

May 13th 1937. Moscow. Kremlin. Stalin's reception room.

At 17:05, Tukhachevsky entered Stalin's giant office. The reason for talking to the 'Red Lord' was very unpleasant, but the 'Red Marshal'[1] was hoping for another victory in the protracted power struggle in the Red Army.

On 10 May, Tukhachevsky received Voroshilov's order to resign from his post as Deputy People's Commissar for Defence of the Soviet Union. The same order appointed him to the post of commander of the provincial Volga Military District. This unexpected news caused the astute and experienced Tukhachevsky complete bewilderment. He fell into an uncharacteristic state of indecision.

In the middle of 1937, the 'Red Marshal' was at the peak of his military career. Having held the key position of Deputy People's Commissar of Defence for Armaments for several years, Tukhachevsky, enjoying Stalin's full confidence, took important steps to reorganise the Red Army. Based on German military ideas, he developed a Soviet doctrine of 'blitzkrieg', based on the massive use of tanks and aircraft. The high-speed wheel-and-track tank type had become a key component of the 'Red Militarist's' offensive warfare doctrine. Based on this strategy, Tukhachevsky determined the structure of the Tank-Automotive Troops Red Army, the nomenclature of Tank Armaments and the key military specifications of the main and special types of tanks. However, in his opinion, this work was far from over. The Red Army still had a huge number of problems to solve.

Tukhachevsky was concerned about the quality of the tanks produced and the lack of Soviet commanders' ability to effectively interact infantry, tanks and aircraft. The large-scale military exercise of the summer and autumn of 1936 confirmed his fears. The boastful propaganda effect of manoeuvres hid the terrible quality of Soviet military equipment and the lack of competence of the commanders. An urgent solution to these problems required Tukhachevsky to obtain new, emergency powers in the Red Army. On the eve of the major war in Europe, the 'Red Marshal' was ready to assume full power in the Red Army.

Stalin warned him several times about possible drastic changes in the People's Commissariat of Defence of the Soviet Union. Moreover, he repeatedly discussed with Tukhachevsky plans for a possible replacement of the incompetent Voroshilov with a more talented military commander. He even vaguely hinted that Tukhachevsky might become the new People's Commissar for Defence. Stalin also often spoke about the danger of internal enemies and 'spies' who had insidiously infiltrated the Soviet government system. Stalin was particularly concerned about the 'spies' who had infiltrated the leadership of the Red Army. In his opinion, preparations for a future major war in Europe required a brutal crackdown on numerous internal enemies.

Stalin's fears resulted in a new wave of repression. Tukhachevsky knew about the arrest by NKVD agents of his closest subordinates: Komkors (Colonel General) Vitaliy Primakov[2] and Vitovt Putna.[3] He understood that as a former tsarist officer, he was also at risk of being arrested by the NKVD and was prepared for such a development. In the Stalinist Empire of 1937, the highest military officials had only two paths: arrest and painful death in NKVD dungeons or a dizzying career. Both options seemed equally likely to Tukhachevsky. The 'Red Marshal' always carried personal weapons with him, and a heavy Mauser C96, given to him during the Russian Civil War, was hidden in his belongings. However, instead of the expected arrest or promotion, he received a demotion and transfer to another position.

What took place on 10 May did not fit into Tukhachevsky's ideas about the possible future. The new appointment meant not only a significant demotion, but also a departure from Moscow to provincial Kuibyshev. That's where the commander of the Volga Military District was supposed to be. The 'Red Marshal' understood that Stalin was behind Voroshilov's decision, and only he could provide the necessary explanations for the mystery of the new appointment. Alarmed and puzzled by such an unexpected change in his life, Tukhachevsky began to reflect on the reasons for Stalin's decision. He was alarmed by the coldness in communication during the last personal meetings in 1936 and the lack of invitations to talks with Stalin in 1937.[4] Finally, Tukhachevsky put aside his gloomy doubts and decided to personally talk to the author of the mysterious outcome. After several unsuccessful attempts, he managed to reach Stalin. The latter assured him in a gentle voice that everything was fine and invited him to meet in his Kremlin office.

However, on the evening of 13 May, an unpleasant surprise awaited the Red Marshal in Stalin's office. Unlike the meeting described above in 1931, Stalin was not alone. His closest servants were present in the office: Chairman of the Council of People's Commissars of the Soviet Union (formal Head of the Government of the USSR) Vyacheslav Molotov, People's Commissar of Railways of the Soviet Union (Minister of Transport) Lazar Kaganovich, People's Commissar for Defence of the Soviet Union (Minister of War) Kliment Voroshilov and People's Commissar for Internal Affairs (Chief Executioner) Nikolai Yezhov. They were here for a reason, and when Tukhachevsky appeared, none of them were going to leave. They were acting as witnesses to an important conversation. In addition, the 'Master' needed loyal servants there for other purposes. Being extremely cowardly and pathologically suspicious, Stalin constantly feared for his life. Although it was impossible to bring a weapon into the office, the physically powerful Tukhachevsky could easily kill the puny Stalin with his bare hands. It would not be easy to do this with so many devoted servants. However, the 'Red Marshal' did not plan to kill Stalin at all. He did not prepare a military plot to seize power in the USSR, which Stalin later accused him of. Tukhachevsky hoped for a frank conversation with the owner of the office without witnesses, but this proved impossible.

Despite some hidden tension, Stalin was friendly. He invited Tukhachevsky to sit at a large table next to the nearest servants. The Master of the office, following his habit, began to walk along the other side of the long table, smoking his favourite pipe. In response to the silent question in Tukhachevsky's eyes, Stalin asked the 'Red Marshal' in a gentle voice to fulfil his request to leave Moscow for Kuibyshev and personally restore order to the troops of the Volga Military District. According to Stalin, the former Commander, now removed from command of the troops, neglected his duties for a long time and led the military units into complete chaos. He again motivated his request with the approach of a major war in Europe. At the end of his explanation, Stalin came closer and, dropping to a whisper, hinted to Tukhachevsky 'in a friendly way' that NKVD agents had arrested one of his lady friends, who had turned out to be a foreign spy. Further, he also quietly said that it would be better for everyone if Tukhachevsky left Moscow for a while. This explanation by the 'Master' of the piquant reasons for the decision instantly relieved the tension. Despite his official marriage, the 'Red Marshal' was not an exemplary family man. He took Stalin's hint of romantic relationships with several women quite adequately.

Somewhat reassured by the arguments given by the 'Master', Tukhachevsky addressed his official questions and reported on the poor state of affairs with the new types of weapons of the Red Army. He hinted to Stalin that his prolonged absence from Moscow could negatively affect the timing of Red Army receiving new models of military equipment. Those present in the office, including Stalin, listened to the report of the 'Red Marshal' in silence. Contrary to usual practice, no one asked him any questions. At the end of the conversation, Stalin, smiling amiably and dropping back to a whisper, mysteriously promised that Tukhachevsky would return to Moscow very soon and be able to continue his business. The cunningly deceived 'Red Marshal' left the office 45 minutes after the start of the conversation.[5]

Tukhachevsky's fate was decided by the 'Master of the USSR' long before this last meeting. Stalin needed this conversation only to confuse the 'Red Marshal' and deprive him of the will to resist. Just as earlier in the power struggle with Trotsky, Stalin disarmed his opponent not with intelligence, but with complete immorality. Tukhachevsky, who believed the treacherous Stalin, was literally and figuratively disarmed.

On 24 May 1937, in Kuibyshev, he meekly allowed himself to be arrested by NKVD officers. Moreover, Stalin kept his word about Tukhachevsky's imminent return to Moscow. That day, the former 'Red Marshal' in a torn uniform with his marshal's stars torn off was escorted to Moscow. He was placed in a cold and dark prison cell in the basement of the NKVD building on Lubyanka. 'The Bloody Dwarf' Yezhov personally interrogated Tukhachevsky. Two days later, bleeding profusely from a bruised face, the former 'Red Marshal' signed a 'confession' about the preparation of an assassination attempt on Stalin. In the last month of his life, while the 'investigation' lasted, Tukhachevsky experienced incredible humiliation and monstrous torture in the basement of the Lubyanka.

The Crushing Defeat of the Red Army Leadership
Seven senior officers of the Red Army (the 'Tukhachevsky Group') were arrested in connection with the preparation of the Tukhachevsky military coup. Among them was Ieronim Uborevich. NKVD

investigators did not have any real evidence of the guilt of those arrested, except for personal confessions obtained under torture. The case was completely fabricated by Yezhov and reflected all the intellectual primitiveness and complete immorality of this pathological man.

The 'Master' was rightly afraid that the unexpected arrest and accusation of 'espionage' of high-ranking military men with great authority would raise questions from the Red Army commanders. A week before the trial of the 'Tukhachevsky Group', Stalin decided to explain the reasons for his decision to the top officials of the Red Army. For these purposes, a special expanded meeting of the Military Council of the Red Army[6] was held on 2 June 1937. In addition to 80 members of the Military Council, 116 invited high-ranking Red Army officers participated in the meeting. The 'Master' himself spoke to the army elite explaining the government's position on the arrested military personnel from the 'Tukhachevsky Group'. He was not at all going to prove the guilt of the arrested military men, which was beyond doubt from his point of view. Stalin only wanted to share with the terrified Red Army commanders some details of the 'military conspiracy' he had exposed. At the beginning of his speech, he emphasised the similarity of the accusations against 'Tukhachevsky's Group' with the circumstances of the military coup in Spain a year earlier. Soviet propaganda attributed the success of General Franco's coup to German spies infiltrating the Spanish armed forces.[7] In his pompous speech, the 'Master' informed the Soviet military:

> I think these people are puppets and puppets in the hands of the Reichswehr. The Reichswehr wants us to have a military coup, and these gentlemen have taken over the preparation of the military coup. The Reichswehr wants these gentlemen to systematically deliver military secrets to them, and these gentlemen to communicate military secrets to them. The Reichswehr wants the existing government to be taken down, slain, and they took up the case, but failed. The Reichswehr wanted everything to be ready in case of war, so that the army would switch to wrecking so that the army would not be ready for defence, the Reichswehr wanted this, and they were preparing this case. This is the agency, the governing core of the military-political conspiracy in the USSR, consisting of ten exemplary spies and three exemplary provocateur-spies.
>
> This is the agency of the German Reichswehr. That's the main thing. Therefore, this conspiracy has not so much an internal basis as external conditions, not so much an internal policy in our country as the policy of the German Reichswehr. They wanted to make a second Spain out of the USSR, and they found and recruited the spies who were preparing the military coup. Here is the situation. Tukhachevsky especially, who

played the role of a noble man, incapable of petty villainy, a well-mannered man. We considered him to be a good military man, and I considered him to be a good military man. I asked him: how could you bring the division's strength to 7,000 people within 3 months? What's it? A layman, not a military man. What is a division of 7 thousand people? It's either a division without artillery, or it's a division with artillery without cover. It's not a division at all, it's a disgrace. How can there be such a division? I asked Tukhachevsky: How can you, a man who calls himself an expert in this business, insist that the number of division be reduced to 7,000 people and at the same time demand that we have 60–40 howitzers and 20 guns in our division, so that we have so many tanks, so much artillery, so many mortars? There's one of two things here – either you have to take all this military equipment to hell and leave only soldiers, or you just have to leave the equipment. He tells me, 'Comrade Stalin, this is a passion'. This is not a passion, this is wrecking, carried out on orders from the German Reichswehr.[8]

Frightened by the repressions, the Soviet military had to listen to such delusional statements by Stalin for more than an hour. He tried with all his might, in his usual rude manner, to discredit the most qualified Soviet military leaders, who had great authority in the Red Army. Stalin especially tried to denigrate Marshal Tukhachevsky. Further, as usual, he tried to remove his personal responsibility for the appointment to senior positions in the Red Army of 'spies' and 'wreckers'. Stalin paradoxically explained his personnel blindness by the unprecedented successes of his domestic policy: 'But the general situation, the growth of our forces, the progressive growth in the Red Army, in the country, and in the party, have dulled our sense of political vigilance and somewhat weakened our visual acuity.'[9]

Despite all the primitiveness and even absurdity of Stalin's arguments, he managed to get the full approval of the senior Red Army officers present at the Military Council. Voroshilov's long-term personnel 'work' has borne fruit. Stalinist slander fell like 'seeds' of lies on fertile ground. Most of the Soviet commanders were semi-literate and incompetent, but absolutely loyal to Stalin. Thanks to Voroshilov's total propaganda, the new generation of Soviet military no longer doubted that Stalin, not Trotsky, was the real creator of the Red Army. The 'Tukhachevsky Group',[10] accused by Stalin of betrayal, had the last surviving Trotsky henchmen. These people possessed undoubted high military competency. The destruction of the most intelligent and educated senior officers who formed the core of the progressive part of the Red Army shifted the balance towards the incompetent and frankly stupid 'Cavalrymen'. However, even unconditional acceptance of any of Stalin's most terrible crimes did not save the semi-literate 'elite' of the Red Army from death. Over the next three years, most of the high-ranking military officers present at the Military Council on 2 June 1937, would be shot on Stalin's orders.

A Special Military Tribunal was created for the trial of the 'Tukhachevsky Group', consisting of eight senior military personnel,[11] including Tukhachevsky's long-time enemy Shaposhnikov. On 9 June 1937, the first meeting of the closed Special Military Tribunal was held. NKVD investigators have not provided any evidence of the guilt of the 'conspirators'. As noted above, the prosecution was based entirely on personal confessions extracted under torture from the defendants. As noted above, the prosecution was based entirely on personal confessions extracted under torture from the defendants. The completely fabricated court case was a ridiculous mix of allegations about the defendants' ties to Leon Trotsky, who lived abroad, previously convicted representatives of the 'opposition' to Stalin in the Communist Party, and the German General Staff. NKVD investigators claimed that the 'Tukhachevsky Group' was preparing an armed 'seizure' of Kremlin with the aim of assassinating Stalin and arresting the leaders of the Communist Party of the Soviet Union and the Soviet government. The judges were not at all confused by the absurdity of the charges. On 11 June 1937, all the accused senior Red Army officers from the 'Tukhachevsky's Group' were found guilty by the Special Military Tribunal and executed.

However, contrary to Stalin's false promises, this trial was not the end at all, but only the beginning of large-scale repression in the Red Army. According to various sources, up to 40,000 Soviet officers were shot during the Great Terror. Despite the scale of the repression, the evil Stalin found the strength and time for petty revenge. He tried to erase any memory of his former favourite Tukhachevsky. In accordance with order No.0114 of the People's Commissar for Defence Voroshilov dated 26 July 1937, the position of Head of Armaments of the Red Army was abolished, and the Technical Staff was transferred to other departments of the Red Army.[12] Any official mention of Tukhachevsky in the USSR was strictly forbidden until Stalin's death in 1953.

The Rise and Fall of Khalepsky

In parallel with Tukhachevsky's rise, Innokenty Khalepsky's career was developing just as successfully. The role of Stalin's favourite, who was in a hurry to please his 'Master' at any cost, brought the Head of the UMM noticeable dividends. On 22 February 1933, Stalin awarded Khalepsky the Order of Lenin 'for his great and fruitful work on the technical equipment of the Red Army'. Furthermore, the number of attentions of the 'Master' to the Head of the UMM continued to grow.

As noted above, after the pompous 'Parade of Steel and Motors' on 9 February 1934, Stalin's servants received a whole 'shower' of awards, titles and privileges. Stalin, who believed in the power of his newly created Mechanised Troops, ordered the renaming of a number of military administrative structures for propaganda purposes. On 22 November 1934, the Red Army's Mechanisation and Motorisation Directorate (UMM) was transformed into the Tank-Automotive Directorate of the Red Army (ABTU). At the same time, Khalepsky retained his position as the Head of this Directorate.

On 4 June 1935, Voroshilov presented him with a personal Ford car (GAZ-A) 'for his energetic work'. On 20 November 1935, Khalepsky received from Stalin the military rank of Komandarm 2nd rank (General of the Army). On 9 April 1936, he was appointed to the position of Head of Armaments of the Red Army, which was vacated by Tukhachevsky, who received a higher position. In his new position, Khalepsky's powers have significantly expanded. In addition to tanks, he gained control over the development of Red Army aviation and artillery. His short tenure as Head of Armaments of the Red Army was the culmination of Khalepsky's military career and the beginning of his fall into oblivion.

In early 1937, Stalin convinced himself that there was a conspiracy in the leadership of the Red Army. After that, he began to carefully and consistently remove the alleged 'conspirators' from all significant positions.

In April 1937, Khalepsky was removed from his position as Head of Armaments of the Red Army and appointed Deputy People's Commissar for Communications. In October 1937, he unexpectedly became People's Commissar for Communications. Khalepsky held this post for only three months. From the outside, such appointments looked like obvious promotions. However, in reality it was only part of Stalin's game of neutralising foreign 'spies' and 'wreckers' in the Red Army.

In August 1937, Khalepsky was removed from his position as People's Commissar for Communications and transferred to the lower position of Special Representative for Communications of the Council of People's Commissars of the Soviet Union. Further, the situation developed in accordance with the typical scenario of Yezhov for the neutralisation of Stalin's 'enemies'. In November 1937, during a business trip, Khalepsky was arrested in a train carriage by NKVD officers. During the 'investigation' he was accused of having links with the 'Tukhachevsky Group' and of participating in a 'military-political conspiracy' against Stalin.

In the NKVD dungeons, the most sophisticated tortures were applied to him. Unable to withstand the monstrous treatment, Khalepsky not only confessed to all the 'crimes', but also gave extensive false testimony against more than a hundred of his colleagues and acquaintances. These false statements became the basis for a new wave of arrests and accusations against the leadership of the Red Army. Few could withstand the torture of NKVD executioners. Many of the arrested high-ranking 'wreckers' and foreign 'spies' also gave false testimony against Khalepsky.

On 29 July 1938, the court found Innokenty Khalepsky guilty of participating in the 'Military-Fascist Conspiracy' in the Red Army. He was sentenced to death by firing squad and executed on the same day. So sadly ended the life of another devoted servant of Stalin, who trusted his 'Master' too much. The name Khalepsky was forgotten for several decades. However, the key decisions he made had a direct or indirect impact on the development of Soviet Tank-Automotive Troops for many more years.

Chain of Arrests and Executions at KhPZ

As noted above, in the spring of 1936, after the BT-7 tank gearbox scandal, the Investigative Commission of the NKVD arrived at the Kharkov Locomotive Factory (KhPZ). The investigators immediately launched an investigation into the discovered fact of 'wrecking'. Afanasii Firsov, the Head of the KhPZ (T2K) Tank Bureau, was suspended from his post during the investigation. He was transferred to a secondary position of senior designer. Instead of Firsov Tank Bureau, his deputy Nikolai Kucherenko temporarily headed it. However, the problems for KhPZ engineers did not end there.

The Investigative Commission of the NKVD found defects not only in the gearbox, but also in many other important tank components. All BT-7 design documents were seized for verification by NKVD investigators. All T2K employees were repeatedly interrogated. The answers of the young engineers to the provocative questions of the NKVD investigators were carefully recorded and put in thick cardboard file folders. Seeing the sinister gleam in the eyes of the NKVD investigators, all the members of the Tank Bureau understood that they were in big trouble. The materials collected by the investigators were enough to send each of them to Gulag for many years. Under these conditions, it was not only about saving their engineering team, but also their lives. The young designers were distracted from their gloomy thoughts only by the intense work that consumed all their time.

In the second half of 1936, T2K was working hard to eliminate defects in the gearbox of the BT-7 tank. To solve the problem, four gearbox variants were developed (two gearboxes were designed by Aleksander Morozov and two gearboxes by Vladimir Doroshenko). Based on the test results, a three-speed gearbox designed by Morozov was selected for mass production. At that moment, it seemed to the factory management that the problem had been solved. The upgraded gearbox began to be installed on the BT-7. On 15 July 1936, production of BT-7 tanks resumed with new reinforced gearboxes.

Gradually, another problem began to be solved. A huge number of immobilised tanks stationed in the grounds of the KhPZ finally got the opportunity to move. These tanks with defective gearboxes did not have time to be sent to the Red Army before the scandal arose and were found to be defective. They stood on the factory grounds for almost half a year, causing sadness and sometimes despair among the workers and engineers of KhPZ. After the defects were eliminated, the staff of the Military Quality Control System for Weapons began to gradually accept refurbished tanks for shipment to the troops. However, the investigation into the 'wrecking' in the design of the BT-7 tank continued.

The factory management sincerely did not understand the reasons for the claims made against them. As with any other Soviet military factory, KhPZ ignored product quality issues. Military Representatives (employees of the Tank-Automotive Directorate of the Red Army (ABTU), who accepted defective tanks for the Red Army received bonuses and privileges from the factory management for their 'blindness'. The current situation suited not only the directors of tank factories, but also the managers of the military industry in Moscow. High quantitative indicators created the illusion of a constant 'growth in production' of modern military products. The dissatisfaction of the Red Army technical services was compensated by special teams of factory technicians. They regularly went on business trips to military units and helped the military repair non-combat capable tanks. This vicious practice of ignoring defects continued for many years.

In 1936, the established order was suddenly disrupted by meticulous NKVD investigators. As noted above, Stalin's mood changed, and he opened another season of hunting for 'wreckers'. In the reports that Yezhov regularly sent to Stalin in 1937, design errors caused by haste and lack of competence turned into terrible crimes against the defence of the USSR. The collusion of the KhPZ leadership and the corrupt military, familiar to all military factories, had now been classified by NKVD investigators as criminal activity by organised 'wrecking groups'. The chain of arrests and executions that followed Stalin's change of mood affected virtually all KhPZ employees, from the director to the lowest unskilled worker.

The Appearance of 'Ardent'

Firsov's removal from office deprived Tank Bureau KhPZ (T2K) of its leader. Although he actually continued to work, everyone understood that his time at the Kharkov Locomotive Factory (KhPZ)[13] was ending. In addition, NKVD had complaints against other T2K employees, half of whom were under the age of 30. Contrary to expectations, Moscow was not sure of the loyalty of the young designers from Kharkov. In their opinion, the long stay of engineers under the influence of 'Wrecker' Firsov had had its 'harmful' results.

Deeper checks of the formal signs of loyalty of young designers had begun. As noted above, to the dismay of the members of the Investigative Commission of NKVD, there were only six Bolsheviks in T2K, and the rest of the young engineers had fairly free political views. Such a small number of Stalin's direct agents seemed to NKVD investigators to be a consequence of a strategic mistake in appointing a former tsarist engineer as Head of T2K.

The only way to remedy the situation was to significantly increase the number of Bolsheviks in the Tank Bureau and appoint a new leader, also a member of the Bolshevik Party. NKVD's total suspicion of 'wrecking' precluded the appointment of someone from Factory No. 183 (Kharkov) to this important position. However, the close-knit team of factory employees and management was strongly opposed to the appointment of a Moscow protege to this position. Kharkov believed that in an attempt to limit or even deprive the plant of independence, Moscow was imposing its own people on them. The city, which was the capital of Ukraine until 24 June 1934, maintained a certain degree of autonomy. The KhPZ leadership had extensive experience in successfully repelling Moscow's attacks and was not going to give up. It was possible to solve this delicate problem only at the highest level.

The main boss of military industry Ordzhonikidze was required to make a compromise personnel decision that could satisfy all interested parties. In order to defend against the attacks of NKVD, it was necessary to find a person with the image of an exemplary Bolshevik, who could not be suspected of 'wrecking' in any way. However, in order to gain the trust of the young but knowledgeable T2K engineers, it required an equally flawlessly competent engineer who could replace Firsov. Fortunately, the wise Ordzhonikidze had a man who satisfied such contradictory demands.

On 25 December 1936, Mikhail Koshkin was appointed head of T2K. From the point of view of the Soviet leadership, Mikhail Koshkin, a 38-year-old loyal Bolshevik and former party functionary, was sent to fulfil an important state task. He had to save the dying Tank Bureau of one of the leading tank factories of the USSR from the destructive influence of the 'wreckers'.

Factory management and designers greeted Mikhail Koshkin, who arrived from Leningrad, very cautiously. In many ways, the story of five years ago was repeated. At the end of 1931, in a similar crisis situation caused by the failure of mass production of the BT-2 tank, Afanasii Firsov was sent from Leningrad to the factory. Brilliantly educated and intellectually gifted, 'wrecker' Firsov was able to overcome the initial barrier of alienation and quickly became his own man in KhPZ. Already in 1932, no one questioned the authority of the Head of the Tank Bureau KhPZ (T2K). Throughout Firsov's tenure at Kharkov, the young designers who made up the majority of the Tank Bureau team perceived him as a kind and wise teacher and father.

Firsov's new accusations of 'wrecking' turned out to be a strong moral blow for the young T2K engineers. They were acutely aware of the monstrous injustice of the Soviet regime. The inability to protest against the actions of NKVD, and hence Stalin, provoked the transfer of negative emotions to a protégé of this unfair authorities who came from Leningrad. To avoid conflict, Koshkin needed to show wonders of communicative competence. Fortunately for the T2K team, in addition to his engineering skills, he had outstanding communication and leadership skills.

Koshkin Becomes Firsov's Successor

For future success as Head of the KhPZ (T2K) Tank Bureau, the first impression made on young engineers was of great importance. On the first day after arriving at the factory, the energetic Koshkin asked Firsov to take him through all the rooms that were related to the development and improvement of the BT tank. He wanted to introduce himself to the staff of the Tank Bureau and Experimental Tank Workshop as soon as possible.

The news of the arrival of a new Moscow protégé spread quickly across the factory. All the employees who met him during the tour of the work premises watched the new boss with great attention. They tried to make the first estimates and forecasts of its potential. In turn, Koshkin tried to make a good impression on his new subordinates.

His appearance and manner of communication looked very natural in the eyes of the employees of Factory No. 183 (Kharkov). Koshkin was modestly dressed and carried himself democratically. He shook hands with all the employees he met and asked for a long time about current affairs.

Over the next few days, Koshkin not only got to know each of the designers, but also learned all the details of their work. The former Head of the Tank Bureau Firsov was by his side all this time. Feeling that his time was running out, he treated the person who came to take his place very kindly. Firsov understood that the future of the design bureau he created depended on the relationship between the new boss and the young engineers. He had no doubt that Koshkin possessed sufficient design competencies and organisational abilities to continue work on improving the BT-7.

Thus, thanks to Firsov's assistance, the employees of the Tank Bureau and the workers of the Experimental Tank Workshop had a very favourable impression of Koshkin. The outgoing Head of the Tank Bureau literally transferred to him some of his influence and authority in the team of young engineers and factory workers. Since January 1937, Koshkin had fully mastered Factory No. 183 and moved around the factory without accompanying anyone. By the way, T2K was soon renamed Design Bureau '190'.

Koshkin managed to get rid of the image of Moscow's henchman very quickly. The new Head of the Design Bureau '190' quickly began to be perceived at the factory as its own. Koshkin continued to study the specifics of the BT-7 tank modernisation and the operation of the factory as a whole. Within a week of his arrival, the new Head knew all aspects of the work of Design Bureau '190' and was ready for full-time work in his position. However, Koshkin did not stop at the first success. The new Head of the Design Bureau '190' used a democratic style of communication with everyone he came into contact with: designers, technologists, workers and Representatives of the Military Quality Control System for Weapons. He sincerely shared their problems, difficulties and worries and, if possible, tried to help them solve them. Koshkin was principled, hardworking and honest. Thanks to these personal qualities, his authority at the factory quickly became very high. Factory No. 183 employee Alexander Zabaykin recalls: 'Koshkin was easy to handle and businesslike. He didn't like verbosity. As a designer, he quickly got into the essence of the design, assessing its reliability, adaptability, and mass production capabilities. He listened attentively to us technologists, and if our comments were well-founded, he immediately used them. Everyone respected and loved him.'[14]

However, the main quality that defined Koshkin's entire mental appearance was his extraordinary energy and determination. He had been working towards his goal for many years. Koshkin dreamed of running his own design bureau, and now, finally, his dream had come true. He understood that the year would be very difficult for the design bureau he headed and for Factory No. 183 in general. Koshkin was not intimidated by the alarming challenges of the beginning of 1937. He was eager for a new activity. It was for this quality of character that Koshkin soon received the nickname 'Ardent' from the designers of the Design Bureau '190' and the workers of the Experimental Tank Workshop.

Biography of Koshkin

Mikhail Koshkin had a typical biography of a representative of the new generation of Soviet designers. He was born on 21 November 1898 in the village of Brynchagi, Yaroslavl Governorate, in a very poor peasant family. The village had only 300 inhabitants. The nearest major city, Yaroslavl, was 145km away. The only opportunity for Mikhail to receive primary education was the parochial school located in the village. After his father's death in an accident, the 8-year-old eldest son was forced to work in parallel with his studies. Despite the help of the eldest son, it was difficult for the mother to support two young children. The only way out of a difficult situation was to send Mikhail to work in Moscow.

The huge city was located about 200km from the village of Brynchagi. In 1909, after graduating from parochial school, 11-year-old Mikhail began his adult life away from home. Due to low pay and lack of rights, child labour was widespread in tsarist Russia. As a rule, children were used in low-skilled jobs, and the pay was barely enough to keep them from starving to death. Mikhail was lucky to get to a confectionery factory in Moscow, where, at least, he was not in danger of starvation. The job was hard, but the factory owner treated him well. The future creator of the T-34 tank worked very hard. Young Mikhail sent most of the money he earned to his mother in the village. In such difficult conditions, he proved himself to be a purposeful and strong-willed person. During his eight years working in Moscow confectionery factories, he worked his way up from a baker's assistant to a qualified operator of a mechanical candy packaging machine. Apparently, it was while working on primitive automata that Mikhail first showed interest in technology. This growing interest in complex technical structures later determined his professional path.

Production of 'Sormovo's freaks' at Krasnoye Sormovo Shipyard No. 112.

Vladimir Lenin delivers a speech on Red Square, Moscow, 7 November 1918.

'Parade of Steel and Motors', 9 February 1934.

Top commanders of the Red Army in 1927.

Captured Renault FT-17 tank at the Krasnoye Sormovo Locomotive Factory in Nizhny Novgorod.

British Mark V tanks in service with the Red Army.

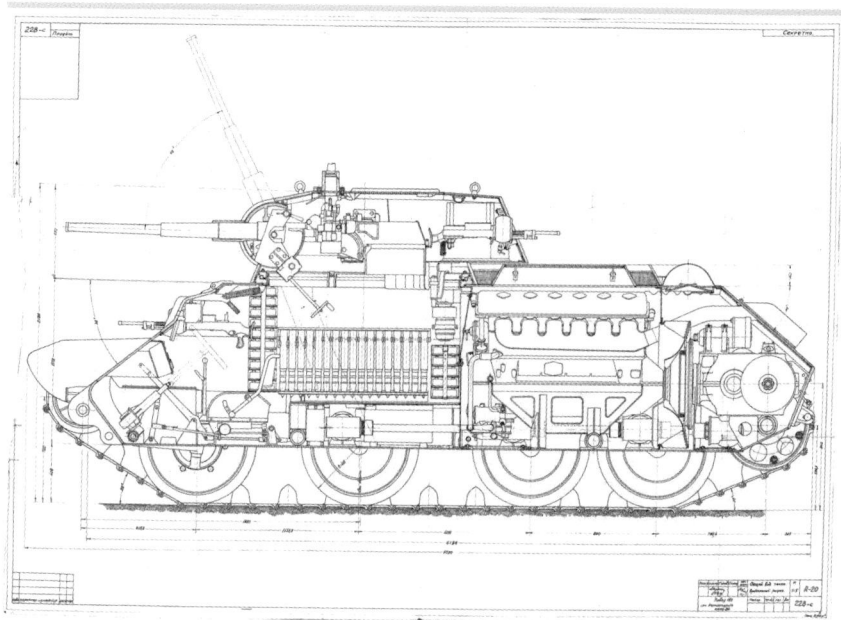

A prototype drawing of the BT-20 (A-20) wheel-and-track tank. March 1938.

Chief Designer of the Factory No. 183
Mikhail Koshkin.

T-32 (A–32) prototype tank, loaded with ballast, simulating the weight of additional armour. Autumn 1939.

T-34 tank No. 1 departs from Kharkov to Moscow.

One of the first mass-produced T-34 tanks.

An abandoned Stalin's 'wonder tank'.

In 1917, under the yoke of endless defeats on the Eastern Front in the First World War, the rotten tsarist regime fell. However, the new Russian republic continued to send young men into the senseless meat grinder of trench warfare. In February 1917, Mikhail Koshkin was mobilised and sent to study at the 58th Infantry Regiment, located in Voronezh. After completing three months of military training, Private Koshkin, part of a march battalion, went to the front line of the Southwestern Front. His service was very short. In August 1917, Koshkin was seriously wounded and sent for treatment to a military hospital located in Moscow. While Mikhail was recovering from his injury, the Bolsheviks led by Lenin and Trotsky seized power in St. Petersburg. On 20 November 1917, Koshkin was demobilised from the Russian army. Soon, due to the revolutionary chaos, the Russian Imperial Army ceased to exist.

Since the moment of the armed coup in Petrograd, Koshkin unconditionally supported the Bolsheviks. The young man, who had experienced all the hardships of the unjust tsarist regime, had enough reasons for this. On 15 April 1918, the future creator of the T-34 tank volunteered to join the Railway Unit of the Red Army formed in Moscow. Military service on improvised armoured trains, which formed the basis of the Railway Unit of the Red Army, fully corresponded to his ever-increasing interest in military equipment.

On 1 October 1919, Koshkin joined the Bolshevik Party. At that time, his military unit participated in the battles at the front near Arkhangelsk. It was there that he first saw British Mark V tanks. The impression they made on him lasted for the rest of his life. They were used in this sector of the front by the Triple Entente Expeditionary Force in battles against the Red Army. During these battles, several Mark V tanks were captured by the Bolsheviks and were in service with the Red Army until 1930.

Koshkin's active participation in the Russian Civil War continued until the beginning of 1921. Military service was suddenly interrupted by a deadly disease – typhus fever. After suffering from a serious illness, Koshkin's health deteriorated so much that he could no longer take part in combat operations. However, during the Russian Civil War, Koshkin showed his talent as a party agitator. His correct speech and frenzied energy effectively motivated the Red Army soldiers. As practice has shown, in this fratricidal war, Bolshevik propaganda proved to be no less effective a weapon than the beloved Koshkin armoured trains.

The military leadership noticed Koshkin's talents. In the summer of 1921, he was sent to Kharkov to attend Courses for Political Agitators for the Red Army. Koshkin's outstanding abilities impressed the courses' teachers, who were used to working with illiterate and tongue-tied cadets. Just two months later, the talented young propagandist was sent to study in Moscow at the Communist University 'Sverdlov'. At this elite Bolshevik university, the future creator of the T-34 studied at the Party faculty until July 1924. In his spare time, Koshkin taught his less educated colleagues the basics of communication competence at the Political Propaganda Club.

After graduating from the Communist University 'Sverdlov', Koshkin was sent to the city of Vyatka. On 20 September 1924, he was appointed director of a local confectionery factory. In five and a half months of managerial activity, the energetic Koshkin was able to modernise and partially automate the technological process at an archaic confectionery factory in Vyatka. Mechanical automata made according to his drawings made it possible to reduce the amount of manual labour and improve the quality of confectionery products. His talent as a political agitator was also of great importance. Koshkin was able to quickly win over the employees of the confectionery factory who were deprived of the attention of the former bosses. This activity also contributed to the growth of labour productivity. However, Koshkin's work as director did not last long.

Soon, the valuable Soviet manager was transferred to the position of party propagandist in the local branch of the Bolshevik Party. During several years of party work, Koshkin was able to significantly advance in the Bolshevik hierarchy. In 1929, he assumed the important position of Head of the Propaganda Department of the Provincial Committee of the CPSU(b). In parallel with his party work, Koshkin was engaged in self-education. He aspired to fulfil his long-held dream and receive a tertiary technical education.

In 1928, Stalin began to carry out the total militarisation of industry. To achieve his goals, he needed loyal young engineers and managers. The most capable members of the Bolshevik Party were most suitable for this. They should have been sent urgently to receive a tertiary education at the technical education institutes. Stalin trained them to replace the tsarist engineers, who aroused in him a pathological suspicion of disloyalty.

On the orders of the 'Master', an active propaganda campaign was launched to find and recruit young Bolsheviks with technical abilities. From that moment on, 30-year-old Koshkin had a chance to realise his dream. By this time, he had completed his secondary education courses and received a secondary education certificate required for admission to the tertiary technical education institute. However, Koshkin had to make great efforts to prepare for the Leningrad Technological Institute entrance exams. According to his wife's memoirs, he worked during the day and studied textbooks at night.

Soon, the necessary 1,000 candidates were recruited to launch the pompous accelerated training programme for future Stalinist engineers. As a rule, they came from the lower ranks of archaic Russian society. Before the Bolsheviks came to power, they had virtually no chance of self-realisation in the engineering profession. Blinded by the intense propaganda, they willingly agreed to a deal with the Red Devil. Not all young people who chose the difficult path to engineering were capable and motivated. However, later several real engineering 'diamonds' appeared among them, one of which was undoubtedly Mikhail Koshkin.

In August 1929, the future creator of the T-34 entered the Leningrad Technological Institute at the Mechanical Faculty. In the spring of 1930, an able student named Koshkin was transferred to the Leningrad Machine-Building Institute. This new Institute was established on 25 April 1930 by personal order of Ordzhonikidze. It was intended to train engineers for numerous military factories. In parallel with his studies at the Institute, Koshkin continued to engage in active party work. This allowed him to establish personal contact with the leader of the Leningrad Bolsheviks, Sergei Kirov, and the People's Commissar of Heavy Industry (Ministry of Industry of the Soviet Union), Gregory (Sergo) Ordzhonikidze. These acquaintances played a big role in his future professional career.

In May 1934, Koshkin successfully graduated from the Leningrad Machine-Building Institute on speciality 'Cars and Tractors' and qualified as a 'Mechanical Engineer'. However, under the guise of obtaining a civilian specialty, Koshkin was preparing to work on designing military equipment. His real specialty was tanks. The content of his thesis, the 'Medium Tank Gearbox', which he defended in 1934, was classified. It was such talented and loyal young designers as Koshkin who were needed by the People's Commissar of Heavy Industry to implement Stalin's fantastic plans for the total militarisation of the USSR industry.

By order of Ordzhonikidze, Koshkin and three other top graduates of Leningrad Machine-Building Institute were sent to work at Factory No. 185 'S. M. Kirov' (Leningrad). Admittedly, the young engineer fully justified the trust of his high patron. In just two years, Koshkin has made a brilliant career at the plant. He rose through the ranks from an ordinary designer to Deputy Head of the Design Department. In a relatively short period of work, Koshkin gained significant experience in design and organisational work. During this time, he participated in the modernisation of serial T-28, T-35 and T-37 tanks and in the development of experimental T-46 and T-29 tanks. He also gained extensive practical experience leading a team of designers in designing wheel-and-track tanks. During this period, Koshkin has studied the main problems of the tank industry well. He knew exactly what specifications a new type of medium tank should have, suitable for mass production.

For his active participation in the creation of the T-29 wheel-and-track tank at Factory No. 185 'S. M. Kirov' (Leningrad) in April 1936, Koshkin was awarded the Order of the Red Star. Meanwhile, Ordzhonikidze closely monitored the promotion of his favourite and made plans for his further use in higher positions.

Ordzhonikidze fell on hard times at the end of 1936. Due to the conflict with Stalin, he was rapidly losing his influence in the military industry. With each passing day, the People's Commissar of Heavy Industry found it increasingly difficult to protect its people from the attacks of Stalin's bloodthirsty favourites Yezhov and Beria. The scandal at the Kharkov Locomotive Factory (KhPZ) with BT-7 tanks led not only to Firsov's dismissal from the post of Head of the Tank Bureau KhPZ (T2K), but also to the complete disorganisation of the factory. Stalin accused Ordzhonikidze of poor control over the factory and 'blindness' in the selection of managers. According to the 'Master', there were too few Bolsheviks working at KhPZ, and the Tank Bureau was run by former tsarist engineers, whom he considered 'wreckers'. At the end of 1936, the situation at the factory escalated so much that Ordzhonikidze could no longer save Firsov. However, if a worthy replacement was found for the 'wrecking' Head of the T2K, the People's Commissar of Heavy Industry had a chance to save the main staff of the design bureau in Kharkov.

Meanwhile, the 38-year-old Koshkin was fully ripe for independent work as the Head of the Tank Bureau and dreamed of creating a high-speed medium tank. As noted above, Koshkin was sent to Factory No. 183 (Kharkov) to replace Firsov. Moreover, Ordzhonikidze sent him there not only as an experienced designer who could solve the gearbox problem of the ill-fated BT-7, but also as a crisis manager who could restore Stalin's trust in the leadership of Factory No. 183. Thus, Koshkin had the opportunity to test himself as the Head of the Tank Bureau of one of the two main Soviet tank factories. To do this, he had to complete the first super-difficult task of the demanding 'Master'.

'Holy Grail' of the Soviet Tank Industry

In addition to the many manufacturing defects, the wheel-and-track BT tanks had a major design flaw that significantly limited their combat capability. Due to the one-axle drive, the ability to move with the tracks removed was limited by the quality of the roads. When driving on wheels, the wet dirt roads were completely impassable for BT tanks. In the USSR, where paved roads were very rare, the use of BT tanks on wheeled drive was severely limited. With caterpillar drive, the tanks' cross-country capability was good, but their track life was very low. After 500km of movement, the fragile caterpillar track was completely out of order, and their complete replacement was required. Thus, the main advantage of wheel-and-track tanks, which consisted in the ability to carry out lightning raids deep into the enemy's defences, was limited

Such tanks could move on wheels at high speed only in Western Europe, where there was an extensive network of good paved roads. Stalin, who closely followed the development of Soviet tanks, knew about these shortcomings from the reports of Khalepsky and other tank experts. The 'Master' demanded that his servants immediately eliminate these significant disadvantages of wheel-and-track tanks.

The first time such an instruction was given by Stalin was on 13 August 1933. At the meeting of the Defence Commission at the Council of People's Commissars of the Soviet Union, where the new Tank Armament System of the Red Army[15] was approved, it was decided to eliminate the shortcomings of BT tanks. After the parade on 1 May 1934, Stalin again reminded his servants of the need for further constructive improvement of the BT tank. In particular, he pointed out the need to modernise the wheel drive of the tank while maintaining all the main components of the tank and creating a three-axle drive. These improvements, according to Stalin, were supposed to significantly increase the combat value of wheel-and-track tanks.[16]

Finally, after another reminder from the 'Master', on 19 June 1935, at a meeting of the Council of Labor and Defence, it was decided to fix the shortcomings of the wheeled drive of wheel-and-track tanks.[17] However, one very important reservation was made when making this decision. The document was about improving the wheeled drive of experimental tanks only. If the tests of the upgraded prototypes were successful in the end of the 1930s, it was planned to mass-produce new types of wheel-and-track tanks based on them. In particular, the changes required by Stalin were provided for in the specifications for the experimental T-46 and T-29 wheel-and-track tanks. In order to increase the manoeuvrability of tanks on wheels, it was planned to create a two-axle drive for the T-46 tank and a three-axle drive for the T-29 tank. It was also supposed to improve the procedure to remove or install the tracks. Usually, on mass-produced BT tanks, it took about half an hour for experienced tankmen to carry out the procedure to remove or install the tracks. The main disadvantage was that in order to carry out this tedious procedure, the tankmen had to leave the tank and remain unprotected for a long time possibly under enemy fire.

Despite Stalin's repeated reminders, no serious work was carried out to improve the wheeled drive. The mass-produced BT-5 wheel-and-track tank had undergone no changes. There were also no plans to modernise the wheeled drive on the projected BT-7 tank. Such persistent disregard by Soviet designers of the requirements of the all-powerful Stalin is explained by the extreme technical complexity of the multi-axle drive design. Mass production of tanks with such complex drives at Soviet tank factories was simply impossible at that time. However, in 1935, none of his servants could tell Stalin such a bitter truth. The time when technical experts told the 'Master' unpleasant information without fear of endangering their lives ended in the beginning of the 1930s.

Technically incompetent and simply stupid, Stalin did not understand why he was constantly being 'deceived'. For several years, he persistently demanded improved wheel-and-track tanks from Ordzhonikidze and his followers. The 'Master' believed that if his engineers promised him in 1933 to make a new 'wonder tank' with a three-axle drive and a diesel engine,[18] and did not do it within three years, then this was the result of deliberate 'wrecking'. The development of experimental tanks with an improved wheeled drive had been underway for several years, but prototypes suitable for mass production had not been created.

After many years of unsuccessful attempts, installing a diesel engine and three-axle drive on a tank became a kind of 'Holy Grail' for Soviet tank designers. Following the example of the legendary knights, in order to obtain it, the designers had to go on a long 'journey' involving a high risk of being shot in the NKVD dungeons. In turn, managers of the Soviet tank industry were forced to constantly postpone the start of mass production of wheel-and-track tanks with multi-axle drive. No one wanted to directly admit Stalin's mistake in choosing the main type of tank drive. The servants hoped that the technical level of the Soviet tank factories would gradually grow and the problem could be solved in the future.

There was a simple alternative solution to the problem of tanks moving through cross-country and wet dirt roads. Its implementation did not require many years of experimental work and the creation of new technologies and equipment. However, this option contradicted Stalin's directive and was stubbornly ignored for a long time. Thus, until the creation of the T-34, this simple solution was not implemented.

Exactly the same situation was observed with numerous attempts to install diesel engine on serial tanks. And the reason for this state of affairs was not at all the machinations of 'spies' and 'wreckers'. Because of Stalin's ambitions and stubbornness, reasonable solutions to complex technical problems were blocked. The most technically complex and difficult tank designs to organise mass production were persistently chosen for implementation. Feverish haste and constant changes in assignments provoked wrong decisions and prevented engineers from focusing on systematic work.

Stalin's accumulated irritation naturally resulted in large-scale repressions against Soviet tank industry designers and managers in 1937. Someone had to answer for the constant failures of the military industry caused by the stupidity and incompetence of the 'Master'.

Voroshilov's New 'Wonder Tank'

Despite the unfortunate failures with Grote's and Dyrenkov's 'wonder tanks', Voroshilov's desire to please his 'Master' had not diminished. However, in 1932, an almost insurmountable obstacle appeared on this path. Tukhachevsky, who shone with intelligence and broad technical knowledge, completely captured Stalin's attention. Although Voroshilov did not outwardly show irritation, his hatred for the brilliant 'Red Aristocrat' grew every day. The jealous servant of the 'Master' was grieved by such a humiliating position. Whenever he met Tukhachevsky, he suffered the most severe torments from his inferiority complex.

For the former locksmith, who graduated from only two classes at the parochial school, the level of competence of the 'Red Aristocrat' was completely unattainable. Voroshilov, appointed by Stalin to the high position of People's Commissar for Defence, had no authority among the top Red Army military. Studying at the Military Academy 'Frunze' seemed to him like a way out of the impasse of professional incompetence. However, in response to plaintive requests for a referral to study at the Academy, Voroshilov always received an unequivocal answer from the 'Master' – no, never! After that, the offended servant had no choice but to play the role of the most incompetent man in the

Red Army and patiently wait for his chance to take revenge on the 'Red Aristocrat'.

Besides Tukhachevsky, Voroshilov had other competitors on the difficult path of gaining Stalin's attention. Ordzhonikidze and Khalepsky closed the last opportunities for him to show tank ambitions. Voroshilov's role in the development of Soviet Mechanised Troops was limited only to signing endless documents. They were compiled by his mortal enemies and approved by Stalin. The humiliated People's Commissar for Defence had to look for his lucky chance literally on the fringes of the Red Army.

In the summer of 1934, Voroshilov met a young 'inventor' Nikolai Cyganov. He served as a technician for the 4th Tank Regiment Ukrainian Military District. This very active young man effectively demonstrated a special automatic coupling device to the naive Voroshilov. It allowed two tanks to overcome obstacles or evacuate immobilised military equipment from the battlefield. Moreover, to use the automatic coupling device, the crew members did not need to leave the tank under enemy fire.

The People's Commissar for Defence was so excited about his new toy that Cyganov was awarded a gold watch and promoted to platoon commander. Later, during the tests, the specialists of the Tank-Automotive Directorate of the Red Army (ABTU) found out that the vaunted automatic coupling device did not work at all. However, Voroshilov, who believed in Cyganov's natural talent, did not pay attention to such 'little things'. He did not notice that the 'inventor' had no technical education, but had a pronounced tendency for manipulation and deception. Voroshilov really liked the fairy tale about the 'people's designer' and he decided to once again try his hand at creating a 'wonder tank'.

Since a candidate for the role of the tank 'people's designer' was found, a primitive propaganda performance typical of that time was played out. In a speech to the soldiers of the 4th Tank Regiment, Voroshilov ordered the improvement of the wheeled drive of the BT tank. Inspired by the high level of trust, 'people's designer' Cyganov volunteered to solve this problem quickly. Attending the 'performance', Commander of the Ukrainian Military District Komandarm 1st rank (General of the Army) Iona Yakir promised to provide the 'young talent' with everything necessary for work. Thus, all the 'characters' of this play performed their roles with the diligence of provincial actors.

Soon, a small group of military technicians led by Cyganov was created on the basis of the repair shop of the 4th Tank Regiment. In the spring of 1935, they began experimental work to modernise the wheeled drive of the BT tank.

Voroshilov believed that this young technician would be able to easily solve the problem that the best tank designers of the USSR with a diploma of tertiary technical education had been unsuccessfully trying to solve for several years.

Tank of the 'Latest Design'

Voroshilov approved all Cyganov's ideas to improve the wheeled drive of the BT-2 tank. Admiring the work of his favourite, he used all his power to promote the 'ingenious invention'. On 25 April 1935, managers of the Soviet tank industry were instructed to produce six prototypes of the tank of the 'latest design'. This decision was agreed with the People's Commissar of Heavy Industry Ordzhonikidze and, as a result, was binding on tank factories. On 4 May 1935, the order for the manufacture of six Cyganov tanks was equally distributed between the two largest centres of the tank industry: Kharkov and Leningrad.

Thus, in 1935, the story of the Dyrenkov 'tanks' was repeated. Once again, the skilful manipulator, using the trust of a technically incompetent but influential patron, received huge resources to implement his absurd 'inventions'. However, leading Soviet tank designers did not share the optimism of the People's Commissar for Defence regarding the tank of the 'latest design'. All tank experts considered Cyganov's 'ingenious' inventions to be technical garbage. However, no one was able to directly deny the incompetent Voroshilov the manufacture of Cyganov 'wonder tanks'. The design of the tank, named after Stalin, simply could not be rejected due to the technical illiteracy of its designer. However, Soviet engineers and managers found other safer reasons to ignore the order to produce BT-IS prototypes. Citing the workload, the management of the Kharkov Locomotive Factory (KhPZ) categorically refused to manufacture Cyganov's 'wonder tanks'. Cyganov received exactly the same refusal at Factory No. 185 'S. M. Kirov' (Leningrad).

In this impasse, Voroshilov had to use the technical resources of Red Army under his control to solve the production problem of tank of the 'latest design'. It was decided to manufacture the BT-IS prototype at the repair shops of the 45th Mechanised Corps Kharkov Military District. Although Cyganov was formally in charge of manufacturing the BT-IS, a large number of qualified army technicians were involved in the work. It was only thanks to such professional help that the project was implemented in metal. The assembly of the only BT-IS was completed by early June 1935. The serial BT-2 was used as the base for its creation, which underwent modernisation. The only difference between the Cyganov tank and the serial BT was the improved driving characteristics of the tank when using the wheeled drive. In particular, an 8×6-wheel convertible drive was made.[19]

Next, the prototype of the BT-IS tank was tested, which lasted with some interruptions until the autumn. Thanks to Voroshilov's patronage, the large number of defects identified during the tests of the 'wonder tank' did not prevent it from being recognised as successful and very promising.

On 15 November 1935, Cyganov officially reported on the 'brilliant' test results of the BT-2-IS to Voroshilov and Ordzhonikidze. Based on this distorted information, they made a joint decision to continue further work on the BT-2-IS tank. However, in 1936, the BT-2-IS was no longer relevant. Voroshilov proposed to continue work on the creation of the tank of the 'latest design' based on the commercially available BT-5. Another joint order from Voroshilov and Ordzhonikidze to provide the Cyganov group with all necessary assistance to create the BT-5-IS, addressed to the leadership of the Kharkov Locomotive Factory (KhPZ), soon followed.

At the beginning of 1936, the Cyganov group, encouraged by the support of their high patron, began work on a new BT-5-IS project. As part of the project, it was planned to increase the cross-country capability of the three-axle drive, increase the range by installing an additional fuel tank in the rear of the tank and increase the hull armour. Another feature of the 'wonder tank' was the special synchronisation mechanism of the wheeled and tracked drives, which allowed it to continue moving, even if the tank lost one of the track. In such a situation, there was a wheeled drive on one side of the tank, and a caterpillar drive on the other. At the same time, the movement of the track on one side was synchronised with the rotation of the road wheels on the other side of the tank.

Despite orders from Moscow, the KhPZ leadership continued to ignore the Cyganov group. KhPZ engineers and managers stubbornly refused to engage in both the manufacture of the BT-5-IS series of tanks and the design work on adapting the upgraded wheeled drive used on it to the BT-7 tank. The Head of the KhPZ (T2K) Tank Bureau, Firsov, considered the development of Cyganov's 'innovative' ideas a waste of money and time. He has already started work on a new promising tank to replace the BT-7. KhPZ management fully supported Firsov's uncompromising stance towards tank of the 'latest design'.

Voroshilov, offended by such a reaction from professional designers and KhPZ management, began to look for an alternative production site. Soon, Tank Repair Factory No. 48 was proposed for the manufacture of 'wonder tanks'. It was repurposed from a former sugar factory and had extremely limited production capabilities. This small factory was located in the suburb of Kharkov and was engaged in the repair of BT tanks. Unlike the influential leadership of KhPZ, the director of Tank Repair Factory No. 48 could not resist Moscow's pressure, and had to comply with the demand. According to optimistic plans, in 1936, ten BT-IS tanks were supposed to be manufactured on the basis of the BT-5 tank. Voroshilov ordered to allocate the necessary funds for the construction of BT-IS.

The production of BT-5-IS prototypes was carried out by upgrading serial BT-5s located at Factory No. 48 under repair. This work was accompanied by noisy conflicts and scandals. Cyganov, just like Dyrenkov a few years earlier, blamed factory engineers and managers for his failures due to technical incompetence. Taking advantage of the urgency of the fight against the 'wreckers', he constantly wrote complaints and denunciations against the leadership of Tank Repair Factory No. 48 to all higher authorities, including Stalin.

The assembly of ten BT-5-IS at Tank Repair Factory No. 48 was completed in the autumn of 1936. Tests of the experimental tank soon began. Cyganov's test progress reports were sent personally by Voroshilov. Thanks to a high patron, the BT-5-IS tank was again hastily declared very promising. However, just a year later, the BT-5-IS would be called the 'Wreckers' Tank', and its 'genius' creator Cyganov would be arrested by NKVD agents.

The New Head of the ABTU

On 9 April 1936, Stalin promoted Khalepsky to the position of Head of Armaments of the Red Army. Komdiv (Lieutenant General) Gustav Bokis, his deputy, became the new Head of the Tank-Automotive Directorate of the Red Army (ABTU). There is no doubt that he was the ideal candidate for this post. Bokis was a competent specialist with a tertiary technical education and extensive management experience. He did not need to spend time getting acquainted with the activities of the ABTU. Together with Khalepsky, he was actively involved in the creation of this Directorate of the Red Army, providing it with qualified personnel and implementing all Soviet tank projects of the 1930s.

Since its inception, the ABTU had served as an intermediary between the highest level of military leadership and the Soviet tank industry. All strategic decisions on tank types were made by Tukhachevsky and Stalin and were formalised in the form of decisions by the Defence Committee at the Council of People's Commissars of the Soviet Union (commission under the Government of the Soviet

Union) and other senior administrative structures. The task of the ABTU was to translate Stalin's directives into detailed specifications of new tanks. However, in reality, most of Khalepsky's subordinates' time was spent overseeing the mass production of tanks and the development of new prototypes at tank industry factories.

During Khalepsky's tenure as head, the influence and staff of the UMM, later renamed ABTU, grew significantly. As part of this administrative structure, several departments appeared, each of which solved its own specific tasks. In addition to the increase in staff, the technological and scientific level of the ABTU employees had significantly increased. By the mid-1930s, based on Western experience, special procedures for formulating specifications for prototype tanks and complex test protocols for experimental armoured fighting vehicles had been developed. The Military Quality Control System for Weapons had become an important tool for monitoring the activities of the tank industry. Each of the tank factories had a fairly large staff of ABTU specialists, formally independent of the plant management.

Despite the sometimes tense relations between ABTU specialists and managers of the Soviet tank industry, in most cases Khalepsky managed to reach compromises with them on controversial issues. However, after Khalepsky's transfer to a new position and especially Ordzhonikidze's death, this balance was disrupted. Nevertheless, the powerful foundation laid by Khalepsky allowed the ABTU to function as a precise and well-established mechanism in the second half of the 1930s.

In addition to the external well-being of the administrative structure of the ABTU, Khalepsky left big problems to his successor. The rapid development of the combat capabilities of serial tanks, characteristic of the early 1930s, had slowed down significantly or completely stopped by 1935. Tank designers are bogged down in a swamp of endless production problems and the elimination of design flaws. The main task of the ABTU under Bokis continued to be to stimulate the tank industry to solve two main problems. As noted above, in order to comply with Stalin's order, all wheel-and-track tanks designed in 1937 had to be equipped with an improved wheeled drive with multi-axle drive. The second problem was the development and installation of a diesel engine on tanks.

Bokis saw his main mission in the accurate and professional performance of his work. In 1936, the Head of the ABTU was determined to work methodically. Bokis continued to implement the Concept of Mechanisation of the Red Army Tukhachevsky. 'High-speed' wheel-and-track tanks and amphibious tanks were the main means of implementing this doctrine of aggressive warfare. Due to the light weight of thin armour and the 'convertible' drive, these 'high-speed tanks' were able to raid deep behind enemy lines. Gustav Bokis literally worshipped wheel-and-track tanks. He was confident in their bright future, and did not even want to hear about any other types of tanks. He threw all the strength of his Directorate into fulfilling the promises made to Stalin by Khalepsky back in 1932.

However, as noted above, the capabilities of mass-produced tanks of this type were significantly limited by their design features. New tank models developed in the experimental workshops of tank factories were endlessly tested and refined. Due to the extreme technical complexity and archaic equipment of tank factories, the serial production of wheel-and-track tanks with a new multi-axle drive and diesel engine was constantly postponed. Despite Stalin's dire warnings and repeated postponements, the prospects for mass production of a new generation of Soviet tanks looked very dim. Many senior Red Army officers, in particular the influential Shaposhnikov, had accumulated significant claims against ABTU.[20] Stalin received regular reports of serious defects in mass-produced tanks. Despite the numerous promises of Ordzhonikidze and the directors of the tank factories, defects and design flaws continued to be a chronic problem of new tanks coming from factories to the Red Army.

However, the new Head of the ABTU Bokis was also not without his drawbacks. Unlike Khalepsky, he had no direct contact with Stalin. However, the Head of the ABTU, like his predecessor, could not stay away from the usual top-level intrigues of the Red Army. Bokis, who was not allowed to see Stalin, was forced to show his qualities of a flattering and obsequious courtier in relation to the secondary Voroshilov. It seemed to him that at the beginning of the relatively calm year of 1936, this was quite enough for a quiet life. However, the events that took place during the bloody year of 1937 showed that Voroshilov's patronage did not save him from arrest, torture and execution.

The BT-9

At the beginning of 1937, the Design Bureau '190', under the leadership of Koshkin, continued routine work to eliminate numerous shortcomings in the BT-7 design. In addition, experimental work was underway to install a diesel engine, a 76.2mm gun and many other equally complex projects on this tank. Despite the limited number of employees, the volume of work was constantly increasing. The Red Army needed a new generation of wheel-and-track tanks to gradually replace the ill-fated BT-7 tank.

On 28 February 1937, specifications for the design and manufacture of the new wheel-and-track BT-9 tank [21] were sent to Factory No. 183 (Kharkov) from the Tank-Automotive Directorate of the Red Army (ABTU). It represented a further development of the BT line. The new 'Super BT' was supposed to be the 'wonder tank' in which all Stalin's expectations were finally to be realised.

Many of the parameters of the 'Super BT' were similar to those of the serial BT-7. It was assumed that the tank, weighing 12–13 tons, would be armed with a 45mm tank gun, three 7.62mm DT machine guns and a flamethrower. The tank's crew was supposed to consist of three men. The main attention of the designers was supposed to focus on eliminating the long-known disadvantages of this type of tank: thin armour, a flammable engine and insufficient cross-country ability of the wheeled drive. It was supposed to strengthen the hull tank's protection by using sloped armour up to 25mm thick. Due to its conical shape, the turret of the tank was also supposed to have better protection. Experimental heterogeneous (cemented or carburizing) armour was supposed to be another way to increase the tank's protection. For a long time, attempts were unsuccessfully made to copy the technology of its manufacture in the West, primarily in Germany. It was also planned to install a BD-2 (V-2) diesel engine on the tank. To increase the cross-country ability on wheels, it was supposed to introduce a three-axle drive. The procedure to remove or install the tracks should not have exceeded 10–12 minutes, including the time on the stowage of the tracks above the fenders. In addition, a special synchronisation mechanism was to be installed on the tank, ensuring the synchronicity of wheeled and tracked drives. This allowed the tank to move normally even with the loss of one track.

For the designers of Factory No. 183, the task of developing the 'Super BT' did not come as a surprise. There was already a preliminary agreement between the factory management and ABTU on the further development of the BT tank line. Work on the new tank, which was supposed to replace the BT-7, has been underway at Design Bureau '190' for a long time. However, the BT-7 gearbox scandal, and especially Firsov's dismissal and arrest, significantly slowed down this work. Under pressure from Stalin, Bokis demanded that the designers of Factory No. 183 create a 'Super BT' as soon as possible. The new Head of the Design Bureau '190' urgently needed to mobilise his team to fulfil a new responsible government task. However, the problems for Koshkin did not end there. Just two days later, another surprise awaited him in the form of an order to develop another tank. The new order appeared thanks to the intrigues of Cyganov and his patron Voroshilov.

The BT-7-B-IS

On 2 March 1937, Design Bureau '190' received another order from the Tank-Automotive Directorate of the Red Army (ABTU). It was urgently necessary to design and manufacture a prototype of the BT-7-B-IS wheel-and-track tank. According to the specifications obtained, the new tank was supposed to have a three-axle drive and special synchronisation mechanism, which made it possible to 'increase the tank's cross-country ability when moving it to road wheels, as well as preserve the ability to move when one of the tracks breaks'.[22]

According to the military, this tank was supposed to combine the advantages of the BT-7 serial tank and an improved multi-axle drive type tank of the 'latest design' BT-IS of Cyganov. In many ways, the specifications of the new tank ordered by the ABTU repeated the characteristics of the BT-9 ordered two days earlier. As noted above, this project appeared under pressure from Voroshilov, who tried to promote the ideas of his favourite. After several years of ignoring Cyganov, the management of Factory No. 183 (Kharkov) was forced to conclude a contract with the ABTU for the production of a tank with a multi-axle drive of his design. However, the most 'talented inventor' was still not allowed to work at the factory.

The almost simultaneous order from Cyganov for the development of two tanks with very similar specifications is surprising. However, in 1937, such a dangerous topic, in order to avoid arrest and execution, could only be discussed in whispers with very reliable people. Koshkin, who understood well who he was dealing with, meekly obeyed the new order and began to look for resources to fulfil the new ABTU order. Moscow ordered the development of new tank designs as soon as possible. Koshkin's reasonable proposal to combine these two similar tank designs (BT-9 and BT-7-B-IS) was rejected by the leadership of the ABTU.

Despite the catastrophic lack of time and people, the disciplined Koshkin began to complete two new Bokis assignments. However, the unpleasant surprises from Moscow did not end there for Kharkov. Soon, on Stalin's initiative, the third 'Super BT' project appeared, the specifications of which were formulated based on the experience of combat use of Soviet tanks in Spain.

Unexpected Combat Experience

The combat experience gained by tankmen in Spain, on the contrary, greatly interested Stalin. On his initiative, on 5 February 1937, a large military meeting was held in the Oval Hall of the Kremlin Senate Palace. It was attended by a group of participants in the battles in Spain, managers of the tank industry, chief designers and senior officers of the Red Army. The People's Commissar for Defence Kliment Voroshilov chaired the meeting. The participation of the 'Master' gave the meeting a high status, and Stalin's servants put a lot of effort into its preparation.

In accordance with the established rules of the carefully directed 'performance', specially selected and trained participants of the battles in Spain performed 15-minute reports in front of the audience. Of the tankmen who spoke, Stalin was naturally most interested in the Hero of the Soviet Union Pols Armans. The 'Master' was very interested in the details of the use of Soviet tanks in combat. A brilliantly educated young officer who had showed outstanding courage in battle, Armans presented a very detailed analysis of the fighting and spoke quite frankly about the advantages and disadvantages of Soviet tanks.

The suspicious Stalin, who did not trust the optimistic reports of his servants, consistently asked Armans one provocative question after another. The 'Master' asked the speaker in detail about the comparative specifications of Soviet and foreign tanks and about suggestions for improving tanks in the future. In his report, Armans emphasised that when designing new tanks, attention should be paid to protection against the use of petrol bombs. This primitive anti-tank instrument was actively used by Franquistas in Spain. Since Stalin had photos of burnt-out Soviet T-26 tanks on the table in front of him, he was especially excited by this fact. After reporting on the effectiveness of petrol bombs, Armans' 'interrogation' became more intense. As a result, the Soviet tankman's 'brief' report lasted more than an hour. Stalin was pleased with the brilliant tankman. It seemed to those present at the meeting that the Hero of the Soviet Union, who spoke to Stalin, had a bright future ahead of him. However, shortly after this meeting, Armans was arrested on charges of espionage. He spent a year and a half in NKVD prison and was released only in June 1939. Fortunately, Armans[23] was among the few who managed to survive the Great Terror and get out of Stalin's prison alive.

However, despite Armans' arrest, his report at the meeting with Stalin had a great influence on the further development of Soviet tanks. He managed to tell the 'Master' more about the features of tanks than the multi-page reports compiled by his numerous servants reported.

During the dialogue with Armans, the chief tank 'specialist' of the USSR managed to utter several phrases concerning the specifications for the design of new tanks. Since the early 1930s, any words uttered by the 'Master' at official events were perceived by his servants as explicit directives, binding for execution. All of Stalin's wishes for the design of new tanks, voiced at a meeting on 5 February 1937, were carefully recorded in official documents and sent for action to the Tank-Automotive Directorate of the Red Army (ABTU). It was these directives, transformed into specifications for a new tank, that Koshkin unexpectedly encountered when, on 2 March 1937, he received an ABTU order to develop a BT-7-B-IS tank design.

'...a tank designed for urban combat'

In addition to the technical problems that plagued Soviet tanks everywhere, the Spanish Civil War revealed new flaws in them. Soviet tanks turned out to be completely defenceless against the fire of anti-tank guns and even heavy machine guns. As experience had shown, rapid-firing anti-tank guns of 25–47mm calibre easily penetrated the thin armour of the T-26 and BT-5. An attempt to break through the enemy's defences, which had even a small number of such anti-tank guns, inevitably led to fatal losses for armoured fighting vehicles.

The list of disadvantages of Soviet tanks was not limited to thin armour. The fighting in the cities of Spain brought another surprise to the Soviet military. The tanks turned out to be completely unsuited to fighting in populated areas. Petrol bombs dropped from roofs or windows of houses on narrow streets turned out to be terrible weapons. During the battles in the cities, the number of tanks burned out by petrol bombs exceeded the number hit by artillery. Even if such a threat was detected, the tanks could not fight it. The limited-elevation tank gun did not allow Soviet tankmen to fire on the upper floors of buildings where enemies with incendiary devices were hiding.

Information about this failure of the Soviet tankmen in the form of photos of burnt-out tanks reached Stalin. He was outraged by the vulnerability of Soviet tanks. The 'Master' believed that in a future major war in Europe, saturated with cities, his tanks should have an advantage over the enemy. The Bolshevik leader, who was incompetent in engineering matters, did not understand that it was impossible to create a tank equally well suited for fighting in any conditions. He instructed his servants to immediately eliminate the identified shortcomings.

In addition to stating the problem of tanks' weakness in urban combat, the chief 'specialist' on tanks in the USSR proposed specific 'measures' to eliminate these shortcomings. Voroshilov carefully wrote down the recommendations of the 'Master', which he expressed during communication with the participants of the battles in Spain, and reflected them in a letter to Bokis.

Stalin's 'brilliant' idea about the fighting qualities of the new tank, as interpreted by Voroshilov, was as follows:

a) The tank should, in my opinion, have great penetrating power. It should destroy not only all kinds of barricades, but also stone barriers – walls, houses, etc., for which it may be advisable to strengthen the front of the tank, giving it the shape and properties of a battering ram, it needs to be carefully considered;

b) it should be possible to conduct machine-gun fire, and preferably gun fire upward, at elevation angles up to 60–70 in order to hit the enemy in the upper floors of houses. This requires good upward and lateral observation;

c) the tank crew must be protected from the ingress of burning liquid from petrol bombs into the tank;

d) it is acceptable to strengthen the reservation, especially in the front of the tank by reducing speed, but while maintaining the necessary turning ability;

e) the rear of the tank must be provided with fire protection from burning liquid;

f) it is advisable to have a wheel-and-track running gear on the tank similar to the BT-IS tank created by Cyganov;

g) it is advisable to protect the tank tracks from the action of bundles of hand grenades.[24]

After receiving Voroshilov's letter, Bokis immediately instructed his subordinates to prepare the appropriate specifications for the creation of a new tank. Stalin's assignment to develop a new experimental tank was, of course, extremely urgent. He was preparing for a major war in Europe and wanted his new tanks to fully meet the conditions of modern warfare. To implement directive of the 'Master', it was proposed to focus all resources. The special tank project had to be implemented even at the cost of freezing other projects.

Voroshilov organised another series of joint meetings between ABTU specialists and representatives of the Soviet tank industry. They discussed urgent measures to improve the combat capability of the projected tanks based on the Spanish experience.

One of these meetings was held on 8–9 April 1937 in Moscow. By order of Bokis, the heads of design bureaus of the leading tank factories in Leningrad and Kharkov arrived at the meeting. During the discussion of Stalin's directive, the meeting participants outlined the main measures for its implementation. Following the meeting at ABTU, general specifications were formulated for the creation of '. . . a tank designed for urban combat'.[25]

The meeting participants decided that such a tank should be armed with a gun with a calibre of at least 76mm and protected by armour capable of withstanding fire from a 45mm anti-tank gun from a distance of 1,000m. Thus, already at the stage of discussing the main parameters, specifications began to appear, which later became distinctive features of the T-34 tank. From that moment on, these parameters of armament and armour became mandatory for implementation in all designed tanks, regardless of their original purpose. In an effort to fulfil the ever-changing requirements of the 'Red Lord', the designers of the leading tank factories of Kharkov and Leningrad were forced to feverishly rebuild their work.

The next meeting on the problem of creating a new tank took place just a month later, on 7 May 1937. Mikhail Koshkin also took part in it. On 4 June Voroshilov approved new specifications for the BT-7-B-IS tank, developed at ABTU. The main reason for the revision of the specifications for the 'Super BT' was the study and description of the experience of combat use of Soviet tanks in Spain. For the first time, two tanks appeared in these requirements: one with a wheel-and-track drive, the other with a caterpillar drive.

The specifications for the caterpillar-drive tank are of the greatest interest from the point of view of studying the history of the T-34:

The purpose of the tank:
a) – is to fight with manpower, artillery, tanks and to break through fortified positions in manoeuvrable conditions.
b) – for action in mountainous conditions and for urban combat.

1. Tank type – only with caterpillar drive.
2. Weight (approximately) – 25-30 tons.
3. Armament: one turret type T-46-5.[26]
   a) According to the first variant of armament:
      – 45mm gun and coaxial machine gun DT on the turret – 1 front;
      – DT machine gun on the rear of the turret – 1;
      – anti-aircraft machine gun DT – 1.
   b) According to the second variant of armament:
      – 76.2mm L-10 tank gun[27] and coaxial machine gun DT in the turret – 1 front;
      – DT machine gun on the rear of the turret – 1;
      – anti-aircraft machine gun DT – 1.
   c) In both armament variants, a flamethrower is additionally installed to protect the rear of the tank – 1.[28]

Upon careful analysis of the specifications for the new tracked tank, the main specifications of the future T-34 tank are noticeable in the second version of the weapon. However, the path to the realisation of this barely-outlined trend in the development of Soviet armoured fighting vehicles turned out to be very difficult and winding. In the summer of 1937, no one expected that the technically complex and incredibly expensive wheel-and-track tanks, which seemed so promising, would soon give way to simple and cheap tracked tanks.

Optimization of the Number of Tank Projects

After the meeting in Moscow, Koshkin returned to Factory No. 183 (Kharkov) very perturbed. The design order for the new 'Super BT' was extremely urgent. On 8 June 1937, the People's Commissar of the Defence Industry of the Soviet Union Moisey Rukhimovich sent an order to his subordinates to implement Stalin's directive: 'Please inform the 8th Main Directorate about all your considerations, the planned work plan, the deadlines for readiness and responsible performers within five days'.[29] Rukhimovich, who had replaced Ordzhonikidze after his suicide, was in a hurry to fulfil Stalin's orders and at the same time please Voroshilov. Based on Rukhimovich's order, the Koshkin team had all two weeks to prepare the preliminary design of the new tank.

Simultaneously with the increased pressure from the bosses of the military industry, another problem arose. The military from the ABTU required Design Bureau '190' to simultaneously work on three tank projects with similar specifications. The resources available to the Koshkin team were extremely limited and allowed to develop only one 'Super BT' project. After agreeing with the director of Factory No. 183 and receiving approval from the leadership of the 8th Main Directorate of the People's Commissariat of the Defence Industry, Koshkin decided to combine the three projects. Thus, instead of three separate tanks ordered by the ABTU (BT-9, BT-7-B-IS and '. . . a tank designed for urban combat'), Design Bureau '190' focused all its resources on designing a single tank, the 'Super BT'.

However, even such a drastic optimisation of the number of projects did not allow Koshkin to avoid a feverish rush. To fulfil Stalin's urgent task, the designers of Design Bureau '190' had to work 12-14 hours a day. Lack of time provoked Koshkin to use ready-made design solutions. Therefore, the preliminary design of the BT-7-BIS tank was based on developments on other experimental tanks that were developed under Firsov.

At that time, Koshkin did not suspect that the tank, the preliminary design of which he was developing in a feverish hurry, had a very stormy and long future ahead. At first, this tank would become the main threat to Koshkin's career and possibly life, and eventually its improved version would glorify its creator all over the world.

Voroshilov's 'Plan'

Since the early 1930s, Voroshilov's main dream was full control over the tank industry. For him, this was another way to influence Stalin, and therefore strengthen his precarious position in the Red Army. However, for the 'Fake Marshal',[30] the realisation of this dream was accompanied only by pain and disappointment. As noted above, for a long time, Voroshilov's tank projects ended in complete collapse, or as in the case of Cyganov, they brought very small dividends. The obstinate bosses of the Soviet military industry had long spoiled his life and constantly prevented him from implementing his 'progressive' tank projects. However, the impending Great Terror created new opportunities for the 'Fake Marshal' to realise his long-held dream.

Although Voroshilov was not the initiator of the bloody repressions, he was directly involved in them. His signatures were on all the numerous execution lists of 1937–8 immediately after Stalin's signatures. This allowed Voroshilov to indirectly influence people's entry into these execution lists, or at least be among the first to receive information about people sentenced to death by the 'Master'. Already in the spring of 1937, he began to receive the first dividends from a new wave of repression. Ordzhonikidze's suicide and the subsequent wave of bloody repression significantly weakened the resistance to the implementation of Voroshilov's tank plans at the highest level of the leadership of the Soviet military industry in Moscow. However, the directors of the largest tank factories in Leningrad and Kharkov, despite their external loyalty to the formal Head of the Red Army, continued to maintain some degree of independence. Voroshilov was keenly interested in changing the management of these plants and appointing his own people to vacant positions.

The object of the first attack by Voroshilov and his favourites was one of the two largest tank factories of the USSR, the 'Kirov' Factory (Leningrad). In May 1937, Voroshilov's young favourite Josef Kotin[31] was appointed Chief Designer of the 'Kirov' Factory, and his adopted son, Petr Voroshilov,[32] was appointed his Deputy. These positions at the factory were vacated as a result of a wave of arrests at the Design

Bureau of the 'Kirov' Factory. Terrified by the death of his former patron Ordzhonikidze and the arrests of his subordinates, Rukhimovich did not dare to object to the actions of the 'Fake Marshal'.

Thus, a combination of intrigue and involvement in repression allowed Voroshilov to seize full control of the 'Kirov' Factory in the spring of 1937. This success contributed to the emergence of a powerful new force that began to have a decisive influence on the development of the Soviet tank industry – 'Voroshilov's group'. For a short time, there was an illusion that Voroshilov and his favourites could compete with Stalin in their power. However, an attempt by members of 'Voroshilov's group' to seize power in Kharkov at Factory No. 183 proved fatal to their existence.

'Voroshilov's Group'

In early 1937, as a result of Stalin's de facto dismissal of Tukhachevsky, the role of Technical Leader of the Red Army became vacant. The 'Master' didn't have anyone who could replace the 'Red Militarist'. Uborevich and Khalepsky had lost Stalin's trust, and candidates from the new generation of the Soviet military were not yet ready to take up such an important position. For some time, Stalin tried to independently determine the development strategy of Soviet Tank-Automotive Troops. However, his complete technical incompetence and intellectual limitations have reduced all his directives in this area to a stupid repetition of the ideas of the 'Red Militarist'.

A new impetus for changing the general ideas of the 'Red Lord' about tanks was the unsuccessful experience of using armoured fighting vehicles in the Spanish Civil War. Stalin reacted to the failure with the idea of modernising existing tank types. He borrowed the main directions of modernisation from the Soviet tankmen who fought in Spain. However, on this difficult path, the chief Soviet tank 'specialist' faced insurmountable obstacles.

It was not possible to install thicker armour and 76mm gun on the extremely overloaded wheel-and-track running gear of the Christie tank. Stalin felt that in the event of a very likely failure, he would have no one to shift responsibility to. In this situation, he hurried to get rid of the 'difficult child', passing the solution to the tank problem to the nearest servants.

In this situation, Voroshilov assumed the role of Technical Leader of the Red Army by default. It was he who had to fulfil the mission of taking into account the bitter Spanish experience in the development of the 'Super BT'. The incompetent People's Commissar for Defence was unable to handle such highly complex technical issues. When determining the vector of further development of Soviet tanks, Voroshilov was forced to rely on his more competent favourites. One of them was the aforementioned Head of Tank-Automotive Directorate of the Red Army (ABTU) Gustav Bokis. The second was the Head of Academy Mechanisation and Motorisation of the Red Army 'Stalin' (VAMM), Ivan Lebedev.[33] He was named to this position in June 1936, when, under pressure from Voroshilov, Tukhachevsky's protege was removed from this position. Through the appointment of Ivan Lebedev to the post of Head of the VAMM, the People's Commissar for Defence strengthened his position, and the 'Red Marshal' lost another channel of influence on the development of Soviet Tank-Automotive Troops.

Bokis and Lebedev became key figures in the newly formed 'Voroshilov's group'. Their intelligence and abilities have become a kind of 'crutches' for the incompetent and intellectually limited Voroshilov. This combination of the influence of the 'Fake Marshal' and the abilities of his favourites ensured 'Voroshilov's group' a great but short-term success.

After the execution of the 'Red Militarist', his functions in determining the strategy for the development of tanks finally passed to the triumvirate of Voroshilov, Bokis and Lebedev that had formed in early 1937. Although the favourites of the 'Fake Marshal' had the necessary experience and competencies, they did not become a full-fledged replacement for Tukhachevsky. The main difference between the chaotic actions of Bokis and Lebedev and the purposeful activities of Tukhachevsky was their limited horizons and shallow goals. Voroshilov, Bokis and Lebedev dreamed of absolute power in the Red Army only for the purpose of their own well-being, but nothing more. They had nothing like the strategy of the ideologist of Soviet militarism, Tukhachevsky, who dreamed of the world domination of Bolshevism. Also, unlike the 'Red Marshal' they were not independent figures and could not withstand the constant interference of the incompetent Stalin. That's why the suspicious 'Master' eliminated the ambitious Tukhachevsky, so he was in no hurry to deal with the members of 'Voroshilov's group'.

Stalin wanted the future 'Super BT' to remain highly mobile while increasing its firepower and armour protection. This is exactly what the surviving Soviet commanders advised him based on the Spanish experience. The task of Bokis and Lebedev was to find reasonable ways to implement these unreasonable directives from the 'Red Lord'. It was these two who found a simple solution to the problem posed by Stalin. This decision eventually became one of the factors in the emergence of the T-34. However, the gradual definition of the specifications of Stalin's future 'wonder tank' was carried out chaotically. Bokis and Lebedev did not have any purposeful strategy for creating a new medium tank. Finding the key specifications of the future T-34 happened by accident, rather in spite of than because of their actions.

Although Voroshilov dreamed of defining the future of Soviet Tank-Automotive Troops for many years, he failed to effectively and, most importantly, in the face of unprecedented repression, safely realises these new opportunities. In the end, Voroshilov, Bokis, and Lebedev became mired in petty intrigues and missed most of the wide-ranging opportunities that opened up to them.

'Cavalryman' Voroshilov's 'Trojan Horse'

On 21 June 1937, a special commission from Tank-Automotive Directorate of the Red Army (ABTU) arrived from Moscow to review the preliminary design of the BT-7-B-IS tank at Factory No. 183 (Kharkov). It was quite a rare event. Usually, the head of the Design Bureau Factory No. 183 presented the preliminary design of the tanks he developed in Moscow. In the 1930s, Afanasii Firsov made such trips many times. His successor, the Head of Design Bureau '190', Koshkin, also regularly visited Moscow and made reports and presentations at various meetings. The fact that a commission from Moscow came to Kharkov to review the preliminary design of the new tank was both alarming and caused a sense of pride among the employees of Factory No. 183. Koshkin also felt similar emotions. He was particularly concerned about the composition of the commission, which included people who aroused negative emotions among many key employees of Factory No. 183. Koshkin understood that during the presentation he would face another serious test of will and character.

Instead of Director Ivan Bondarenko, who went on a long business trip abroad, the important guests from Moscow were greeted by Acting Director of Factory No. 183 Fedor Lyasch. The commission of several ABTU specialists was headed by Brigade Engineer (Major General) Vasily Sviridov. He was an experienced member of the Khalepsky team, who had done a lot to buy the Christie tank in the USA. Sviridov worked at the ABTU as an assistant to Bokis.

The preliminary design presentation took place in a small meeting hall, which could comfortably accommodate members of the ABTU Commission and the audience. To emphasise the status of the members of the high Moscow commission, they, along with the factory administration, were seated at a long table on a small elevation. Several dozen employees of Factory No. 183 were present as spectators in the hall. Since the meeting had a secret status, only those who were directly involved in the development of the new tank project were allowed to attend. Thus, almost the entire Design Bureau '190' team gathered in the meeting hall.

Based on the experience of previous presentations, those in the meeting hall expected a fairly routine event. Preliminary design represented the very first stage of tank design. Usually, this kind of presentation involved considering the general concept of a new tank, while avoiding making serious decisions. Only some members of the ABTU Commission and the astute Koshkin knew that in this hall, under the guise of discussing preliminary design, the fate of Design Bureau '190', and possibly Factory No. 183, would be decided.

The beginning of the presentation did not foreshadow a future big scandal. Koshkin went to a large stand on which several drawings of the future tank on a large scale were fixed and began his report. The members of the ABTU Commission listened attentively to the speech, sometimes writing something down in their notebooks. Most of Koshkin's report did not elicit any noticeable emotional reaction from the audience.

The main parameters of the new tank practically did not differ from the specifications of the serial BT-7 and were well known to those present in the hall. However, when Koshkin began to talk about the wheel-and-track running gear of the future tank, the members of the commission and the audience in the hall noticeably perked up. Their relaxation, and sometimes even drowsiness, has completely disappeared. All eyes turned to the stand, where a detailed drawing of the tank's running gear appeared. Koshkin began to describe the tank's wheel-and-track running gear to the audience. He explained that when the tank was moving on road wheels, the torque was transferred from lateral clutches to three-axle drive through two lengthwise drive shafts and six telescopic cardan shafts. This design caused an ambiguous and very violent emotional reaction among the members of the ABTU Commission.

Fierce disputes between several groups of Soviet designers about various multi-axle wheeled drive schemes have been going on for several years. The hall was attended by prominent representatives of two competing points of view on possible design options for the wheel-and-track drive tank. A tall young engineer with glasses expressed his emotions especially loudly. He was sitting at the table next to the speaker Koshkin and allowed himself to interrupt the speaker several times with loud exclamations.

It was Adolf Dik, a member of the Moscow commission and adjunct professor at the academic department 'Tanks and Tractors' of the Military Academy of Mechanisation and Motorisation of the

Red Army 'Stalin' (VAMM). He was well known at Factory No. 183, called him the 'Moscow upstart' and treated with extreme hostility. Dik first appeared at the factory in 1934, when, as a student at VAMM, he underwent practical training in Kharkov. Despite his long stay at the factory, Dik, unlike Koshkin, did not become his own man at Factory No. 183. As early as 1934, his German neatness and arrogance caused acute irritation among young engineers from the Tank Bureau KhPZ (T2K). Thus, the factory management and the young designers had a very negative opinion about him.

Once again, Adolf Dik was remembered at Factory No. 183 in November 1936. In the midst of the crisis caused by the defective gearbox BT-7, an engineering project by Dik was sent from Moscow, accompanied by a note from Bokis. It contained drawings and calculations of an alternative gearbox for the BT tank. A note from ABTU strongly recommended that the designers of Factory No. 183 familiarize themselves with the graduation project Dik, and use it as an example of brilliant design that deserves their special attention. In the crisis situation of 1936, when the designers were feverishly looking for a way out of the impasse, such a demonstration of engineering excellence from yesterday's student Dik was perceived by the employees of Factory No. 183 as a personal insult. The factory management did everything possible to ensure that gearbox, designed by the 'Moscow upstart', never entered mass production. After this incident, Adolf Dik became literally hated at Factory No. 183.

The next appearance of Dik occurred in 1937, which was even more difficult for Factory No. 183. He was sent to Kharkov on a business trip as a direct agent of Bokis. Dik carried out hos mission at Factory No. 183 from 1 March to 24 April 1937. His duties were actually limited to overseeing the work of the new Head of the Tank Bureau, Koshkin, and his team. Dik carried out his work with German thoroughness and accuracy. He recorded and sent to Moscow all the actions of Koshkin and his design team. Dik's reviews of Design Bureau '190' were highly critical, and their negative content was well known at Factory No. 183. Against this unfavourable background, the degree of hatred towards the 'Moscow upstart' has reached its limit.

However, the negative opinion of Factory No. 183's management and designers about him did not bother Dik at all. Sometimes it seemed that he was deliberately reinforcing his negative image. While fulfilling another Bokis assignment in Kharkov, Dik met and became friends with the 'inventor' Cyganov and tank tester Captain Kulchicky. These people were no less hated at Factory No. 183, and perhaps even more than Dik. Together, these three ambitious outcasts formed a cohesive team of competitors to Koshkin and his Tank Bureau. Kharkov knew about their plans to seize power at the factory. Thus, the very fact of being present on 21 June 1937 at a report in Kharkov by Adolf Dik did not promise anything good to the staff of Design Bureau '190'. Dik's outrageous behaviour during the presentation fully confirmed Koshkin's concerns.

The Koshkin report was completed, and according to the preliminary design review procedure, it was time for questions and discussion of what was heard. The main topic of discussion was expected to be the drive of the experimental wheel-and-track tank. It was the most complex unit of the tank. The features of its design clearly reflected the degree of competence of its creator and belonging to one of the competing approaches to the design of the wheeled drive. Koshkin used the main elements of the multi-axle wheeled drive of the experimental T-29 tank, which he worked on at Leningrad, in the design of the drive of the future tank. According to its specifications, it was similar to the drive scheme developed by the Cyganov team. This design has been well tested and, despite its complexity, has proven effective on the PT-1 and T-29 tanks. As noted above, there was an irreconcilable struggle between the representatives of these approaches. At the same time, two recognised young Soviet experts in the field of wheel-and-track tank design were present in the hall: Koshkin and Dik.

Instead of the friendly discussion accepted at such events, Koshkin was subjected to a veritable barrage of criticism from the ABTU Commission. The members of the Moscow commission focused in their statements on the weaknesses of the multi-axle wheeled drive of the experimental tank. The presented design was particularly sharply criticised by Adolf Dik, who was a proponent of the alternative concept of designing wheeled drive of the wheel-and-track tanks. Koshkin skilfully countered his opponent's attacks, justifying the chosen solutions and agreeing with a number of shortcomings of the proposed design.

Gradually, the hard-to-contain negative emotional tension between representatives of Moscow and Kharkov began to make itself felt. In addition to reasonable comments, which were absolutely normal at the preliminary design discussion stage, some members of the ABTU Commission began to openly express doubts about the design competence of the Head of Design Bureau '190'. Under the influence of such statements, factory employees present at the discussion began to get the well-founded impression that the main purpose of the arrival of the ABTU Commission was not the desire to improve the design of the new tank, but to remove Koshkin from office.

'Ardent' could not stand such undeserved rudeness and, with all his characteristic energy, began to defend his authority. He felt absolutely confident in his territory and was ready to repel any attack by Moscow emissaries from ABTU. The forces of the opposing sides were approximately equal. Koshkin was supported by members of his design team, and the Head of the Moscow Commission, Vasily Sviridov, was expected to side with Dik. Soon, the 'discussion' turned into an open verbal altercation, in which the warring parties could hardly restrain themselves from physical contact with their opponents. In the dispute over the choice of the type of drive, there was no neutral party capable of acting as an impartial arbitrator. All the representatives of the older generation of designers were either arrested or had already been executed, and there was no one recognised authority among the younger generation. In this conflict situation, the degree of expression of negative emotions was increasing by the minute. Passions had heated up to such an extent that the young engineers were almost ready to prove their case with their fists.

As a result, the consideration of the preliminary design 'Super BT' instead of a constructive discussion ended in a noisy scandal. Acting Director Lyasch and Head of the ABTU Commission Sviridov managed with great difficulty to cope with the heated emotions of the opposing sides. Finally, after shouting their fill, the young representatives of the two concepts of wheeled-drive design, gesturing noisily and shaking their fists, went their separate ways. However, the confrontation between Moscow and Kharkov did not end with this emotional episode at all. It was only a short pause in the deadly conflict that was raging.

The Adolf Dik Report

After the scandal at the presentation, the members of the ABTU Commission, led by its Head Sviridov, hurriedly left for Moscow. However, Adolf Dik remained in Kharkov to prepare a report on the results of the discussion of the preliminary design of the BT-7-B-IS tank. This was a big risk for him, as the young engineers from Design Bureau '190' were determined to beat him up. Dik took refuge from them in the ABTU representative office located at the factory. There, under the reliable protection of the military, he did his job safely. On 27 June 1937, the completed report was sent to Moscow. The following was written in the document prepared by Dik:

1. The designed BT tank is not an upgrade of the BT-7-B-IS tank, as stipulated in the ABTU contract and specifications, but is a new BT-type wheel-and-track tank with a three-axle wheeled drive. Of the serial

units of the BT-7 tank, the project provides for the use of only the following components: main clutch, lateral clutches, cooling system fan and steering mechanism.

2. The project also does not meet the specifications for the BT-9 tank.
3. The design of the torque transmission from the engine is based on the example of the BT-5-IS, which proved to be better than other schemes of our tanks, since the wheeled drive and tracked drive branch out behind the lateral clutches, which provides ease and convenience of tank control, eliminates wheelspin wheels on the track in turns, reduces the number of brakes to two and increases turning ability when driving on a single track. On a wheeled drive, the tank with this torque transmission scheme from the engine obeys the steering wheel worse due to the lack of a differential, but when using lateral clutches and brakes, manoeuvrability on solid ground does not differ from manoeuvrability when driving on a caterpillar drive.[34]

In total, the Dik report listed sixteen comments on the design of the 'Super BT' proposed by Koshkin. Almost all of them concerned the device of an extremely complex wheel-and-track multi-axle convertible drive. The essence of these remarks was clear only to a very well-trained expert. However, any layman could feel the general accusatory trend of Dik's verdict. Having devoted most of the report to the devastating criticism of its opponent, the 'Moscow upstart' offered his way out of the impasse of designing 'Super BT'.

Dik's main proposal was to develop a new design for the torque transmission from the engine to the second, third and fourth pairs of road wheels using a special gear reduction drive ('guitar'). At the same time, the drive design variant proposed by Dik was to be developed in parallel with the drive variant proposed by Design Bureau '190' (using telescopic cardan shafts). During the re-examination of the preliminary design 'Super BT', the commission had to choose the best of the designed drive variants for implementation in the prototype. This best option, of course, had to be the one that Dik was developing. The noisy discussion around the BT-7-B-IS drive was just a good reason for Koshkin's removal and the appointment of the 'Moscow upstart' in his place.

After receiving the Dik report, Voroshilov decided that everything was going according to plan and approved all the proposals of Koshkin's opponent. The management of Factory No. 183 was ordered to provide 'Moscow upstart' with equal conditions and resources with Koshkin to develop an alternative version wheeled drive of the BT-7-B-IS tank.

A Mennonite[35] in the Service of the Red Army

The revolution of 1917 turned the social foundations of the Russian Empire upside down. The eldest son, the mainstay of a traditional deeply religious family of German immigrants, grossly violated its centuries-old traditions. Adolf Dik not only took up arms, but also began to create the most formidable weapon of the time – tanks. In October 1925, the former Mennonite Dik voluntarily joined the Red Army, and in June 1926 he became a member of the Bolshevik Party.

Although suffering a similar fate, Dik, unlike Dyrenkov and Cyganov, was not a fraud and an impostor. He had received a tertiary technical education. At the end of 1931, Adolf Dik entered the Red Army's Military-Technical Academy 'Dzerzhinsky' in Leningrad. In June 1932, together with other students of the Faculty of Mechanics and Motorisation, he was transferred to the newly established Military Academy Mechanisation and Motorisation of the Red Army 'Stalin' (VAMM) in Moscow.

In the autumn of 1936, Adolf Dik graduated from VAMM with honours and continued his military service in the Kharkov Military District as an engineer with the 5th Tank Brigade. His brilliant abilities and high level of technical competence were noticed by Voroshilov's favourites: Bokis and Lebedev. As mentioned above, in March–April 1937, Adolf Dik was on a business trip to Kharkov to fulfil a 'special assignment' by Gustav Bokis, Head of the ABTU. He watched the design of the BT-7-B-IS wheel-and-track tank at Design Bureau '190'. At the same time, Dik studied the design of the BT-5-IS Cyganov tank at Tank Repair Factory No. 48. In May–June 1937, Dik took part in the troop testing of three BT-5-IS tank prototypes in the area of Kharkov. Thus, Adolf Dik had extensive practical experience in creating and upgrading gearbox, drive and running gear wheel-and-track tanks.

After returning to Moscow in the summer of 1937, Military Engineer 3rd rank (Senior Lieutenant) Adolf Dik was hired as adjunct professor at the academic department 'Tanks and Tractors' of the VAMM. As noted above, on 21 June 1937, Dik arrived as part of the ABTU Commission to review the preliminary design of the BT-7-B-IS tank and was the author of a negative review of the Koshkin design.

The patronage of the 'Fake Marshal' promised him a brilliant career and fame as the creator of the future T-34. However, the ethnic Georgian Stalin would never have approved of an ethnic German in the place of the chief designer of the most numerous Red Army tank. The 'Red Lord', just like the 'Brown Lord', experienced a monstrous inferiority complex due to lack of belonging to the main nation of his empire. For this and many other reasons, the career of the talented tank designer Adolf Dik in the USSR was initially doomed to collapse.

A New Attack on Koshkin

Although the ABTU Commission left Kharkov, the passions around the BT-7-B-IS tank flared up with renewed vigour. The scandal surrounding the various tank drive variants became the reason for the continuation of the Voroshilov people's attack on Koshkin. Before leaving, the Head of the ABTU Commission, Sviridov, agreed with the Acting Director of the Factory No. 183 Fedor Lyasch, that Adolf Dik would remain at the factory to provide 'qualified assistance' to the designers from the Koshkin team.

As mentioned above, the 'Moscow upstart' was supposed to create an alternative drive option for the BT-7-B-IS tank. To ensure Dik's design activities succeeded, factory management had to create favourable conditions and provide him with several assistants from among the designers of Design Bureau '190'. Despite the protests of factory employees, Lyasch, under pressure from Moscow, was forced to accept such an unpleasant decision. The 'Moscow upstart', who was aware of his privileged position, tried to make the most of this decision. Dik demanded from the management of Factory No. 183 to place at his disposal three of the most highly qualified designers from Design Bureau '190'.

Such impudence of the 'Moscow upstart' caused a violent backlash at the factory. Moscow was far away, and in Kharkov, all power was concentrated in the hands of Acting Director Lyasch and Head of Design Bureau '190' Koshkin. They knew the 'art' of intrigue and organising bureaucratic tricks no less than the bosses of the military industry in Moscow. Under the pretext of excessive workload, the Head of Design Bureau '190' was in no hurry to give Dik scarce designers. Koshkin's authority was so great that none of the young designers at Design Bureau '190' wanted to work with Dik, even under threat of punishment. As a result of such mild opposition, instead of the three best designers, Acting Director Lyasch allocated only two of the youngest and most inexperienced engineers to help the 'Moscow upstart' – one on 1 July, the second on 17 July 1937.

Dik tried to complain about the actions of Lyasch and Koshkin Military Representative ABTU in Kharkov Military Engineer Dmitry Saprygin. On 20 August 1937, Saprygin sent a written complaint to Moscow against the management of Factory No. 183. In the letter, he complained that the ABTU employee Dik at the factory was not receiving the necessary assistance. His constructive comments were ignored and not taken into account in the development of the tank design. He further stressed that Koshkin was actively opposing Dik's efforts to create an alternative project wheeled drive for an experimental tank. Allegedly, the Head of Design Bureau '190' 'is trying to demoralise young designers by saying that Comrade Dik is engaged in fruitless design, and that Dik will not succeed. Therefore, these already weak designers are giving up'.[36] In conclusion, Military Representative Saprygin regarded Koshkin's actions as deliberate sabotage of a government assignment and even accused him of 'wrecking'.

Bokis, who received this letter from Kharkov, tried to influence the plight of his favourite Dik and punish the Head of Design Bureau '190'. However, despite the peak of the 1937 repressions and influential enemies, Koshkin was not removed from office or arrested. Moscow's reaction boiled down to a new round of correspondence between the ABTU and the factory.

In August 1937, in response to an angry letter from Bokis, the management of Factory No. 183 provided the Dik Design Group with an additional (third) designer. As a result, by the end of August 1937, a small group of young engineers led by the Moscow upstart it was possible to develop the preliminary design special gear reduction drive ('guitar') and suspension of the BT-7-B-IS tank.

Thus, despite all the intrigues of Moscow, Dik was unable to create serious competition for the leader of Design Bureau '190'. As further developments have shown, all the efforts of the 'Moscow upstart' and his young assistants (Dik Design Group) turned out to be completely in vain. At the same time, the Factory No. 183 design team, led by Koshkin, completed the refinement of its preliminary design of the BT-7-B-IS tank. The Head of Design Bureau '190' took into account all the previously expressed comments and, thanks to the additional time, was able to significantly improve the initial version of the 'Super BT' project.

New Design Group

Meanwhile, the confrontation between Factory No. 183 (Kharkov) and the Tank-Automotive Directorate of the Red Army (ABTU) intensified. Taking into account the earlier scandal at Kharkov, a second review of the preliminary design of the new tank in early September 1937 took place in Moscow at the ABTU office. In addition to the Design Bureau '190' project, created under the leadership of Koshkin, the meeting also reviewed the developments of the Dik Design Group. Judging by the fact that the review of the submitted design materials took place over three days, unprecedented pressure was exerted on Koshkin in Moscow.

The improved preliminary design of the 'Super BT', developed by Design Bureau '190', was once again subjected to scathing criticism. However, Koshkin again disagreed with the criticism of the ABTU staff. Bokis was enraged by this reaction and was forced to file a complaint against Koshkin with his boss Voroshilov. The 'Fake Marshal' organised a meeting of the triumvirate of conspirators, inviting Bokis and Lebedev to his office. At the meeting, the conspirators adopted an adjusted plan of attack on Koshkin and immediately began to implement it. Meanwhile, the situation for the seizure of Factory No. 183 for 'Voroshilov's group' had worsened. In early September 1937, director Ivan Bondarenko returned to Kharkov from a long business trip abroad.

On 11 September 1937, after coordinating with Voroshilov, Bokis launched a new attack on Koshkin. He sent letter No. 182987 to Kharkov with the following content:

> Considering that the existing organisation of the new design at Factory No. 183 did not provide the required quality and pace of work, I consider it necessary to create a New Design Group under Department '100' with its direct subordination to the director factory. The New Design Group should consist of the best designers of Factory No. 183, consisting of at least 20 people.
>
> For my part, I agree to send Military engineer 3rd rank Comrade Dik to the Kharkov for the leadership of the New Design Group. In addition, 20 5th year students of the Military Academy Mechanisation and Motorisation of the Red Army 'Stalin' (VAMM) may be sent to the factory in October.[37]

Despite his formal writing style, Bokis was essentially blaming the leadership of Factory No. 183 for the failure of Stalin's assignment. Such an accusation in the autumn of 1937, at the height of a new wave of repression, could have had deadly consequences. After the veiled threats, Bokis moved on to specific measures that, in his opinion, factory management should have taken to remedy the crisis situation. Although the director of Factory No. 183 Bondarenko did not answer to the military, Bokis directly ordered him to change the staff structure of the factory, create a new department and transfer all work on the BT-7-B-IS tank there. Thus, if the factory management had followed the order from Moscow, Koshkin would have automatically lost his entire design team. All the best designers of Design Bureau '190' had to be transferred to this new department. In addition, the absence of mention of Koshkin in the letter meant an unspoken recommendation for his removal from work on the new tank. On the contrary, designer Adolf Dik was mentioned as the uncontested Head of the New Design Group.

The Bokis letter was drafted in such a way that if it fell into Stalin's hands, the situation in Kharkov was presented in a favourable light for the Head of the ABTU. From the direct content of the letter, it followed that Bokis did not exceed his authority, but took urgent measures to save the new tank project.

Despite the force of the new attack, the management of Factory No. 183 once again withstood Moscow's pressure. Director Bondarenko, who returned from a long business trip abroad, had given new strength to the resistance to Moscow's dictates. He fully approved of all the counteraction measures taken in his absence by Acting Director Lyasch and Head of Design Bureau '190' Koshkin. Moreover, with his characteristic boldness, he was preparing a counter-attack on key members of 'Voroshilov's group'. To do this, he needed extra time, and he skilfully used his experience in managerial intrigue. Under various bureaucratic pretexts, Bondarenko did not allow Voroshilov's protege Adolf Dik to create a New Design Group and take the place of the head of this new department.

Separate Design Bureau (OKB)

After Bondarenko's return, the beneficial period for the seizer of Factory No. 183 ended. Voroshilov, Bokis, and Lebedev decided to indirectly influence the tank factory through the leadership of the military industry in Moscow. There they quickly found a new reliable ally. People's Commissar of the Defence Industry Rukhimovich also had a strong dislike for the independent Bondarenko. Besides, after Ordzhonikidze's suicide, he was very afraid for his life and wanted to maintain a good relationship with the powerful People's Commissar for Defence.

Rukhimovich responded very quickly to Voroshilov's requests. He ordered the management of Factory No. 183 to immediately fulfil all the requirements of the Head of the Tank-Automotive Directorate of the Red Army (ABTU) Bokis. On 28 September 1937, a list of mandatory actions addressed to Director Bondarenko was sent from the People's Commissariat of the Defence Industry. It said the following:

> By Government Decision No. 94ss of 15 August 1937, the 8th Main Directorate of the People's Commissariat of the Defence Industry proposed to design, manufacture prototypes and prepare production

by 1939 for serial production high-speed wheel-and-track tanks with synchronised wheeled and tracked drive.

This work should be done at your factory.

Due to the extreme seriousness of this work and the extremely tight deadlines set by the Government, the 8th Main Directorate of the People's Commissariat of the Defence Industry considers the following measures necessary:

1. Create a Separate Design Bureau (OKB) for tank design at Factory No. 183, directly subordinate to the Chief Engineer of the Factory.
2. By agreement with the Heads of VAMM and ABTU, appoint adjunct professor VAMM Military engineer 3rd rank Comrade Adolf Dik as the Head of the Separate Design Bureau (OKB). To allocate 30 5th year VAMM students to work at the Separate Design Bureau from October 5 and an additional 20 people from December 1. 5th year VAMM students arriving at the plant must be provided with housing and all conditions for normal work.[38]

The Head of the ABTU was confident that this time Bondarenko would not be able to escape the execution of a direct order from his Moscow superiors. On 29 September 1937, Gustav Bokis ordered the Head of the Academy of Mechanisation and Motorisation of the Red Army 'Stalin' (VAMM) Ivan Lebedev to send adjunct professor of the 'Tanks and Tractors' Department Military Engineer 3rd Rank Adolf Dik on a business trip to Factory No. 183. He was convinced of his victory over the obstinate Bondarenko and Koshkin. However, contrary to expectations, the 'Moscow upstart' was met with great hostility at the factory in Kharkov. Despite the fact that Dik had a legitimate reason to be at the factory, he was unable to fulfil Bokis' instructions. The factory management continued to ignore him and did not provide any access to the management of the design work on the design of the 'Super BT'. Dik's business trip to Kharkov lasted a very short time – from 1 to 18 October 1937 – and ended with another scandal. The young designer sent from Moscow again failed to cope with the role of Voroshilov's 'Trojan Horse'.

The Collapse of the 'BT-20' Special Operation

In early October 1937, by order of Bokis, the ABTU developed 'Specifications for the design and manufacture of high-speed wheel-and-track tank BT-20'. In 1937, this was the fourth version of the specifications 'Super BT' and it was created specifically for Dik.

The specifications for the new tank were practically the same as those for the BT-9, BT-7-B-IS and the '...a tank designed for urban combat'. Some minor details related to the attempt to introduce combat experience of using Soviet tanks in Spain were added to the previous versions of the 'Super BT' specifications. The 'BT-20' project was another excuse to dismiss Koshkin and replace him with Dik. To achieve their goal, the members of 'Voroshilov's group' have performed wonders of organisational and managerial efficiency. The usually rather slow bureaucratic procedures for approving specifications in numerous higher authorities were carried out with lightning speed this time.

On 11 October 1937, the specifications for the BT-20 tank were approved by the chief of the ABTU Komdiv (Lieutenant General) Bokis. On the same day, they were sent to the director Ivan Bondarenko. However, the brilliantly planned 'BT-20' special operation was not destined to come to fruition. The events at Factory No. 183 were intervened in by 'higher forces' in the form of the People's Commissar for Internal Affairs (Head of the NKVD) Yezhov, acting on Stalin's instructions. From that moment on, further events began to develop with lightning speed.

On 15 October 1937, People's Commissar of the Defence Industry Rukhimovich was unexpectedly removed from office and arrested the next day. Thus, another favourite of the late Ordzhonikidze was eliminated from the leadership of the military industry. This situation caused a shock in the People's Commissariat of the Defence Industry. Prior to the appointment of a new People's Commissar, the work of all departments of the People's Commissariat was completely paralyzed. As a result of these events, Voroshilov completely lost control of the situation in Kharkov. Sensing that the situation had changed dramatically, Dik was forced to hastily flee from Kharkov to Moscow. After 'returning' from a business trip, the 'Moscow upstart' again appealed to Bokis with a complaint against the management of Factory No. 183. However, in the new conditions, it was much more difficult to influence the director of Bondarenko.

Meanwhile, after agreeing with Stalin, the vacant position of People's Commissar of the Defence Industry was given Mikhail Kaganovich.[39] He was the older brother of Stalin's closest servant Lazar Kaganovich. The new People's Commissar worked for the People's Commissariat of Heavy Industry for a long time and was one of Ordzhonikidze's closest favourites. Despite his profession as a locksmith, Mikhail Kaganovich was an experienced schemer and was in no hurry to respond to Bokis' complaints. While the top leadership of the military industry was recovering from the shock of Rukhimovich's arrest, the business of the raiding of Factory No. 183 slowed down. Voroshilov and Bokis had to negotiate for a long time with the new People's Commissar Mikhail Kaganovich about putting pressure on director Ivan Bondarenko.

On 20 October 1937, Bokis sent another letter to Kaganovich, complaining about Factory No. 183's two-month disregard of orders to create a New Design Group to designing a new version of the 'Super BT'. However, the cautious Kaganovich, weighing his chances of salvation in the face of repression, remained silent. Meanwhile, the People's Commissariat of the Defence Industry saw arrests of military industry bosses on an almost daily basis. They were accused of having criminal ties with the arrested former People's Commissar Rukhimovich.

As a result of Yezhov's actions, the staff of the People's Commissariat of the Defence Industry was almost completely replaced. On 27 October 1937, Brigade Engineer (Major General) Vasily Sviridov was appointed Head of the 8th Main Directorate of the People's Commissariat of the Defence Industry to replace his predecessor, who was arrested by the NKVD. Previously, he worked as an assistant to Bokis and headed the ABTU Commission, which came to Kharkov at the end of June 1937. The Head of the ABTU believed that the appointment of his man to the position of Head of 8th Main Directorate of the People's Commissariat of the Defence Industry, responsible for the development and production of tanks, would guarantee the result he needed at Factory No. 183. Bokis did not know that he had less than a month left to lead ABTU. The clouds of Stalin's anger began to gather over him. The next execution list of high-ranking Red Army commanders with the surname Bokis had already been prepared by Yezhov and was only waiting for Stalin's signature.

Koshkin's Victory

At the end of October 1937, Kaganovich finally responded to Bokis' appeal. People's Commissar has scheduled a special meeting to resolve the issue of creating the Kharkov Separate Design Bureau (OKB) for the design of the 'Super BT' on 29 October. The warring parties in Kharkov and Moscow immediately began preparations for a decisive battle for control of Factory No. 183.

On 25 October 1937, by order of Bokis, the ABTU drafted documents regulating the establishment of the Separate Design Bureau (OKB) at the factory in Kharkov. The author of these documents was Adolf Dik.[40] His proposals for the organisation of OKB were as follows

1. Create a Separate Design Bureau (OKB) at Factory No. 183, unrelated to the mass production of tanks and subordinate directly to the factory Director.
2. To ensure faster design, it is necessary to allocate the best factory tank designers to work at OKB.

3. For the effectiveness of design work, in addition to the previously
   planned 20 designers, allocate 10 more factory engineers and to be
   allowed to work at OKB 40 5th year students Academy of Mechanics and Motorisation of the Red Army 'Stalin' (VAMM), trained for
   design work.[41]

According to this document, the OKB and Experimental Tank
Workshop that was being created actually turned into an ABTU
branch under the overall leadership of Adolf Dik. All the best
designers, including Koshkin's deputy Aleksander Morozov, were
to be transferred to the OKB. Dik did not forget and his partner in
the conspiracy, Captain Kulchicky. He assigned him the important
role of a permanent consultant on the design of a new tank. Dik's
ambitions also extended beyond Factory No. 183. In particular, he
wanted to get the right to attract and pay for consultations and work,
both individual specialists and the entire staff of military scientific
institutions (VAMM, TsAGI,[42] NATI,[43] etc.).

Three days before the special meeting on the creation of OKB in
Kharkov, Bokis and Dik were absolutely confident of their victory. All
decisions have been made, and the necessary documents have been
worked out in great detail.

A special meeting for which these documents were prepared was
held on 29 October in Moscow at the ABTU office. The meeting
was attended by Gustav Bokis, Head of the ABTU, director of
Factory No. 183 Bondarenko, and Vasily Sviridov, Head of the 8th
Main Directorate of the People's Commissariat of the Defence Industry.
The balance of power was clearly not in favour of director Bondarenko.
However, instead of the planned victory of Bokis and Dik, the meeting
in Moscow again ended in a deafening scandal.

Bondarenko was not against the organisation of OKB, but he
categorically disagreed with the appointment of the 'Moscow upstart'
as Head of OKB and the transfer of all authority to design a new tank
to him. According to the director of Factory No. 183, the team for
the design of the new BT-20 tank should be led by a 'proven' design
engineer who reported directly to the factory management, and not
to Moscow. This position of Bondarenko did not surprise Bokis and
Sviridov at all, however, Kaganovich's reaction, who was informed
about the results of the meeting, turned out to be completely unplanned.

Quite unexpectedly for the confident Voroshilov people, People's
Commissar of the Defence Industry (Minister) Mikhail Kaganovich
fully supported the obstinate director of Factory No. 183. The cautious
Kaganovich felt that Bondarenko could show such incredible resistance

only if he relied on Stalin's opinion. At the end of 1937, the People's Commissar, who had almost all his subordinates arrested, could not afford to object to the opinion of the 'Master'.

It was a complete victory for Koshkin and his young design team! Bokis was stunned and depressed by such an unexpected decision by People's Commissar Kaganovich. This unexpected blow was a harbinger of his imminent fall and death.

The Secret Design Bureau for Designing Stalin's Secret Tank

On 1 November 1937, a new design team was created at Factory No. 183 (Kharkov), called Design Bureau '24'. This is how the hypothetical Separate Design Bureau (OKB) was created, which the losers Bokis and Dik fought for so long. Mikhail Koshkin was expectedly appointed Head of Design Bureau '24', and Nikolai Kucherenko, one of the followers of the late Firsov, was appointed to the vacant position of Head of Design Bureau '190'.

As noted above, Koshkin emerged as the absolute winner in the power struggle at the tank factory. The close-knit team of factory employees proved to be too tough for 'Voroshilov's group'. Thanks to the failed intrigues of Bokis and Dik, Koshkin was able to focus all his efforts on working on 'Super BT'. The new design bureau was relieved of work on other projects that took up so much time and effort from Koshkin and his best designers. All the numerous BT-7 tank modernisation projects were left at Design Bureau '190'.

Although work on Stalin's new secret tank was fraught with deadly risks during a period of unprecedented repression, Koshkin enthusiastically embarked on the project of a new version of the 'Super BT'. He appointed Aleksander Morozov as his deputy and project manager for the BT-20 tank. Together, they began to form the staff and organisational structure of the new design team. In the atmosphere of total secrecy and espionage mania at the end of 1937, this proved to be a very difficult task. Candidates for the new Koshkin team were thoroughly vetted by NKVD officers. Those who passed the filter of Stalin's special services were invited to an interview with Koshkin and Morozov. They carefully checked not only the abilities and degree of design competence of applicants, but also their loyalty to the Bolsheviks.

In total, twenty-one designers from among the employees of Design Bureau '190' and Design Bureau '35'[44] were accepted into the new secret design bureau. Such a small number of employees was insufficient to develop such a complex project, but Koshkin was used to working in conditions of an acute shortage of professional staff. After the formation of the staff, Koshkin and Morozov appointed the most experienced designers to lead the design teams for the main components of the future BT-20 tank. The project of the new tank received the factory index A-20.

The formed Design Bureau '24' team was ready to start working on the new version of the 'Super BT' immediately. However, there was a problem with choosing the location of the new division's employees. This problem was not related to the shortage of suitable facilities for design work. There were quite enough such rooms at the giant tank factory in Kharkov. In addition, the work of such a small team did not require large premises or any special conditions. The problem when choosing a room to accommodate the Design Bureau '24' team arose with ensuring secrecy.

The psychosis that accompanied the total repression reached its peak by the end of 1937. NKVD employees who were constantly present at the plant were seriously afraid that the secret specifications of the wonder tank would be stolen by foreign spies. To ensure the strictest secrecy of Stalin's assignment, the staff of Design Bureau '24' was placed in a large room on the second floor of the main office building of Factory No. 183. Stalin's agents did not yet know that in just six months the 'main nest' of foreign 'spies' would be discovered by NKVD investigators in this building, and Director Bondarenko and his deputies would be the leaders of the 'spies'.

Although there were no prisoners in the Koshkin team, the operating mode of the designers resembled the conditions of an NKVD special prison (Sharashka). An armed NKVD officer was constantly on duty at the door of the room where the designers of Design Bureau '24' worked. The entrance to the premises was carried out only with special passes. Stalin's idiotic secrecy limited the communication of the Koshkin team's designers with other employees to the utmost. Even colleagues from Design Bureau '190', who also worked on secret tank projects, were barred from entering Design Bureau '24'. The working hours of the Koshkin team also differed little from the work in the Gulag. The designers worked 16 hours a day. Although no one formally restricted their freedom, Koshkin and his staff, overwhelmed by the sheer volume of work, often stayed overnight in the room where they worked.

As compensation for their work in prison conditions, the young designers who made up the majority of the Koshkin team received higher salaries than their colleagues from other design teams and additional bonuses. However, the main motive stimulating the employees of Design Bureau '24' was the prestige and high importance of their work. In turn, Koshkin provided young engineers with creative freedom and encouraged innovative solutions to complex problems. Forgetting about the strict supervision of NKVD and the constant threat of arrest, the employees of Design Bureau '24' worked with youthful enthusiasm.

The deadlines for the project work were very tight. All the resources of the factory had to be concentrated to work on the new version of the 'Super BT'. Full project readiness The BT-20 wheel-and-track tank project was scheduled for 15 March 1938. Despite all the efforts of the young engineers, the deadline for the preliminary design of the new tank variant was missed.

The End of the Epoch of Wheel-and-Track Tanks

Meanwhile, Yezhov's punitive machine continued its bloody work. As noted above, on 13 November 1937, Khalepsky was arrested by NKVD investigators. This was followed by arrests of all those who were associated with him during his leadership of the Tank-Automotive Directorate of the Red Army (ABTU). On 23 November, ABTU head Gustav Bokis was arrested on charges of participating in the 'Anti-Soviet and Terrorist Military Organisation' ('Tukhachevsky's Group'). With his arrest, the last obstacle to abandoning the creation of wheel-and-track tanks was eliminated.

Just one year after the introduction of the preliminary design of the 'Super BT', Koshkin would decisively abandoned the super-complex and unpromising wheel-and-track drive, and as a result, a prototype of the legendary T-34 would appear. However, it would take another year for Stalin and the bosses of the Soviet tank industry to recognise a fait accompli. The extreme rigidity of the Red Army leadership was reinforced by the inertia of Soviet military industry. In the end, the period of abandonment of wheel-and-track tanks in the end of the 1930s turned out to be as long as the period of preparation for their mass production in the beginning of the 1930s.

In 1938, the bloody repression continued. On 8 July 1938, the Head of the 8th Main Directorate of the People's Commissariat of the Defence Industry, Vasily Sviridov, was arrested. On 7 August 1938, adjunct Professor Adolf Dik was dismissed from the Military Academy of Mechanisation and Motorisation of the Red Army 'Stalin' (VAMM), and then arrested by NKVD officers. His name, like the names of other arrested designers, was forgotten. Dik miraculously survived nine years of imprisonment in Stalin's Gulag. Many times during his stay at the Siberian labour camp, he came close to death from starvation and overwork. Only his youth and hard work helped him survive. Although Dik was released after Stalin's death and worked as an engineer for many years, he never again engaged in the design of military equipment. He died in Moscow in 1979.

Chapter 5

TANK OF THE 'NEW TYPE'

People Who Will Work Miracles

As noted above, in the autumn of 1936, Stalin decided to intervene militarily in the Spanish Civil War (Special Operation 'X'). The dictator's pragmatic desire was hidden behind the beautiful words 'providing active military assistance to Republican Spain'.[1] Stalin, like Hitler, was preparing for a major war of aggression in Europe. He could not miss the opportunity to test the skills of his military and the combat qualities of new military equipment in full-scale operations.

In the plans to provide 'assistance' to Republican Spain proposed, in addition to supplying forces, sending military 'advisers' to command Spanish troops at all levels, up to the highest. Thus, Stalin had an urgent need to select reliable commanders. Most of the senior officers of the Red Army reported their desires to help the Republicans. The voices of Mikhail Tukhachevsky and Ieronim Uborevich stood out among them. They especially loudly asked to be sent to fight in Spain. Tukhachevsky and Uborevich explained their zeal with a reasonable desire to test their strategic and tactical techniques for using Mechanised Troops in practice. However, the suspicious Stalin categorically refused to send any of the top officers to Spain. Later, after the arrest of members of 'Tukhachevsky's Group', he justified his refusal on the grounds of secrecy. In his speech at the Military Council of the Red Army on 2 June 1937, Stalin noted that the top commanders of the Red Army were too famous in the West to send them on secret missions.[2]

However, the real reason for this decision was Stalin's loss of confidence in his former favourites. In the autumn of 1936, he was already afraid to let Tukhachevsky and Uborevich go abroad. The 'Master' was afraid that, following the example of General Franco,

158

they would return with troops, and with the support of Hitler and Mussolini, they would overthrow him. In this difficult situation, Stalin found an alternative solution to the problem of command of the Red Army Expeditionary Force in Spain. He decided to send young officers of junior and middle rank abroad, whose loyalty he had no great doubts about. According to Stalin's plan, after such a test in battle, the surviving young military men were supposed to replace the favourites from 'Tukhachevsky's Group' who had lost his trust.

The group of 'volunteers', formed from representatives of various military specialties, was dominated by tankmen. They were led by the commander of the 4th Separate Mechanised Brigade, 38-year-old Kombrig (Major General) Dmitry Pavlov (alias 'De Pablo'). His candidacy was proposed to Stalin by the Commander of the Byelorussian Military District, Ieronim Uborevich. The former Head of Armaments of the Red Army considered Pavlov the best tank commander of the Red Army. After careful study of the candidate's biography, the choice of Uborevich was approved by Stalin. Later, giving an official justification for his decision at a meeting of the Main Military Council of the Red Army, Stalin said:

> And we sent inconspicuous people, they are doing wonders there. Who was Pavlov? Was he famous? No, let's send people without names, our lower and middle officers. They have power, and it's connected to the army. These people will work miracles, I assure you. It is from these people that boldly nominate for high positions! They'll rebuild everything, and they won't leave a stone unturned. Push people more boldly from below. Be brave – don't be afraid![3]

The reasons for Stalin's decision are obvious. In the midst of the 'Purge' (Chistka) of the Red Army command staff, he was in dire need of new military leaders. The 'Master' was constantly looking for loyal people among the military. He clearly sympathised with people like him who came from the bottom of Russian society. It was much easier for Stalin, the son of a shoemaker, to communicate with the sons of peasants and workers. In such capable and motivated people as Pavlov and Koshkin, the 'Master' found a new foothold in the Red Army and military industry. In response to Stalin's attention, a new generation of young favourites actively demonstrated their loyalty. Their worldview was formed in conditions of total propaganda, and their extremely limited education, due to their social background, did not allow them to critically perceive the leader of the Bolsheviks and the essence of his criminal activities. These young people perceived the 'Master' as a great leader who did not make mistakes, and were ready to give their lives to carry out his orders.

The Main Opponent of Wheel-and-Track Tanks

During his eight months in Spain, Dmitry Pavlov successfully commanded the International Tank Brigade. This military unit fought bravely during the repulse of the breakthrough of the Republican front near the city of Majadahonda[4] (January 1937), in the Battle of Jarama[5] (February 1937) and in the Battle of Guadalajara[6] (March 1937). In June 1937, Pavlov returned to the USSR as part of the rotation of Soviet troops.

Despite the deaths of Soviet 'volunteers' and heavy losses of tanks and aircraft, Stalin recognised the participation of the Soviet Expeditionary Force in the Spanish Civil War as a great success. Many of the military survivors were generously rewarded. On 21 June 1937, Dmitry Pavlov was awarded the title Hero of the Soviet Union for successfully completing a special assignment in Spain. However, the main reward was to receive the status of a new favourite and a high position.

In July 1937, after a personal meeting with Stalin, Pavlov was appointed Deputy Head of Tank-Automotive Directorate of the Red Army (ABTU). The views of Stalin's new favourite on the development vector of the Soviet Tank-Automotive Troops differed significantly from those of his boss Gustav Bokis. Pavlov was one of a small group of Red Army commanders who, in battle, were able to evaluate and compare the capabilities of the two most numerous Soviet tanks, the BT-5 and the T-26. And this comparison turned out not to be in favour of wheel-and-track tanks. It was after returning from Spain that Pavlov became an active supporter of tracked-drive tanks. He loudly criticised the shortcomings of wheel-and-track tanks and insisted on the development of classic tanks with track drive. Pavlov's opinion was supported by all tank commanders who had gained combat experience in Spain.

In the spring of 1937, at a meeting of the Technical Council of the People's Commissariat of Defence of the Soviet Union and the Military Council of the Red Army, Pavlov spoke in favour of creating a new medium tank with caterpillar track drive. Unlike Tukhachevsky, Pavlov was not a strategist, so he neglected the capabilities of wheel-and-track tanks to implement the Soviet version of blitzkrieg. He argued his position with the probability of the tank crew's survival in battle. Thanks to caterpillar-track drive, the T-26 tank remained completely stable after stopping. Wheel-and-track tanks experienced prolonged rocking after an abrupt stop due to the suspension design.

Thus, unlike the BT-5, the crew of the T-26 tank had the ability to quickly open accurate fire after a sudden stop. This was an extremely important quality for the crew of the lightly armoured Soviet tank mid-1930s. As the experience of the Spanish Civil War has shown, the inability to fire accurately from a tank during a short stop meant almost guaranteed death in battle.

However, the Head of the ABTU Komdiv Gustav Bokis, relying on the concept of Tukhachevsky, categorically disagreed with this point of view of tank commanders who had received combat experience in Spain. While acknowledging the individual disadvantages of wheel-and-track tanks, he emphasised their strategic advantages. Based on this, Bokis considered it necessary to create an improved BT-type wheel-and-track tank based on the experience of fighting in Spain. On 15 August 1937, Stalin put an end to this dispute between the two tank experts. His opinion was formalised by Resolution No. 94ss of the Defence Committee at the Council of People's Commissars of the Soviet Union 'About new types of tanks for arming Red Army tank forces'. It stated that to equip Mechanised Troops and mechanised cavalry regiments, it is necessary to have a wheel-and-track BT type tank (Christie tank) weighing 13–14 tons with a 400 hp diesel engine, with one 45mm tank gun with stabiliser or with one 76mm tank gun and two DT machine guns.[7] As a result of this decision, it became necessary to create a new version of the 'Super BT'. This new tank was to become the basis of the Soviet Tank-Automotive Troops for the coming years. Thus, in this round of intense struggle between supporters of the two main types of tanks, Bokis proved to be the winner. However, the main opponent of Head of the ABTU continued to fight. It took Pavlov more than two years to reverse this erroneous decision of Stalin. The path to victory for the uncompromising proponent of tracked tanks began with the arrest of an opponent, an event that became common during the Great Terror period.

On 28 November 1937, shortly after Bokis' arrest, Stalin appointed Komkor (Colonel General) Dmitry Pavlov to the post of Head of the ABTU. Thus, Pavlov confirmed his status as Stalin's new favourite. He was supposed to replace the executed Tukhachevsky, Uborevich and Bokis and become the new Technical Leader of the Red Army. As with other favourites, as confidence in his loyalty grew, 'Master' gradually increased Pavlov's influence in the Red Army. In March 1938, on Stalin's recommendation, he became a member of the Main Military Council of the Red Army. The influence and authority of the new favourite continued to grow rapidly, and Pavlov had a dizzying career ahead of him. His biography will tell how the son of peasants became Stalin's favourite.

Biography of Dmitry Pavlov

Dmitry Pavlov was born on 23 October 1897 in the village of Vonyuh, Kostroma Governorate, in a poor peasant family. The head of the family dreamed of giving his children at least some kind of education. However, in a remote village located in the north of the European part of the Russian Empire, it was very difficult to fulfil this desire. There was only an elementary school at the local church for education. In it, peasant children were taught to read and write.

Extreme poverty proved to be an insurmountable obstacle for Dmitry continuing his studies at a paid gymnasium in the nearest major city. A free alternative to gymnasium for a peasant's son was Realschule (a type of secondary school). The number of places in them was limited, and the duration of study (two years) did not allow students to receive a full secondary education. However, thanks to his abilities and diligence, Dmitry was able to enrol in Realschule in the village of Sukhoverkhovo. It was located just 4km from the village of Vonyuh.

Dmitry walked to school every day and returned home in the evening. Despite his academic achievements, two completed classes were not enough to receive secondary education. To continue his studies, Dmitry had to take exams at the Spaso-Krasnogorsk Forestry Realschule. This Realschule was located in the village of Gorchukha, 200km from his home. They trained specialists in forest resource management, which were very rich in Kostroma Governorate.

After successfully passing the exams and two months of training, the future Technical Leader of the Red Army was expelled from the Realschule. The reason for the expulsion was not Dmitry's poor studies, but his father's lack of money. Although studying at the Forestry Realschule was free, you had to pay for accommodation and uniforms. The father of the future Komkor could not find 130 rubles for this. It was a fantastic sum for a poor peasant. The hope of receiving a life-saving state scholarship also proved futile. Instead of continuing his studies, Dmitry had to return home. He began helping his father run the farm, doing primitive peasant labour. However, Dmitry did not give up on his dream and continued to study on his own.

A few years later, his dedication and diligence allowed him to take the external exams for four classes at Rostov Men's Gymnasium. Soon he received the long-awaited certificate of secondary education. In the Russian Empire, where the majority of the population was illiterate, the certificate of secondary education gave its holder a number of privileges. However, soon all of Dmitry's life plans were destroyed by outbreak of the First World War.

In 1914, under the influence of patriotic hysteria that swept the Russian population, 17-year-old Dmitry Pavlov volunteered to join the Imperial Army. For a peasant's son from a very poor family, military service opened up great opportunities for improving social status. The secondary education he received gave him privileges during military service and the hope of becoming a junior officer.

In the first two years of his service, it seemed to the young man that his plans were being successfully implemented. Dmitry Pavlov served in rear units and quickly received the military rank of Senior Unteroffizier (non-commissioned officer). However, the heavy losses of soldiers and junior officers caused by a number of major defeats on the Eastern Front forced the tsarist generals to send more and more young men into the bloody meat grinder of the war. Soon, Dmitry Pavlov, as part of his military unit, was sent from the safety of the rear to the front line.

In June 1916, he was slightly wounded and captured by the Germans. Russian peasants, who had unwillingly become soldiers, were quite willing to surrender to the Germans in the third year of the war. The soldiers of the Russian Army suffered from the unbearable conditions of trench warfare and the officers' poor attitude towards them. The growing flow of Russian prisoners turned out to be an unpleasant surprise for the German command. The POW camps were overflowing with Russians and the Germans had great difficulty providing them with food. To solve the problem, they were forced to send Russian prisoners of war to perform heavy labour far in the rear. Usually, Russians did not show aggression towards the Germans and worked hard for a modest meal. For example, Dmitry Pavlov, a prisoner of war, first worked at a German factory, and later was engaged in loading coal.

After Germany's defeat in the war, Russian prisoners of war began to return home. On 1 January 1919 Dmitry Pavlov returned to his native village of Vonyuh. Eight months later, on 25 August 1919, he was mobilised into the Red Army to participate in the Russian Civil War. His service as an ordinary soldier did not last long. At the end of 1919, Pavlov's abilities and military experience were noticed and he was sent to study at Command Courses in the city of Kostroma. Thus, in the Red Army, he continued his successful career as a professional soldier, interrupted by German captivity.

While serving in the cavalry, Dmitry Pavlov continued his career from platoon commander to battalion commander. In 1922, he was sent to study at the Omsk Infantry School 'Comintern'. After his graduation, Pavlov was named commander of one of the cavalry regiments of the 10th Cavalry Division.[8] The end of the Russian Civil War and the demobilisation of most of the Red Army did not interrupt their military career Dmitry Pavlov. In October 1925, he was sent to study at the elite Military Academy 'Frunze'.

In June 1928, after successfully graduating from the Military Academy, Pavlov was appointed commander of the 75th Cavalry Regiment, 5th Separate Kuban Cavalry Brigade, stationed in Transbaikal.[9] In 1929, his regiment took part in the war with China. On 1 January 1931 Pavlov was sent back to study in the European part of the USSR.

In the late 1920s, Stalin had begun implementing fantastic plans to create numerous Mechanised Troops. A large number of commanders with technical expertise were urgently needed to command the new mechanised military units. To train Soviet officers, at the suggestion of Tukhachevsky, Leningrad organised short-term Academic Courses for technical improvement of the commanding staff (AKTUS VTA) at the Military Technical Academy 'Dzerzhinsky'. From January to August 1931 Pavlov completed his training at these Courses.

After graduating from AKTUS VTA, Pavlov was appointed commander of the 6th Mechanised Regiment, stationed in the city of Gomel (Belarus). From that moment on, the career of a competent commander of a new type of troops accelerated significantly. Pavlov began to move up the military hierarchy quite quickly. In February 1934, he was appointed commander of the 4th Separate Mechanised Brigade (4th OMB), stationed in the city of Bobruysk (Belarus). The 4th OMB was equipped with T-26 and BT tanks, HT-26 flamethrower tanks, T-37A light amphibious tanks, T-27 tankettes, BA-27, FAI (Ford A Izhorskiy), BA-I (Ford AA Izhorskiy) and BA-3 armoured cars, and regimental guns and anti-aircraft machine guns. As a result of Pavlov's skilful command, the 4th OMB quickly gained the status of one of the best mechanised brigades in the Red Army. He was awarded the Kombrig (Major General) military unit for his successful command of the troops. On 16 August 1936, Pavlov received the Order of Lenin.

From 7 to 10 September 1936, the 4th OMB of Kombrig Dmitry Pavlov, took part in the Byelorussian Military District manoeuvres. It was a grandiose military performance, the main purpose of which was to show the invited foreign military the increased power of the Red Army. In total, the Byelorussian Military District deployed 85,000 soldiers and officers, 1,136 tanks, 580 artillery pieces and 638 aircraft for military exercise. The overall leadership of the troops in the manoeuvres was carried out by Byelorussian Military District Komandarm 1st rank (General of the Army) Ieronim Uborevich. In general, this militaristic performance was quite successful. Numerous problems, caused primarily by the low technical reliability of Soviet armoured fighting vehicles, managed to be hidden from the eyes of foreign military attaches.

Stalin was quite satisfied with the propaganda effect produced by the manoeuvres. He decided that his best mid-level commanders were well suited to carry out secret missions abroad. As noted above, Stalin personally approved Pavlov's candidacy for a new responsible government assignment in Spain. The best commander of of a Red Army Mechanised Brigade, who returned from a business trip abroad in 1937, was ready to fulfil Stalin's new responsible task.

Cleaning the Augean Stables

Having tested his new favourite in action, as he once did with Khalepsky, Stalin decided to entrust Pavlov with the responsible task of correcting the long-term 'wrecking' of members of 'Tukhachevsky's Group'. According to the 'Master', the leadership of the Tank-Automotive Directorate of the Red Army (ABTU) has been deceiving him for many years, and putting obstacles in the implementation of his 'brilliant' ideas. Having received complete freedom of action from Stalin, Pavlov finally began solving many of the long-standing problems of Soviet Tank-Automotive Troops left over from his predecessors.

He began by solving the same problem as his predecessor Tukhachevsky in the early 1930s, namely by reviewing the state of work on the creation of experimental tanks. Despite considerable progress in the development of Soviet Tank-Automotive Troops, Pavlov's predecessors had driven themselves into another tank impasse by the middle of the 1930s. Khalepsky and Bokis were unable to fulfil Stalin's task of creating wheel-and-track tanks (T-46 and T-29) and converting the BT to three-axle drive and diesel. Almost five years after the start of design, the T-46 and T-29 prototypes were not ready for mass production. All this time, Soviet tank designers were stuck in a swamp of endless technical problems.

The new wheel-and-track tanks were supposed to replace the tracked T-28 and T-26 tanks. However, the advantages of experimental new-generation tanks over their outdated predecessors turned out to be very conditional. For example, with the same armament and armour as the mass-produced T-28 tank, the prototype T-29 wheel-and-track tank had a higher speed and significantly higher cross-country ability off-road. Tests showed that the T-29 moved better on a ploughed field and on snow than the T-28. However, exactly the same result could have been achieved by simply equipping the T-28 tank with wider tracks.

The special synchronisation mechanism of the wheeled and tracked drives allowed the experimental T-29 tank to continue moving in the event of the loss of the track from one of the sides of the tank. However, such a very dubious advantage turned into a great constructive complexity of the tank. A large number of drive shafts, coupling and skew gears, providing synchronisation of wheeled and tracked drives, significantly increased the cost and complicated the design of the tank, as well as created problems during its maintenance. With the primitive technological level of the Soviet industry and the low skill of the workers, the already extremely high probability of breakdowns of such a complex wheel-and-track running gear increased significantly. In addition, the extreme complexity of the design led to fantastic costs for the production of a single tank. For example, almost two million rubles were spent on the creation of the first prototype of the T-29 wheel-and-track tank. According to the documents, the cost of the second reference copy of the T-29 was supposed to be one million rubles. According to very optimistic estimates, it was assumed that during mass production the cost of the tank should have decreased to 300,000 rubles. However, even with such a significant reduction in production costs, the price of one copy remained excessive.

The plans for mass production of the extremely complex and expensive T-46 and T-29 tanks turned out to be pipe dreams. With the archaic level of development of the Soviet tank industry, this task set by Stalin back in 1932 was absolutely impossible even at the end of the 1930s. The repression finally finished off the experimental tank projects. All the designers who worked on the T-46 and T-29 in Leningrad were arrested, and some of them were shot. Pavlov, in this situation, could only accept the fait accompli of the failure of these tank projects. On 7 August 1938, he closed the T-46 and T-29 tank projects. Also, due to the execution of the lead designer, experimental work on the creation of the promising AT-1 and SU-14 self-propelled guns stopped.

Then Pavlov finally solved the long-standing problem of the first serial T-18 (MS-1) light infantry tanks. Due to complete wear and permanent defects, they were rusting immobile in the warehouses of the Red Army. The order prepared by Pavlov contained the following instructions:

1. When satisfactory modernisation results are achieved, the existing 862 T-18 tanks should be used in fortified regions as mobile anti-tank defence systems. Work on the modernisation of the T-18 is underway. If the modernisation results are unsatisfactory, the T-18 should be withdrawn from the Red Army and sent for remelting. There are absolutely no spare parts for the T-18, and they are not being manufactured.[10]

Thus, first of all Pavlov had to eliminate the accumulated damage from the activities of his predecessors Khalepsky and Bokis. The 'Peasant's Son' ruthlessly hacked down problems with an axe that his more competent but less determined predecessors could not solve. However, all these decisions were just a warm-up for the upcoming 'big game'. Pavlov was faced with much more difficult problems. The chronic tank stalemate of 1937, which resulted from the constant interference of the incompetent Stalin in the development of Soviet Tank-Automotive Troops, required an urgent exit.

Audit of the Soviet Tank-Automotive Troops

The new Head of the ABTU, who had unlimited confidence from Stalin, found it easier to objectively assess the results of the ten-year development of Soviet Tank-Automotive Troops. One of Pavlov's most important activities as Head of the ABTU was to analyse the current state of tanks used in the Red Army. It took him two months to carry out this important activity against the background of the ongoing unprecedented repression.

NKVD investigators continued to search for 'enemies of the people' in the ABTU. In addition to the former ABTU chief Gustav Bokis, many of his subordinates were arrested during the first few months of 1938. It's hard to even imagine the terrible conditions Pavlov's employees were working in. They were constantly expecting new arrests. However, by mid-February 1938, the surviving ABTU specialists still managed to complete an assessment of the condition of the tanks used in the Red Army.

Pavlov had the opportunity to compare the information obtained during the audit, as well as numerous critical reports from high-ranking military personnel on tank deficiencies, with his personal experience in command of the Mechanised Brigade and combat experience in Spain. In addition, Pavlov not only commanded, but also perfectly knew all types of Soviet tanks. One day, he impressed Stalin by sitting down at the levers of a T-26 tank himself during one of the presentations and demonstrating the highest skill in controlling it.

As a result of the analysis, Pavlov, like many other competent senior Red Army commanders, came to depressing conclusions. Despite the huge number of tanks produced, their combat qualities were very low. The reality of using tanks in numerous local conflicts turned out to be very far from the pretentious Stalinist parades on Red Square. The thin armour that poorly protected mid-1930s Soviet tanks, even from heavy machine guns, was completely insufficient in modern warfare. The presence of numerous 37mm anti-tank guns in the potential enemy led to catastrophic losses of BTs and T-26s. With the level of combat capability demonstrated by Soviet tanks in Spain, it was impossible to implement Stalin's plans for an aggressive war in Europe.

Based on this information, Pavlov realised the need for an urgent radical revision of the Soviet Tank Armament System and the creation of fundamentally different tanks of the 'New Type' to urgently replace the 'Wreckers' tanks of the 'Old Type'. At the beginning of 1938, it seemed to him that this could be done quickly enough. Pavlov did not expect that it would take so much time and effort to solve this problem, and the result of his efforts would be completely unexpected for him.

The 'Peasant's Son' at the Head of the Soviet Tank-Automotive Troops

Pavlov was a typical representative of the new generation of military men selected and tested by Stalin. By age and attitude towards the 'Red Lord', this group of young military men acted as his many 'sons'. They were mostly fairly capable and motivated Red Army mid-level commanders. However, compared to the Tukhachevsky generation, their level of education and military experience was incomparably lower.

In many ways, the new Technical Leader of the Red Army Pavlov was the exact opposite of Tukhachevsky and Uborevich. Unlike the 'Red Marshal', who commanded large military formations such as the front (army group) in the Russian Civil War, Pavlov's command and control experience was limited to commanding a tank brigade in a local conflict. Tukhachevsky, defining the strategy of using the Red Army, was inspired by the problems of the global First World War. Pavlov, due to the fragmented nature of his education and narrow horizons, focused on the tactics of using tanks in local conflicts. Once in the position of Technical Leader of the Red Army, he could only use the experience of the local Spanish Civil War. Having experienced tank battles, having survived numerous military engagements, Pavlov knew exactly what was needed to succeed in battle when capturing a small town or village. Such tactical awareness was sufficient for the tank brigade commander's level, but it was not sufficient for the strategic level of military command to which 'Peasant's Son' stubbornly promoted Stalin.

Tukhachevsky considered the strategy of the Soviet version of the German blitzkrieg to be the most effective tool for waging a future aggressive war in Europe. In his opinion, a well-coordinated ensemble of tanks, planes and self-propelled guns was supposed to break through deep gaps in the enemy's defences and rapidly develop an offensive in his deep rear. The main role in this offensive strategy belonged to tanks of various types. As Head of Armaments of the Red Army, Tukhachevsky contributed to the creation of many types of specialised tanks. Each of them carried out their task in a general rapid offensive.

Pavlov doubted the viability of the Soviet version of blitzkrieg, and was sceptical about the thesis of the leading role of tanks in a future major war. The strategic plans of the 'Red Militarist', who planned the occupation of Europe, were not available to Pavlov. He was also strongly opposed to the use of multiple types of specialised tanks in the Red Army. His personal experience of using tanks in the Spanish Civil War testified to the impossibility of practical implementation of the Tukhachevsky approach. As noted above, due to a number of circumstances, his professional development stopped at the tank brigade commander level. The practical 'Peasant's Son' decided to ignore Tukhachevsky's strategy, which he did not understand, and focus his efforts on solving the most pressing problems of Soviet Tank-Automotive Troops.

On 21 February 1938, Pavlov sent Voroshilov a report on the current state of tanks used by the Red Army. In his introductory part, for the first time, he directly stated one of their main problems to the Soviet Tank-Automotive Troops:

> Currently, the Red Army has nine types of tanks in service (T-27, T-37, T-38, T-26, BT-2, BT-5, BT-7, T-28, and T-35). According to the Resolution No. 94ss of the Defence Committee at the Council of People's Commissars of the Soviet Union,[11] since 1939, seven new types of tanks have been additionally introduced (light amphibious tank, STZ light wheel-and-track tank, wheel-and-track reconnaissance tank, BT with diesel, BT with three-axle wheeled drive, T-29 wheel-and-track tank, T-35 with reinforced armour and a 1,000 hp engine).
>
> In fact, the number of tank types is much larger, since the above list does not include special-purpose tanks (artillery, flamethrower, military engineering, remote control tanks).[12]

According to the new Head of the ABTU, such a large number of different types of tanks created great difficulties in managing Soviet Tank-Automotive Troops, complicated operation and repair, supply of spare parts and training of tankmen. Differences in the military specifications (speed, cross-country ability, armour and armament) of these tanks, operating in the same compound, led to the impossibility of their joint combat use. Pavlov, rightly noting the difficulties of manufacturing and combat use of such a diverse armoured fighting vehicles, proposed to reduce all types of tanks to three main ones. At the end of the 1930s, this proposal by the new Head of the ABTU was quite progressive. However, the complete rejection of Tukhachevsky's ideas became one of the factors of the strategic and tactical weakness of the Red Army tank units in a future clash with the Panzerwaffe.

It must be admitted that the problem of the multiplicity of tank types, which became acute in the late 1930s, was a direct consequence of total distortion in the implementation of the Tukhachevsky doctrine. In the process of accelerated production, strange 'Frankenstein' tanks appeared in improvised 'tank factories' based on American and British tanks. Stalin's endless interference, Voroshilov's intrigues, the struggle for control of the Soviet military industry between different factions, design defects, terrible production quality, and finally, Tukhachevsky's own mistakes led to another tank impasse at the end of the 1930s. Tank 'Freaks' were the result of temporary compromise solutions for the sake of a feverish pursuit of Stalin's plans. Thus, the logically constructed 'Red Marshal' scheme of using many types of tanks turned into a pathetic parody of itself.

When defining the development strategy of Soviet Mechanised Troops, Tukhachevsky actively used advanced German military experience. The 'Red Marshal' personally communicated with German generals and constantly improved strategic techniques for using innovative military equipment. As noted above, Pavlov was virtually devoid of contact with Western military experience. As a result of this and many other reasons, he did not make any progress in understanding the strategy of using tanks. As noted above, his level of intellectual development and military competence was completely insufficient to fully fulfil the role of Technical Leader of the Red Army. Despite his extensive life experience, Pavlov remained a man with the world view of a peasant's son and the experience of a tank brigade commander. He didn't care about anything except the tactics of using tank troops. However, even here Pavlov's range of professional interests was significantly limited. He thought little about the interaction of tanks with aviation and did not pay enough attention to the development of promising assault guns.

Such narrow horizons of Pavlov and other representatives of the new generation of the military suited Stalin perfectly. He needed absolutely loyal military and technical specialists without political ambitions, obedient executors of his evil will. Stalin considered questions of military strategy to be his prerogative and was ready to accept the opinions of his new favourites in the Red Army only as material for decision-making. And in this aspect, the expectations of the 'Master' were fully justified. Prior to his execution in July 1941, Pavlov was a diligent executor of Stalin's orders. But his loyalty was still not unlimited. Pavlov did not share his 'Master's' paranoia about 'enemies of the people'. He calmly but consistently opposed the widespread repression in the Red Army. However, one should not attribute humanistic traits to Pavlov on this basis. As a true Bolshevik, he was absolutely ruthless towards the 'enemies' of the Soviet system. The 'Peasant's Son' was only worried about the catastrophic loss of combat capability of his tank forces caused by the destruction of thousands of competent commanders.

Tanks of the 'New Type'

Khalepsky, and Bokis who replaced him, acknowledged individual defects of the Soviet wheel-and-track tanks, but categorically denied their total shortcomings. Prior to Pavlov's appointment as Head of the Tank-Automotive Directorate of the Red Army (ABTU), the Red Army was firmly convinced that the concept proposed by Tukhachevsky and approved by Stalin could not be changed. It was believed that the 'Red Lord' by definition could not be wrong. However, in the era of the Great Terror, responsibility for Stalin's mistakes could be shifted to the executed high-ranking military from 'Tukhachevsky's Group'.

Pavlov was the first to dare to report to Stalin on the need to completely change the concept of using Tank-Automotive Troops and, accordingly, switch to new types of tanks. However, as long as there was at least one supporter of wheel-and-track tanks in high positions in the Red Army, all activities to change the Tank Armament System of the Red Army were limited only to heated discussions. It took some time for the fanatical 'The Bloody Dwarf' and his NKVD executioners to 'clear' a place for new ideas for the development of tank forces.

Finally, after the arrest of Bokis, Pavlov, who received his position, had a free hand to carry out total reforms in the field of development and production of armoured fighting vehicles. The 'Peasant's Son' acted very decisively in these circumstances. Pavlov recognised all previously produced tanks as obsolete and declared the need to create fundamentally new tanks. For them to appear, he needed to completely rethink ABTU's strategy and overcome serious resistance to changes in the Red Army and military industry.

Having practiced solving a lot of long-standing tank problems, Pavlov embarked on fundamental reforms. Based on an analysis of the condition of the tanks used in the Red Army, the 'Peasant's Son' came to the conclusion that it was necessary to make changes to the existing Tank Armament System. He needed to immediately stop the development of tanks of the 'Old Type' and prepare the tank industry to stop their production. Pavlov's decision was like trying to use a paper fence to stop a 'thousand-ton train' travelling at breakneck speed. It soon became clear to him that it was impossible to quickly overcome the inertia of the tank industry management and the Red Army leadership. Pavlov was forced to act in small steps, gradually reducing the speed of the 'thousand-ton train' of the Soviet tank industry and changing the activities of numerous military and civilian bureaucratic structures responsible for the design and production of tanks.

One of his first initiatives was to propose a revision of Resolution No. 94ss of the Defence Committee at the Council of People's Commissars of the Soviet Union 'On new types of tanks for arming Red Army tank forces and on tanks for production in 1938'. These changes assumed that the Soviet designers, in parallel with the work on improving tanks of the 'Old Type', would begin to create fundamentally new tanks with new military specifications. By that time, most of these specifications had already been formulated by Pavlov's predecessors. First of all, it was about the parameters of armour protection and armament of tanks of the 'New Type'.

During numerous experiments at the artillery range firing a 37mm anti-tank gun with standard armour-piercing shells from a distance of more than 500m of armour plates of different thicknesses, it was found that 45mm armour was not penetrated. Based on this, for guaranteed protection, medium tanks of the 'New Type' had to have at least 45mm armour. Pavlov added the classic tracked drive and 76.2mm (3in) tank gun to this hull and turret tank armoured parameter.

Thus, he got the preliminary parameters of the medium tank of the 'New Type'. The magnitude of these parameters seemed to him sufficient to gain dominance on the future battlefield in Europe. However, the path to the creation and mass production of tanks of the 'New Type' turned out to be very long and thorny. The real embodiment of Pavlov's new tank doctrine, the T-34 tank, appeared in metal only at the end of 1940.

The BT-20 (A-20) Tank Design has been Approved by ABTU!

While Pavlov was in Moscow, on Stalin's instructions, repairing the damage caused by 'wreckers' and 'spies', work on the design of the new BT-20 (A-20) wheel-and-track tank was completed at the Design Bureau '24' in Kharkov. A meeting to review the preliminary design of the BT-20 tank was held on 25 March 1938 in Moscow at the office of the Tank-Automotive Directorate of the Red Army (ABTU).

The BT-20 (A-20) design presented by Koshkin to ABTU specialists was an upgraded version of the BT-7, which implemented many of the ideas presented by Firsov. The fully welded hull tank was designed in two versions: with a narrow and wide nose. In both versions, the separate DT machine gun was placed in the frontal armour plate next to the driver. In the hull variant with a wide bow, a fourth crew member was supposed to be placed in the control compartment for maintenance of the separate machine gun. The design of many of the elements of the running gear in the preliminary design of the BT-20 (A-20) wheel-and-track tank was also borrowed from the serial BT-7. In both versions of the project, the bow, stern and upper side armour plates (underwing plates) of the tank hull were positioned sloping. The lower hull armour plates (two-thirds of the height of the tank hull) were positioned according to the BT-7 type, that is, vertically.

The preliminary design of the BT-20 tank was reviewed in a calm and businesslike atmosphere. After Bokis was arrested and Pavlov was appointed in his place, the tension between ABTU and Koshkin completely disappeared. The new Head of the ABTU had no complaints about the Head of Design Bureau '24'. Two staunch supporters of tracked tanks found a common language very quickly.

Following the meeting at ABTU, Pavlov approved the preliminary design of the new 'Super BT' variant. To continue the design, a variant of the BT-20 (A-20) tank with a wide hull nose, four-speed transmission and torque transmission to road wheels using transverse cardan shafts and wheel reduction gears was selected. This is exactly the design drive Koshkin originally proposed for all variants of the 'Super BT' in 1937. No alternative options for transferring torque to a wheeled drive were considered. Also, in accordance with the requirements of the ABTU, it was supposed to increase the BT-20 crew to four people. With these minor comments in mind, Koshkin was given the task of developing the final technical design and manufacturing a prototype tank.

Pavlov also developed quite a constructive relationship with the obstinate director Bondarenko.

With Pavlov's approval, the Design Bureau '24' team, led by Koshkin, has begun the next stage of designing the BT-20 (A-20) wheel-and-track tank. The young designers were very enthusiastic about their small victory, but new difficulties awaited them on the way to creating a new tank.

New Tank Armament System of the Red Army
In the spring of 1938, in Moscow, Stalin and his closest servants discussed the problem of radically changing the Tank Armament

System of the Red Army. In the few years since the beginning of the 1930s, the basic principles of the development of Mechanised Troops, initially put forward by Tukhachevsky, had become firmly established in the practice of the Red Army. However, what happened in reality was significantly different from the original ideas of the 'Red Marshal'. The results of the idealistic plans were significantly distorted by the realities of the constant interference of the incompetent Stalin, the shortage of trained commanders and the archaic Soviet tank industry. However, this ugly tank reality of the end of the 1930s proved to be very resistant to attempts to change it. Under the influence of total propaganda, the position of Stalin's wheel-and-track tanks seemed completely unshakable.

The Tank Armament System, which had developed over the years, had provided significant resistance to Pavlov's attempts to make drastic changes to it. The military and the bosses of the military industry were not interested in dangerous and painful reforms. Pavlov had to overcome tremendous inertia in the Red Army and military industry to fulfil his mission. However, Pavlov's opponents, who were resistant to change, had objective reasons for this.

The 'Old Type' tanks were mass-produced and had trained crews. There was extensive experience in the use of BT and T-26 in local military conflicts, which showed their weaknesses and strengths. On the contrary, the tanks of the 'New Type' parameters that Pavlov proposed to replace them with were still very vague. Military specifications, which later became distinctive features of the T-34 tank, had yet to be determined. Thus, there was no certainty that the archaic Soviet tank industry would be able to produce tanks of the 'New Type', and Soviet tankmen would be able to successfully fight in them in a future major war in Europe.

Pavlov had both allies and opponents on the difficult path of creating tanks of the 'New Type'. The bloody Stalinist repressions had the strongest impact on this process. On the one hand, no matter how sad it is to note, the repression significantly accelerated the overcoming of tank patterns that seemed unshakable until recently. Almost all the high-ranking supporters of the previous views on the development of Mechanised Troops were simply destroyed by the employees of the 'Bloody Dwarf'. As a result, as noted above, all work on the T-29 and T-46 wheel-and-track tanks was discontinued.[13] Thus, proponents of new views on the strategy and tactics of using tanks have more opportunities to implement them. However, supporters of tanks of the 'New Type' also suffered severely from the repression. The destruction of competent managers and qualified engineers slowed down the process of change and worsened the already poor quality of Soviet tanks. For example, after the execution of their creators, the entire line of self-propelled guns (AT-1 and SU-14) and semi-tracked tractors projects completely disappeared.

The result of Stalin's controversial policy was a very strange situation. Paradoxically, the only tank of the 'Old Type' that continued intensive design work was the BT-20 (A-20) tank. No matter how much Pavlov wanted to order the construction of tracked tanks only, he had to come to terms with the fact that work on the 'Super BT' wheel-and-track tank ordered by the 'Trotskyist' Bokis needed to continue.

In the situation of the upcoming big changes in the Tank Armament System of the Red Army, the 'Cavalrymen' prudently took a back seat. Their leader, the cautious schemer Voroshilov, did not dare to contradict Pavlov, who had Stalin's full support. After Bokis arrest, the 'Fake Marshal' immediately changed his views to diametrically opposed ones. From an ardent supporter of wheel-and-track tanks of the 'Old Type', he turned into a 'progressist' and even tried to lead the general direction of tank innovations. Having lost his key favourites due to the repression, the 'Fake Marshal' stopped trying to take over Factory No. 183 (Kharkov) and was satisfied with the dominant influence at the tank factories in Leningrad.

Big Tank Conference

On 20 April 1938, the Big Tank Conference was held in Moscow. The main issue of this secret meeting was the change of the Tank Armament System of the Red Army and the approval of the designs of tanks of the 'New Type'. This long-awaited event was extremely important for the new head of the Tank-Automotive Directorate of the Red Army (ABTU) Komkor (Colonel General) Dmitry Pavlov. The 'Peasant's Son' spent a lot of time preparing for the Big Tank Conference.

Admittedly, this large-scale meeting, which brought together hundreds of military personnel, military industry bosses and tank designers, was organised for only one person. Stalin was the main listener to Pavlov's proposals for the creation of tanks of the 'New Type'. The helpful Pavlov prepared a carefully directed performance for the 'Master', which was played out in full accordance with the script.

Stalin played the role of a wise ruler in it, through which he wanted to strengthen his image as the main 'tank expert'. Despite the importance of the role, it turned out to be very short. All the changes to the Tank Armament System prepared by Pavlov were accepted by the 'Master' without much discussion. During the Tank Conference, Stalin made a few banal remarks about the design of tanks of the 'New Type' and left feeling pleased with himself. The job was done and it seemed that the numerous participants could disperse on their important business. However, in accordance with Soviet traditions, the Big Tank Conference continued for quite a long time without Stalin.

The participants of the performance strenuously created the appearance of a real discussion and even 'voted' for making certain decisions. As a result, all Pavlov's requirements and suggestions for improving the design of the projected BT-20 (A-20) wheel-and-track tank were unanimously accepted by the meeting participants.

Based on the results of the Big Tank Conference, a document was prepared reflecting the following decisions:

> To recognise the design of the BT-20 tank proposed by Factory No. 183 as acceptable. However, it is necessary to increase the thickness of the armour in the frontal part of the tank. Simplify the electrical equipment of the tank installation scheme. To develop a second variant of the turret for the installation of a 76mm tank gun. The tank's crew should consist of four people. Place the whip antenna on tank hull. The radio operator must be located next to the driver. The radio set must be moved from the turret to the tank hull. Communication between the tank commander and the radio operator is carried out using the speaking tube. The elevation of tank gun must be increased to 45°.[14]

In addition, the installation of a flamethrower for self-defence on the tank, provided for in the previous version of the specifications for the BT-20, was cancelled.

On 2 June 1938, after a month of bureaucratic approvals and clarifications, the modified specifications for the BT-20 (A-20) wheel-and-track tank were approved by Voroshilov. Next, the official documents reflecting the new requirements for the Stalin's 'wonder tank' were sent from Moscow to Kharkov.

Meanwhile, the secret Design Bureau '24' team continued to work, unaware of the new upheavals that awaited them in the next few months. Against the background of these shocks, the need to redo the 'Super BT' project once again in accordance with the new tank specifications sent from Moscow would seem to them only minor troubles.

Arrest and Death of Factory No. 183 Management

In 1937, the designers at Kharkov had to work in very difficult conditions. Constant changes in specifications for the different 'Super BT' variants significantly hampered the already difficult work of the

Koshkin team. In fact, in 1937, all the efforts of the young Koshkin team were spent resisting an attempt to seize the factory by members of 'Voroshilov's group'. Due to the combined effect of these factors, the productivity of the actual design work at Factory No. 183 in 1937 was extremely low. During the year, Koshkin failed to complete a single 'Super BT' project. In addition, all these events took place against the backdrop of permanent Stalinist repression. However, the creation of the secret Design Bureau '24' inspired the young designers and they had hopes for a better future.

After the end of the bloody 1937, the residents of the USSR who survived the repressions had the illusion that the most terrible times were already over. However, the new 1938 did not bring the long-awaited relief. Soon, Stalin's Great Terror descended on Soviet citizens with renewed vigour, not excluding the employees of Factory No. 183.

This time, the main target of Stalin's anger was the director of Factory No. 183, Ivan Bondarenko. For a long time, this favourite of Stalin escaped the bloody clutches of the NKVD. It seemed to others that the numerous denunciations and accusations sent to Moscow by his enemies and competitors were not working. However, in the spring of 1938, the attitude of the 'Master' towards the management of factory changed dramatically and the 'Teflon' director fell. On 25 May 1938, Ivan Bondarenko was arrested. Following him, Stalin's executioners arrested several dozen managers and designers, including Fedor Lyasch, Deputy Director of Factory No. 183.

Those arrested were accused of every conceivable crime, from 'violating secrecy' to 'organising an explosion at a factory'. For example, NKVD investigators charged Bondarenko with leading the non-existent Trotskyist Anti-Soviet Organisation and collaborating with German Intelligence. All these utter fantasies of NKVD officers, framed in the form of extensive investigative materials, had nothing to do with reality. The real reason for the arrest and subsequent execution of Factory No. 183's management was the V-2 diesel engine scandal.

As noted above, Stalin wanted to get a tank diesel engine back in 1931. However, the development of the V configuration twelve-cylinder BD-2 piston diesel engine (high-speed diesel engine), which became the development of the German BMW VI aircraft engine, was extremely slow. The technical complexity of the new engine was so great that even the numerous informal consultations received by Soviet engineers from German and American designers did not give the desired result. Intellectually limited, Stalin believed that solving the problem required an energetic manager who could cheer up 'lazy' designers and speed up the process of creating a tank diesel engine.

According to the will of the 'Master', solving the diesel problem became the main mission of Ivan Bondarenko, who was appointed director of the Kharkov Locomotive Factory (KhPZ) on 1 January 1934. With all his inherent energy, he tackled the tank diesel engine problem and quickly made significant progress. By the end of 1934, several prototypes of the BD-2-1 engine (the future V-2 diesel engine) had been tested on an artillery tractor prototype, two high-speed military boats, and two BT-5 tanks.

One of the BT-5 tanks with a BD-2 diesel engine was sent to Moscow to be shown to Stalin. The presentation of the new 'toy' turned out to be very successful. The tank with the diesel engine was very liked by the 'Master', and it seemed to him that the problem had been solved. On 27 March 1935, by order of Stalin, Director Bondarenko and the designers who created the tank diesel engine were awarded the Order of Lenin.

Progress in the development of the tank diesel engine meant the need to prepare for its mass production. To equip the Soviet tank armada, Stalin needed a factory capable of producing thousands of diesel engines per year. Bondarenko understood that the experimental prototype workshop of tank diesel engines at KhPZ could not cope with such a volume of production.

After the presentation of the BT-5 with the BD-2 engine, Bondarenko had a long conversation with Stalin on the topic of organising serial production of the diesel engine. Understanding the technical complexity of the production of the new tank diesel engine, Bondarenko got the 'Master' to make an important decision. It consisted in building a special factory for the serial production of tank diesel engines and allocating huge financial resources to equip the future factory with foreign equipment.

In 1934, construction of a new huge factory capable of producing 10,000 engines per year began at KhPZ. The new Diesel Engine Factory was one of Stalin's main secrets. Equipping it with foreign machine tools and other complex equipment turned out to be a very difficult technological and logistical problem. Solving this problem required no less effort than developing the engine itself.

Soviet engineers, led by Bondarenko, went on long business trips abroad several times to purchase sophisticated imported equipment. They needed precision machine tools to manufacture crankcases, cylinder heads, crankshafts and fuel injection systems for the diesel engine. The atmosphere of secrecy surrounding the tank diesel engine did not allow Moscow to disclose the real purpose of the industrial equipment purchased from foreign partners. When purchasing machine tools in Europe and the USA, Soviet engineers did not report or indicated completely different goals for their acquisition. As a result, the machine tools arrived in separate batches, which turned out to be poorly compatible with each other. The formation of processing lines at the future Diesel Engine Factory required tremendous efforts.

The usual practice of inviting employees of supply companies from the United States, Germany, and Austria to assist was strictly prohibited. The foreign machine tools were excellent, but because of the stupid Stalinist secrecy, their installation and commissioning in Kharkov were carried out by unskilled Soviet workers and engineers. Some of the valuable equipment was hopelessly damaged.

Despite all the difficulties created by Stalin, the problem was nevertheless solved. In 1937, the huge Diesel Engine Factory in Kharkov was ready to begin mass production. However, it soon became clear that there was simply nothing to produce. There was no ready-made prototype of the tank diesel engine for mass production. Despite the success of the presentation in Moscow in 1934, subsequent tests of the diesel engine revealed numerous design defects. The work on improving the prototype of the tank diesel engine stretched over many years. All this time, the tank diesel engine promised to Stalin existed only in the form of several experimental samples. The engineers of Factory No. 183, led by Bondarenko, feverishly continued to refine and correct all the newly identified defects of the highly complex diesel engine.

Meanwhile, Stalin's dissatisfaction with the delays in the start of production grew, and NKVD began collecting denunciations and complaints for the future arrest of Bondarenko. There had been more than enough such 'investigative materials' accumulated over several years of improvements to the diesel engine. For example, Nikolai Gikalo,[15] the Head of the Kharkov Bolsheviks, wrote in a denunciation of Bondarenko: '. . . in 1936, NKVD investigators exposed and liquidated a number of Anti-Soviet Fascist and Terrorist Groups totalling 67 people at the Factory'.[16] Responsibility for such a large number of internal 'enemies' was accordingly assigned to the factory director.

Despite all the efforts of the Factory No. 183 management, things were going badly with the new diesel engine. During 1937, due to constant breakdowns, the deadline for the final testing of the V-2 was postponed several times. If successful, a decision should have been made to start mass production of the diesel engine. Finally, the date of the final testing was set for the beginning of 1938, but this deadline was also missed. After this failure, testing of the modified prototype was scheduled for May 1938. The final testing of the V-2 engine, which took place in April and May 1938, ended unsuccessfully.

After receiving information about the repeated failure of the testing diesel engine, the patience of the pathologically suspicious Stalin ran out. He ordered the NKVD to investigate the activities of the 'wreckers group', consisting of factory management and employees of the Military Quality Control System for Weapons. After a month of torture in NKVD dungeons, Ivan Bondarenko was shot. The same terrible fate befell many employees of Factory No. 183 who participated in the implementation of the tank diesel engine project. This event had a very strong and lasting negative impact on all factory employees.

Fortunately for the future of the T-34 tank, some of the arrested designers survived and, after their miraculous release from Stalin's prison at the end of 1938, continued work on the tank diesel engine. However, the consequences of Stalin's repressions increased the completion period of the diesel engine by another year. Despite all efforts, the designers again made only minor progress in the stable operation of the prototype diesel engine. But Stalin could not wait any longer. On 1 September 1939, it was decided to start mass production of the tank diesel engine. As a result of Stalin's strong-willed decision, the frankly defective engine began to be produced in large quantities. By this time, the designers and technologists of Diesel Engine Factory No. 75 have not been able to rid the V-2 of its key shortcomings.

The V-2, long anticipated by Stalin, became widespread in the Red Army. This engine was used in the BT-7M and the 'Voroshilovec' artillery tractor, and later the T-34 tank. In addition, a more powerful version of the engine began to be installed in KV-1 and KV-2 heavy tanks.

Engine defects became the main problem of units that received new tanks. Since 1939, the Red Army technical service was busy with endless repairs of the V-2. A few years later, tanks of the 'New Type', on which this engine was installed, caused open horror among Soviet technicians. Gradually, the technical services of the Red Army got used to the endless problems of the diesel engine V-2, and began to treat them as an inevitable evil. Despite its active use, the painful elimination of structural defects in the mass-produced V-2 diesel engine continued until the end of the 1940s.

In the decades that have passed since the creation of the V-2 until the collapse of the USSR, Soviet engineers were unable to create an acceptable alternative to the Stalinist diesel engine. Several attempts to add new engines, including the gas turbine engine, ended in an unfortunate failure. Currently, the upgraded version of the V-2 is the main tank engine in the comprehensive armament of the Russian Federation. It is important to note that a number of defects in the upgraded version of the V-2 still have not been eliminated.

Chaos at Factory No. 183 Due to Mass Repressions

The arrest of almost the entire management in May 1938 caused chaos at Factory No. 183. It resonated with the ongoing chaos caused by the repression of the leadership of the military industry and the Red Army. The temporary factory management, who replaced the arrested Bondarenko, desperately tried to continue working. However, all their efforts came to nothing. In fact, NKVD investigators became the main owner of Factory No. 183. They fanatically collected 'investigative materials' for new arrests, completely ignoring the problems arising from their actions. As a result, the activities of the giant tank factory were completely disorganised. All decisions of the interim management of Factory No. 183 had to be coordinated with NKVD officers. In many ways, the situation was repeated at the end of 1936, when the gearbox scandal of the BT tank paralyzed the factory for six months. However, in some aspects, the situation in May 1938 was even worse than in 1936.

Despite the shock and general chaos, the small Design Bureau '24' team tried to continue working on the design of the BT-20 (A-20) wheel-and-track tank. Thanks to Mikhail Koshkin's leadership qualities, the team of young designers maintained minimal efficiency. Aleksey Moloshtanov, one of the creators of the T-34, recalled:

> I can't help but say that Mikhail Koshkin was a born organiser. His energy was bubbling up, he was obsessed with the new tank, and he managed to convey this obsession to all of us. Despite the extreme complexity of the task that had to be solved, we never doubted its reality for a minute and did not spare ourselves in order to achieve our goal.
>
> I was tasked with developing a drawing of a conical turret with the largest possible tilt angle of armour plates of the side armour. Like all members of the Design Bureau team, I worked with great enthusiasm and was proud of the honour.[17]

Meanwhile, Stalin demanded that the design of the 'Super BT' be accelerated. In response to the fair complaints coming from Kharkov about the lack of qualified designers, Moscow made emergency decisions. At the end of April 1938, by order of the Head of the 8th Main Directorate of the People's Commissariat of the Defence Industry Sviridov, the team of the secret Design Bureau '24' was increased to twenty-nine people. The 'new designers' were transferred from other design bureaus in Factory No. 183. It was planned to increase the Design Bureau '24' team to thirty-seven people, but it was not possible to find such a number of qualified tank designers at the factory, drained of blood by mass arrests.

Inspections and the inevitably violent repression that followed led to a constant change in the heads of military factories. NKVD agents were constantly engaged in this bloody 'work' at tank factories from 1937 to early 1939. Under these conditions, the position of director or chief designer at military factories had become deadly. For any real, and often imaginary, mistake or failure, the person holding these positions was threatened with prison and execution. The events in Kharkov were a vivid illustration of this ominous trend. For example, the NKVD arrested many people who were directly or indirectly involved in the creation of the prototype of the T-34 (A-34) tank: Afanasii Firsov, Nikolai Cyganov, Adolf Dik and Ivan Bondarenko. Mikhail Koshkin, the Chief Designer of the T-34 tank, was able to escape this sad fate with great difficulty. His communication skills again played a significant role in this. He was able to establish constructive relations even with Stalin's NKVD executioners. This 'dialogue' with the killers largely saved him and the young members of the Design Bureau '24' team.

In the context of the ongoing repression, it was deadly dangerous to make decisions on your own without coordination with Moscow. NKVD investigators constantly intervened in the work of Design Bureau '24'. They closely monitored the precise execution of orders emanating from Moscow. However, the constant changes in specifications to the 'Super BT' and the lack of permanent management of Factory No. 183 greatly complicated the work. The chaos caused by the arrests at the People's Commissariat of the Defence Industry disrupted Moscow's interaction with Kharkov. It was almost impossible to obtain documents confirming the numerous changes in the design of the experimental tank. For example, the modified technical requirements for the BT-20 (A-20) tank were approved by Voroshilov on 2 June 1938, but the text of these new technical requirements could not be received in Kharkov until the end of the summer. As a result of the chaos and NKVD interference, the design of the secret tank was carried out on the basis of a huge number of clarifying documents and even verbal instructions. This caused a lot of delays in the work of Design Bureau '24', and most importantly, the huge risks of the arrest of the designers by NKVD investigators. In these unfavourable conditions, a small team of designers at Kharkov tried their best to fulfil Moscow's assignment. As Mikhail

Koshkin rightly noted in his letter, 'in the process of developing the BT-20 (A-20) tank design, all this required redesigning the same tank components several times and re-calculating their strength'.[18]

With the ongoing Great Terror, there was no way to solve the key design problems of the secret BT-20 (A-20) tank. Koshkin's team members often bitterly stated that most of the working time in 1938 could be just as pointlessly lost as in 1937. Moscow also realised that the interim management of Factory No. 183, who replaced the arrested managers, was not coping with their duties. The situation at the factory was desperate. All employees of the tank industry, both in Moscow and Kharkov, could only hope that they would survive and later be able to solve all the accumulated problems. However, not all the participants in the described events lived to see the end of the mass repressions.

Degradation of the ABTU

In 1938, the staff of the Tank-Automotive Directorate of the Red Army (ABTU) also continued to be subjected to repression. Many of them became victims of the NKVD's bloody harvest.

As noted above, as a result of the repression, communication between peripheral tank factories and Moscow was disrupted. The strict system of sending orders and receiving reports has almost stopped working. The new Head of the ABTU Pavlov received only scraps of information about the work on designing a secret tank in Kharkov. Due to the lack of information, he was very worried about the situation at Factory No. 183. Bombarded by constant requests from Stalin, Pavlov urgently left for Kharkov. Thus, ABTU degraded to the level of the beginning of the 1930s, when the late predecessor Pavlov Khalepsky was almost constantly located not in Moscow, but at one of the tank factories.

On 7 July 1938, an ABTU commission headed by Komkor (Colonel General) Dmitry Pavlov arrived at Factory No. 183. The commission was at the factory on 7 and 8 July 1938. During these two days, Pavlov personally tried to find out the state of affairs on the production of BT-7 tanks and the development of mass production of the V-2 diesel engine and the BT-7M tank with this engine. He was also interested in the state of affairs with the design of the secret 'wonder tank'. When meeting with Koshkin, Pavlov had a long conversation with him about the state of development of the BT-20 (A-20) wheel-and-track tank project. He looked sceptically at the tall stacks of drawings shown to him by the designers of Design Bureau '24'. The complexity of the design of the convertible drive wheel-and-track tank caused him to feel close to despair. Pavlov was sure that by creating a new wheel-and-track tank, the designers were wasting precious resources. Not daring to disobey the 'Master', the new Head of the ABTU painfully searched for any acceptable ways to abandon the wheel-and-track tank. Finally, he managed to find an acceptable solution, giving hope for a change in Stalin's position. It was the discussion of this decision that was one of the reasons for his trip to Kharkov.

Following a personal meeting, Pavlov agreed with Koshkin on significant changes to the 'Super BT' project. They made a joint decision to create two variants of the BT-20 (A-20) tank in parallel. The first version of the tank would have a wheel-and-track convertible drive, that is, it would comply with the specifications adopted by the Big Tank Conference and approved by Stalin. The second variant of the BT-20 (A-20) tank would be equipped only with the classic caterpillar drive. This variant was named tank 'A-20 with caterpillar drive' in the internal documents of Factory No. 183. Under the NKVD's total control, such a decision, which did not have the approval of the USSR top management, was extremely risky and could be regarded as 'wrecking'. Pavlov, aware of this danger, promised Koshkin to legalise the tank specification changes in the near future and soon kept his word.

After Pavlov left for Moscow, Design Bureau '24' began parallel work on the second version, 'A-20 with caterpillar drive'. By spending scarce resources on developing a tank design without an official order, Koshkin took a lot of risks. If NKVD investigators had found out about this, he would have been arrested immediately. However, it was not by chance that Koshkin received the nickname 'Ardent' from his subordinates. He was willing to take reasonable risks to realise his long-held dream of creating a new medium tank with caterpillar drive. However, the implementation of this sensible decision, the direct result of which was the creation of the T-34, was postponed, and even threatened with cancellation by another arrest in the top management of the tank industry.

On 8 July 1938, the Head of the 8th Main Directorate of the People's Commissariat of the Defence Industry, Vasily Sviridov, was arrested. This former Bokis deputy oversaw all issues related to the development of experimental tanks at the Commissariat of the Defence Industry. As a result of this wave of arrests, the activities of the 8th Main Directorate of the People's Commissariat of the Defence Industry were paralyzed for more than a month.

Only on 21 August 1938, the People's Commissar of the Defence Industry (Minister) Mikhail Kaganovich signed order No. 335ss, which read: 'Three tank prototypes – two with caterpillar drive and one wheel-and-track tank with 8×6-wheel convertible drive must be manufactured at Factory No. 183 and transferred to the People's Commissariat of the Defence Industry for testing by 1 June 1939. Need to install flamethrower on one of the caterpillar drive tanks.'[19] After Kaganovich's decision, the threat of arrest of the Head of Design Bureau '24' decreased somewhat. With the legalisation of the tank 'A-20 with caterpillar drive' project, Koshkin and Pavlov very gradually, overcoming one barrier after another, moved towards the future specifications of the T-34.

The priority of the development of the Soviet tank forces is tracked tanks

On 27 August 1938, the Design Bureau '24' team completed the design of two versions of Stalin's 'wonder tank'. On 6 September 1938, a special commission arrived at Factory No. 183 (Kharkov) to review the design results, headed by one of Pavlov's deputies. Koshkin presented the technical design of the BT-20 (A-20) wheel-and-track tank and the 'A-20 with caterpillar drive' to the members of the commission. Moscow's greatest interest was naturally aroused by the tank with caterpillar drive option.

In an explanatory note to the technical design tank, Koshkin noted the following important advantages of the 'A-20 with caterpillar drive':

With the abolition of wheeled drive, the design of the A-20 tank is significantly simplified and a reduction in the overall weight of the tank is achieved. This allows for the installation of more powerful weapons in the turret in the form of 76.2mm L-10 tank gun. At the same time, the weight of the tank does not increase beyond the calculated one.

The simplification of the tank design itself entails the abolition of a number of details that were inherent in the wheel-and-track tank, namely:

1) gearwheels – 30 pieces;
2) gear couplings and plain bearings – 42 pieces;
3) ball bearings – 46 pieces;
4) cardan joints – 12 pieces;
5) steel castings – 14 pieces.

At the same time, along with the relief, the complete interchangeability of all road wheels and suspension arms on the tank is achieved, and there is also no need to manufacture two types of suspension arms – right and left.

Due to the cancellation of the front steering road wheels, the shape of the tank hull in the front part is straightened and the side plates will not have a ledge, and the width of the tank hull in this place increases by 122mm, which provides greater freedom in placing the crew in the bow of the tank.

Ammunition storage on the bottom of the tank acquires a simpler design and provides for the placement of more ammunition. Approximately, we can expect an increase in the number of 45mm shells for tank gun and circular magazines for DT machine gun to (630 cartridges, 10 circular magazines).[20]

These detailed arguments by Koshkin in favour of caterpillar drive were supposed to help Pavlov overcome the remaining doubts of the pathologically suspicious Stalin.

The BT-20 technical design project in two versions: wheel-and-track tank and 'A-20 with caterpillar drive' was approved by the Moscow commission with some comments. After returning to Moscow on 6 September 1938, representatives of the Tank-Automotive Directorate of the Red Army (ABTU) sent an order to Kharkov, which, in particular, stated: 'The Factory needs to produce one wheel-and-track tank with a 45mm gun, two tanks with caterpillar drive with a 76mm gun and one tank hull for test firing.'[21] Thus, as a result of the joint efforts of Pavlov and Koshkin, the emphasis in the BT-20 (A-20) secret tank project gradually shifted from the wheel-and-track tank to the tank with caterpillar drive.

New Director of Factory No. 183

In the autumn of 1938, the situation at Factory No. 183 (Kharkov) continued to be very difficult. Numerous arrests had left workshops and departments without proper management. Production plans were chronically not fulfilled. NKVD teams of investigators were constantly scouring the factory. Mistakes accidentally made by workers or critical statements about the Soviet regime under Stalin's Great Terror were interpreted as 'terrorism' and 'espionage' in favour of unfriendly foreign states. In these unbearable conditions, many skilled workers fled the factory under various pretexts. Former Head of the Bureau of Operation of the Tank Department Factory No. 183 Nikolai Sobol' described the atmosphere at the factory at that time as follows:

The arrests of a number of the most experienced executives at the factory, who enjoyed the authority and respect of the team, caused people to be tacitly wary and nervous, bordering on passivity: 'What is this?', 'What else can we expect?' It was like ordinary people saying in such cases,

'I've lived a day, and thank God, but if we live to see what happens tomorrow, we'll see.'

The emotional tension at the factory and the complexity of production processes for a long time led to the fact that, although it was possible to earn more money than at other factories there were always few people willing to work here. In view of this circumstance, the city authorities have repeatedly had to give orders to enterprises in the city of Kharkov to forcibly send workers to permanent work at Factory No. 183.[22]

After the arrest of Bondarenko and his deputies, there was no fully-fledged management at Factory No. 183 for more than six months. The situation continued to deteriorate, and the temporary management of the factory was powerless to change anything. Only Moscow could appoint a new director of the largest tank factory. However, finding a competent manager to manage the giant Kharkov plant in the face of total repression proved to be a very difficult task. There was simply no one in the People's Commissariat of the Defence Industry to do this. Most of the staff had been arrested. The bosses of the military industry who remained at large were engaged in saving their own lives. Finally, in October 1938, People's Commissar of the Defence Industry (Minister) Mikhail Kaganovich appointed a new director to Kharkov. Yuri Maksarev became it. Prior to his appointment to this position, he was Head of the Special Tank Department at the 'Kirov' Factory in Leningrad.

The new director of Factory No. 183 inherited a very difficult legacy. Amid the chaos caused by the repression, Maksarev tried to somehow stabilise the situation at the factory. During the first two weeks of his stay in Kharkov, Maksarev begged the NKVD leadership to release at least some of the arrested specialists. He justified his requests by the inability to fulfil Stalin's task of designing and manufacturing military products. Fortunately, his attempts to save innocent people coincided with the emerging trend towards easing repression. Soon, Maksarev secured the release of several 'wreckers' who were imprisoned in NKVD and awaiting execution. However, the new director could not save most of the Factory No. 183 specialists. They'd already been shot!

The new director quickly found common ground with the Head of Design Bureau '24' Koshkin. Yuri Maksarev was well aware that the future of the factory, and therefore its future, depended on the success of the BT-20 (A-20) secret project. Survival in the face of total repression has become a common task for Maksarev and Koshkin. They helped each other with everything they could. No one knew how long the repression would last, and the alliance of Maksarev and Koshkin increased their overall chances of survival.

Is This the End of Repression?

Despite the total horror that engulfed the USSR, in the second half of 1938, there were high-ranking Red Army commanders who decided to personally ask the 'Master' to mitigate the Great Terror. They were a group of young favourites of Stalin, whom he had recently appointed to high positions vacated after the execution of their predecessors. Among these few brave men was the Head of the ABTU Dmitry Pavlov. Quite unexpectedly, the 'Master' listened to the opinion of his favourites.

Under the influence of numerous reports and letters about the chaos caused by the repressions, Stalin's mood gradually changed. Having decided that the main tasks of the Great Terror were completed, and that the negative consequences exceeded the 'positive' results, he decided to curtail the repression. However, stopping the bloody machine of Yezhov turned out to be a very difficult task. In these circumstances, Stalin acted in his usual way. He found a new favourite who was supposed to physically destroy Yezhov and his accomplices in committing mass murder.

On 25 November 1938, in preparation for the implementation of Stalin's plan, Yezhov was transferred from his post to another position. Lavrentiy Beria became the new People's Commissar of Internal Affairs. On 10 April 1939, Beria arrested Yezhov. On 6 February 1940, Yezhov was shot on Stalin's orders.

Historians usually define Beria's appointment to the position of NKVD chief as the end of the Great Terror. As an argument, they cite statistics indicating a significant decrease in the number of shootings. For example, if, according to official data, 400,000 people were shot in 1938 on charges of 'Anti-Soviet and Terrorist activities', then in 1939 'only' 2,600 people were executed. As mentioned above, the supposedly awakened 'humanity' of Stalin has nothing to do with reducing the scale of mass killings at the state level. The devastating impact of the repressions turned out to be so total that even such natural-born executioners as Beria began to fear their consequences. It was these rational considerations that forced Stalin and his bloody executioners to take a number of actions to reduce the devastating consequences of repression. In 1939–40, 150,000–200,000 people were released from Stalin's prisons and Gulag labour camp system. Among them were several hundred miraculously surviving designers and managers of the Soviet tank industry. No one apologised to them for the illegal arrests and torture. The NKVD executioners ordered them to keep quiet and thank Stalin for not executing them.

'There is no need to restrict the factory's initiative, I trust its employees. Let them build both tanks . . .'[23]

By December 1938, the technical design of the two variants of the BT-20 (A-20) tank was ready. For Stalin, the end of the development of the secret tank project was not news. The 'Master' was in a hurry to start a major war in Europe, so he demanded constant reports from his servants. From Pavlov's regular reports, he knew the smallest details of the creation of this and all other tanks of the 'New Type' projects. However, for the production of prototypes of the two BT-20 (A-20) variants (wheel-and-track and caterpillar drive) Pavlov and Koshkin needed to receive the highest blessing of the main Soviet 'tank expert', Stalin. The ritual that had developed by that time required a formal approval procedure for tank models before making a decision on the manufacture of prototypes. Stalin loved rituals, so despite his haste, he ordered an official event with his participation.

The tank mock-ups approval ritual took place on 9 and 10 December 1938 in the Kremlin at an official meeting of the Military Council of the Red Army. The meeting was attended by permanent members of the Military Council: Joseph Stalin, Leon Mekhlis,[24] Yefim Shchadenko,[25] Semyon Budyonny, Grigory Kulik,[26] Aleksandr Loktionov[27] and Dmitry Pavlov.

A year and a half had passed since the memorable Military Council meeting in the summer of 1937, at which the 'Master' explained to his servants why he decided to execute the most competent senior commanders of the Red Army. Since that time, the composition of the Military Council had almost completely changed. All those present, except Stalin, Voroshilov and Budyonny, were replacements for the former members who had been executed. In addition to high-ranking military officials, new, as yet inexperienced bosses of the Soviet military industry also took part in the meeting. They also recently replaced their executed predecessors. The permanent chairman of this pompous performance was the 'Fake Marshal' Voroshilov. The purpose of the large-scale presentation was to show Stalin and his closest servants mock-ups of tanks of the 'New Type'. They were prepared in great haste under Pavlov's supervision by Soviet tank designers who survived the repressions in Leningrad, Kharkov and Moscow.

Before the presentation, Dmitry Pavlov, Head of the Tank-Automotive Directorate of the Red Army (ABTU), delivered the main report. His entire speech boiled down to endless thanks to Stalin for his wise leadership in the development of Soviet Tank-Automotive

Troops. Every time the name of the 'Master' was mentioned, loud and prolonged applause rang out in the hall. At the end of the speech, the Head of the ABTU invited the audience to consistently consider the models of tanks of the 'New Type' of three main types: T-100[28] and SMK heavy tanks,[29] BT-20 (A-20) medium tank and T-40 light amphibious tank.[30] Each of the projects was represented by a Chief Designer who supervised the work on its design of the appropriate type of tank.

After reviewing the mock-ups of the T-100 and SMK heavy tanks, the turn came to the presentation of the BT-20 medium tank (A-20) project. It was presented in two versions: with wheel-and-track drive and with caterpillar drive. Mikhail Koshkin, Head of the Design Bureau '24' Factory No. 183 (Kharkov), and Aleksander Morozov, Lead Engineer of the BT-20 (A-20) project, addressed the audience. According to the scenario approved by Stalin, an 'acute' discussion was to take place after each report. Accordingly, after Koshkin talked about two alternative versions of the BT-20 (A-20) tank, a heated 'discussion' of their military specifications began. Most of the military personnel present, including Deputy People's Commissariat of Defence of the Soviet Union Grigory Kulik, preferred the wheel-and-track variant. They justified their position with the greater operational mobility of the 'convertible tank', capable of making long marches on road wheels. Pavlov countered this idea of the late Marshal Tukhachevsky with an argument about the caterpillar drive's greater technical reliability and adaptability for off-road driving. These arguments were expressed quite emotionally by the opponents. Those present had the impression that Kulik, the leader of the wheel-and-track drive supporters, was emerging as the clear winner in this dispute. Koshkin and Morozov, who did not know the scenario of this event, believed under the influence of excitement that their caterpillar drive tank project was under threat. In desperation, Koshkin began to loudly and very emotionally defend the need to manufacture and test two prototypes of the BT-20: with wheel-and-track drive and with caterpillar drive. At this climactic moment, it was time for the performance of the 'main' character. Stalin, after listening to Koshkin's arguments, came to his defence. The 'Master' graciously allowed the production of prototypes of two variants of the presented BT-20 (A-20) tank design. After the opinion expressed by Stalin, the military's attacks on Koshkin's tracked tank immediately stopped.[31] To a naive observer, from among the recently appointed to the posts of the executed predecessors, it might seem that the 'Master' had made this decision under the influence of a request from representatives of Factory No. 183. However, contrary to the claims of some Russian historians, there could be no solution other than that voiced by Stalin at this 'performance'.

Stalin and Pavlov had decided long before this meeting at Kremlin to produce both prototypes of the BT-20 (A-20) tank. At this meeting, the Head of the ABTU was almost able to convince Stalin of the need to abandon the creation of new wheel-and-track tanks. However, the suspicious 'Master' was in no hurry to make a final decision. He believed that it was possible to abandon the wheel-and-track version of the BT-20 tank (A-20) only based on the results of comparative tests of the two prototypes. Pavlov was forced to agree with Stalin, and Design Bureau '24' continued to spend scarce resources and time developing the no longer needed 'Super BT'. The BT-20 (A-20) wheel-and-track tank, which had been under development for many years, ended its history at the prototype stage and was never mass-produced.

Unaware of Stalin's decision, the Head of Design Bureau '24' very reliably played the role of a progressive designer fighting the conservative military. Moreover, he even received unexpected dividends from the 'Master's' compliment towards him. Koshkin, who managed to convince the 'Great' Stalin of his rightness, immediately began to be perceived by a high-ranking audience of the Military Council as a hero and a great authority.

The Birth of the T-32 (A-32) Tank

After returning to Kharkov from Moscow, Koshkin and Morozov congratulated the Design Bureau '24' team on receiving permission to manufacture prototypes of BT-20 tanks. Shortly after, Factory No. 183 received an official order from the Tank-Automotive Directorate of the Red Army (ABTU) for the manufacture of two variants: with wheel-and-track drive and with caterpillar drive. However, before preparing working drawings and submitting them for prototypes production, it was necessary to make changes to the design of the tank with caterpillar drive variant. By personal order of Komkor (Colonel General) Dmitry Pavlov, it was decided to increase the thickness of the hull tank's vertical armour plates from 25mm to 30mm. The Head of the ABTU believed that armour of this thickness would provide reliable protection against 12.7mm armour-piercing bullets that easily penetrated the armour of Soviet tanks in Spain. The increase in armour thickness has again led to the tedious redesign of many important systems of the tank with caterpillar drive.

To speed up the design of the BT-20 (A-20), Yuri Maksarev, Director of the Factory No. 183, wisely decided to increase the number of designers and support staff in the Design Bureau '24' team.

Despite the consequences of the repression, in the staff of the giant factory, which produced not only tanks, but also artillery tractors, locomotives and diesel engines, managed to find several qualified specialists (designers, draftsmen and blueprint copier specialists), which Koshkin needed so much.

On 13 January 1939, the Design Bureau '24' team completed work on the working drawings of the BT-20 (A-20) wheel-and-track tank and began finalising the tank with caterpillar drive project. The changes in the project concerned increasing the hull tank's reservation to 30mm and installing a 76.2mm L-10 gun in the turret.

Meanwhile, Moscow was undergoing lengthy bureaucratic procedures for approving drawings and layouts of two variants of the BT-20 (A-20) tank, approved on 9 and 10 December 1938 by the Military Council of the Red Army.

On 27 February 1939, the specifications of the BT-20 (A-20) tank were officially approved. The BT-20 (A-20) number was used to designate the wheel-and-track tank, and the tank with caterpillar drive was given the official name T-32 (A-32). Thus, everything was ready for the production of prototypes of Stalin's 'wonder tanks'.

Stalin's Rush and Production Hell

In 1939, against the background of increasing military tensions in Europe, Stalin had serious reasons for haste. The 'Master' constantly demanded that the new bosses of the military industry produce prototypes of new tanks in the shortest possible time. He wanted to be able to equip the Red Army with thousands of tanks of the 'New Type' before the start of the big war. However, it was his idiotic decisions and their consequences that became the main reason for the constant slowdown of the military industry.

The development design and production of Soviet tank reached its peak in 1935, followed by stagnation. After the creation of the BT-7, Kharkov failed to create a single fundamentally new tank. The situation was similar in Leningrad, where all attempts to create a replacement for the T-26 failed. Due to the uncertainty and chaos caused by the bloody repression and stupid orders of the 'Master', several years were irretrievably lost. Despite the curtailment of repression, it took several years to eliminate its most devastating consequences. The fear of Stalinist arbitrariness, which paralyzed creative activity, remained with the surviving young designers until the end of their days. The rush caused by fear of punishment and the resulting production hell continued to be an integral attribute of the Soviet military industry.

After Stalin approved Pavlov's plan to create tanks of the 'New Type', work at Kharkov on the production of BT-20 (A-20) and T-32 (A-32) prototypes was carried out in a frenzied hurry (Shturmovshchina). The workers and engineers of Experimental Workshop 500 were forced to work around the clock. Pavlov, who supervised this work, constantly sent Voroshilov reports on the progress of work on the production of prototypes of BT-20 (A-20) and T-32 (A-32) tanks. In reality, these reports were intended for Stalin personally, and the 'Fake Marshal' only played the role of a postman.

As soon as the drawings were ready, they were immediately sent from Design Bureau '520' to workshops at Factory No. 183 or to other factories for the manufacture of parts, assemblies or mechanisms of BT-20 (A-20) and T-32 (A-32) tanks. This parallel method of work of designers and workers in the manufacture of prototypes of military equipment was traditional for the Soviet military industry. However, most of the huge human, material and time resources were wasted. Due to this 'innovative' approach, due to small changes in the drawings, many parts and entire systems of the tank had to be redone several times. As a result, haste did not lead to an acceleration of work, but to its significant slowdown. In the long history of the T-34 tank, this vicious practice has been repeated many times.

Additional problems for the designers were created by the need to simultaneously produce two versions of the wonder tank prototypes at once. In terms of its design, geometric dimensions, as well as the thickness and slope of the armour plates, the turret of the A-32 tank basically did not differ from the turret of the A-20 tank. However, although most of the parts, assemblies and mechanisms of the tank with caterpillar drive had the same design as the elements of the wheel-and-track tank, many elements of the tanks were significantly different. For example, in the frontal armour plate of the turret of the T-32 (A-32) tank, due to the installation of the more powerful 76.2mm L-10 gun, the dimensions of the embrasure were increased.

Due to the fact that the turret, originally designed for the installation of a compact 45mm tank gun, had to be equipped with a larger 76.2mm gun, the working conditions in the turret of two crew members deteriorated significantly.

Both tanks were armed with two 7.62mm DT machine guns (the coaxial machine gun and the separate machine gun mounted in the tank hull's front plate). The main difference between the prototype T-32 (A-32) tank and the BT-20 (A-20) was the simpler design of the running gear.

On 26 May 1939, the prototype BT-20 (A-20) wheel-and-track tank was completed. On the same day, a tank on a wheeled drive made a short trip through the grounds of Factory No. 183. The main weapon was missing from the manufactured prototype for some time due to the fact that the artillery factory had failed to deliver the 45mm gun on time. Finally, on 28–30 May, the tank gun and the coaxial DT machine gun, inherited from the BT-7, were installed in the turret of the tank. An important difference between the fully welded BT-20 (A-20) turret and its predecessor BT-7 was that the turret ring diameter increased by 70mm.

From 2–3 June to 15 July 1939, factory testing of the BT-20 (A-20) prototype took place at the Test Range on the outskirts of Kharkov. According to archival documents, during factory testing, the tank travelled 872km, of which 217km was using wheeled drive and 655km with caterpillar drive. The factory testing programme was not completed. The reason for the testing shutdown was numerous breakdowns, which caused the tank to completely lose mobility. The immobilised BT-20 (A-20) was urgently sent to Experimental Workshop '500' Factory No. 183 for repair. In order for the prototype to continue testing as soon as possible, factory technicians had to work around the clock.

On 15 July 1939, the prototype of the T-32 (A-32) tank was completed and made a short trip through the grounds of the factory. Soon it was also sent for factory testing at the Test Range on the outskirts of Kharkov. During factory testing, the T-32 (A-32) tank was able to travel 235km. After that, the tank completely lost its mobility and was sent to the factory for major repair.

Despite constant breakdowns and complete loss of mobility, factory testing of both variants of the 'Super BT' was recognised by Moscow as successful. Further, the plan provided for the transfer of one BT-20 (A-20) and two T-32 (A-32) prototypes to the military for range testing. However, due to the lengthy major repair and the unavailability of the second copy of the T-32 (A-32), the start date for the test range testing was missed.

Range Testing Aborted

Trials of Stalin's 'wonder tank' prototypes took place from 18 July to 23 August 1939 at the Tank Test Range near Kharkov. Major Evgeny Kulchicky, Head of the 1st Department Scientific and Testing Tank-Automotive Test Range (NIABP), was appointed Head of the Special Testing Commission for testing tanks. Unlike his friends, the conspirators who tried to seize power at Factory No. 183 in 1937, he was not injured during the Great Terror, but on the contrary, received a new high position. Since Kulchicky had a negative reputation at the factory, Koshkin and Maksarev had great doubts that the prototypes tests would be successful.

During the testing, mandatory records of the main parameters were kept: the distance travelled, characteristics of road conditions, time spent on movement and various stops, as well as indicators of the efficiency of the engine cooling system of tanks. After each stage of testing, average speed, average technical and operational speed, fuel consumption and engine oil consumption were determined based on the data obtained. In addition, the members of the Special Testing Commission carefully monitored the working conditions of the crew members. Instrument readings and testing results were recorded in travel logs and test protocols. Subsequently, all the information obtained was used in the preparation of the BT-20 (A-20) and T-32 (A-32) trials report and its appendices.

To a naive observer, it might seem that the testing of tank prototypes was carried out at the level of the highest Western standards. And this is not a coincidence, but the result of the Soviets copying Western experience. It would seem that such an effective approach to prototype testing should have completely eliminated the possibility of mass production of defective tanks. However, as the subsequent history of the T-34 tank has shown, design defects accompanied it to the end of production. Despite the great external similarity with the West, the procedure for testing tanks and deciding on their compliance with accepted specifications in Stalin's totalitarian empire had a number of significant differences. Medieval barbarism was hidden under the beautiful shell of procedures and protocols. The main criterion for the combat qualities of a Soviet tank was the approval of the 'Master'. To obtain this approval from the incompetent and simply stupid Stalin, the competing servants were ready to use any means, including indirect or even direct lies. Under these conditions, the results were either ignored or falsified. And even the fear of the most severe punishment could not change this trend, which flourished in the USSR until the end of its days.

After each test run, the tanks entered a field repair shop specially set up for them at the testing range. Constant repairs had become an integral part of testing. By the end of July 1939, the technical condition of the prototypes had deteriorated so much that they had to be sent back to the factory for major repairs. For two days, on 29 and 30 July 1939, the BT-20 (A-20) and T-32 (A-32) tanks were in the Mechanical Workshop '530' Factory No. 183. During the major repair, almost all important mechanisms were removed from the tanks and replaced with new ones. Only then was it possible to continue the test range testing. However, another important reason for stopping testing soon appeared. This reason turned out to be so important that all procedures were grossly violated, and all testing parameter entries were thrown into the far corner.

The Presentation of the Tanks to Stalin is More Important than Testing

At the end of August 1939, Dmitry Pavlov, together with the new bosses of the military industry, was preparing to show prototypes of tanks of the 'New Type' to Stalin. For the sake of this important event, it was decided to urgently interrupt the test range testing. Showing to the 'Master' prototypes of tanks of the 'New Type' was more important than its testing. Relevant orders were immediately sent to all tank factories.

According to an order received by Yuri Maksarev from Moscow, prototypes of BT-20 (A-20), T-32 (A-32), BT-7M and BT-5M tanks (BT tanks with V-2 engines) had to be urgently transported to the factory for repairs. Next, they were to be sent to the Scientific and Testing Tank-Automotive Test Range (NIABP) near Kubinka railway station for presentation to Stalin and his closest servants. The presentation of the tanks was scheduled for the second half of September 1939.[32]

On 23 August 1939, the BT-20 (A-20) and T-32 (A-32) prototypes were rushed to the factory for major repair. The maximum possible number of technical specialists from the Experimental Workshop '500' was involved in the preparation of prototypes for Stalin's demonstration. Once again, all units and mechanisms were removed from the tanks for a thorough inspection. All the doubtful parts were replaced with new ones. The volume of repair work turned out to be so large that the production of the second prototype of the T-32 (A-32) tank was temporarily suspended.

NIABP employees in Kubinka were also preparing to show tanks to Stalin. The scale of the planned tank show was supposed to be amazing. Pavlov planned to simultaneously show the distinguished guests more than a dozen prototypes of tanks of the 'New Type'. His predecessors Khalepsky and Bokis could not even dream of presenting such a large number of experimental armoured fighting vehicles! However, all these preparations turned out to be completely in vain. Stalin did not come to Kubinka!

A Performance Without the 'Master'

September 22nd 1939. Scientific and Testing Tank-Automotive Test Range (NIABP) near Kubinka railway station. The official demonstration of new and upgraded models of armoured fighting vehicles for the top leadership of the USSR.

Although Khalepsky, the initiator and creator of the institute of spectacular presentations of armoured vehicles, had long been in an unmarked grave, specially organised tank shows for Stalin and his servants continued. During the several years of the Test Range's existence in Kubinka, these theatrical performances have been brought to perfection.

The main audience of the presentation were: People's Commissar of Defence of the Soviet Union Kliment Voroshilov, deputy Chairmen of the Council of People's Commissars of the Soviet Union Nikolai Voznesensky[33] and Anastas Mikoyan,[34] member of the Economic Council of the Council of People's Commissars of the Soviet Union Andrei Zhdanov,[35] People's Commissar for Medium Machine Building (Minister) Ivan Likhachev[36] and People's Commissar for Heavy Machine Building (Minister) Vyacheslav Malyshev. Also on this day, Kubinka had military and military industry bosses, directors and chief designers of the factories who designed and manufactured prototypes of the tanks of the 'New Type'. However, the main intrigue of this show was not who was there and who was not at the presentation. Stalin was not there, the only person for whom this pompous presentation was organised! The 'Master' had been ill for several days now. Excruciating diarrhoea made it impossible for him to attend this important event. Stalin was replaced at the presentation by Voroshilov, who was doggedly devoted to him.

Alexander Vetrov,[37] representative of the Military Department of the Council of People's Commissars of the Soviet Union, who was present at this presentation, recalled:

> Marshal Voroshilov arrived. It was immediately obvious that the People's Commissar of Defence was in a bad mood. After absentmindedly listening to Komkor Dmitry Pavlov's report, he greeted the military leaders and industry representatives who came up, and without hesitation headed with Zhdanov, Mikoyan and Voznesensky to a specially prepared elevated observation platform.
>
> So, the marshal and his entourage headed for the observation platform, and we headed for a small green hillock near it. Here, after looking around, I saw a yellow sand-covered area at the edge of the

forest, on which six brown-painted tanks were lined up. On the right flank, the twin-turreted heavy tank SMK – land dreadnought stood out noticeably with its impressive size. The single-turreted KV heavy tank standing next to it, the model of which we saw at the factory of Josef Kotin at the end of last year, looked almost like a baby.

The BT-20 wheel-and-track tank (A-20) and the very similar tracked tank T-32 (A-32) were distinguished by their unusually compact and beautiful shape. They stood next to the upgraded tanks that still formed the basis of the Red Army BT-7M and T-26 tank forces.

. . .

Voroshilov's voice was heard:

– Why don't you start?

There was a commotion at the command tower. Multi-coloured signal flags began to sparkle. The tank crews, which had been built slightly ahead of the tanks, instantly took their places. And now the dull rumble of engines and the rising bluish-brown cloud of exhaust smoke announced that the tanks were ready to move.

. . .

But before the lively conversations caused by the KV's testing successes had subsided, the T-32 (A-32) tracked tank rushed onto an even more difficult track designed for medium tanks.

. . .

Here it overcame anti-tank ditch, escarp, counterscarp and narrow metal bridge at a good pace and with some grace. Having been a tank driving instructor for a number of years, I was well aware of the skill a tank driver needs to possess in order to flawlessly overcome such difficult obstacles, and how powerful and manoeuvrable a tank must be to withstand such high loads.

At that time, Mikhail Koshkin, seemingly smiling nonchalantly, was talking nearby with Nikolai Barykov.[38] Only his feverish eyes and pale lips betrayed his state of mind. The T-32 (A-32) left the last obstacle astern. It would seem that the tests have been successfully completed. But what is it? The tank suddenly turned to the right and went smoothly towards a rather steep hill. It crawled up its slope . . .

– Stop him! – someone from the audience couldn't stand it.

– There's a rise of more than 30 degrees, it can tip over!

I'm looking at the observation platform in alarm. Surprisingly, everything is quiet there. Komkor Dmitry Pavlov, smiling, talks about something with Voroshilov. He nods his head in agreement. I understand that lifting an experienced tank uphill is not an amateur activity of the tank driver, it is provided for in the test plan. Meanwhile, the T-32 (A-32) has already climbed to the very top of the hill.

That's a tank! – My neighbour has already exclaimed admiringly.

Yes, a really excellent tank! That's what we need! – confirmed the other.

There was a round of applause. And the tank-climber abruptly turned around and went down the slope now. Along the way, the driver directed the tank at a fairly thick pine tree and knocked it down with a blow from the nose of the tank hull, thereby showing the tank's ability to overcome wooded areas.

Then the T-32 (A-32) smoothly entered the river. The waves, rolling in, almost got close to driver's hatch. But the tank is already turning up its nose and, as if nothing had happened, goes to the opposite shore. Crossing the river a second time, he easily climbs onto the sandy shore and only then, amid a general roar of approval, hurries to his place at the finish line.

Marshal Voroshilov's mood has clearly improved. He is already laughing and talking animatedly to Zhdanov, Mikoyan and Voznesensky, who surround him. Then, summoning tank designers Mikhail Koshkin, Nikolai Dukhov[39] and Josef Kotin to the command tower, he warmly thanks them.[40]

On this September day in 1939, the experienced 'actors' who performed the carefully rehearsed roles of tank drivers did their job brilliantly. The tank prototypes that participated in the demonstration of their capabilities suffered no breakdowns. The mechanics who prepared the prototypes of the new tanks for the demonstration also did a great job. The presentation was conducted strictly according to plan without incident. Only one important detail spoiled the mood of the organisers of the presentation – the absence of Stalin.

On the same day, Voroshilov reported very emotionally to Stalin about the brilliant results of the presentation of tanks. Exhausted by frequent bouts of diarrhoea, the 'Master' hardly listened to his servant. However, Voroshilov did a good job as a courier, and Stalin was pleased with the tanks of the 'New Type'.

Medium Tank of the 'New Type' Needs 45mm Thick Armour

Despite the success of the presentation, Pavlov still had one more problem. Stalin's approval was required on the question of the thickness of the armour of the medium tank of the 'New Type'. In 1937, Bokis and Lebedev decided that medium tank needed armour with a thickness of at least 45mm to guarantee protection against 37mm anti-tank guns. As noted above, this parameter was determined based on the study of experimental firing data on armour plates of different thicknesses.

Pavlov fully supported the decision of his predecessors, and many times suggested that Stalin sign a directive on a significant increase in the armour of experimental tanks. Only such armour, in his opinion, could guarantee the protection of the crew and internal equipment of the tank from 37mm anti-tank guns at ranges of more than 500m.[41] However, the 'Master' was in no hurry to approve such a armour option for the medium tank of the 'New Type'. He had good reasons for this delay, due to the unwillingness of tank factories and steel mills to work with thick armour.

By mid-1939, Pavlov was able to coordinate with the bosses of the military industry to increase the frontal armour of the 'Super BT' only to a thickness of 30mm. Based on the experience of the Spanish Civil War, this was clearly not enough. However, the bosses of the military industry begged Stalin many times not to rush into such a large increase in the thickness of the armour of medium tanks of the 'New Type', which was causing concerns among the management of Izhorsky and Mariupol steel mills. They quite reasonably believed that the process of manufacturing armour parts from 45mm thick plates and their subsequent welding would cause huge technological problems. To work with armour parts of this thickness required the development of new technologies and the purchase of special equipment from abroad. Mastering the production of new armour parts always caused enormous difficulties and required a lot of time. However, Pavlov considered the concerns of the steel mills' management to be exaggerated.

The Head of the ABTU was convinced that the main risk in promoting his idea of increasing tank protection was the ability of the T-32 (A-32) to withstand the large additional weight of 45mm armour. Without waiting for Stalin's approval, in mid-August 1939 Pavlov assigned Design Bureau '520' of Factory No. 183 to carry out preliminary calculations of the possibility of installing 45mm armour on the T-32 (A-32). Despite the workload of the designers, Mikhail Koshkin, Chief Designer of the factory, fully supported Pavlov's idea. He believed that making an official decision to increase the thickness of the T-32 (A-32) protection to 45mm would finally allow him to create the medium tank of the 'New Type' that he had long dreamed of.

Pavlov hoped that after completing range testing of the T-32 (A-32), he once again try to convince Stalin of the possibility of increasing the thickness of the armour without decreasing the mobility of the tank. The Head of the ABTU expected to use the results of calculations by Design Bureau '520' as an additional argument to prove his case.

The Tanks are Suitable for Use in Red Army Tank Units

After the spectacular presentation, the tanks returned to Kharkov to continue the range testing. Despite the rush, it was not possible to conduct testing within the time limits specified in Dmitry Pavlov's order. In fact, the test range testing was conducted between mid-July and October 1939 with a long break, during which the BT-20 (A-20) and T-32 (A-32) tanks took part in the presentation of tanks of the 'New Type' in Kubinka.

In a report for Moscow, members of the Special Testing Commission made an optimistic conclusion: 'Tanks, prototypes BT-20 (A-20) and T-32 (A-32) meet specifications. Both the BT-20 (A-20) and T-32 (A-32) are suitable for use in Red Army tank units.'[42] Given the constant breakdowns, such a statement looked rather strange. However, the members of the Special Testing Commission, who had miraculously survived the Great Terror, simply could not make any other conclusion than recognising testing as successful. For the sake of Stalin's desire to have new tanks as soon as possible, the numerous design defects discovered during range testing were ignored by them.

However, there was still some connection with reality in the report. The members of the Special Testing Commission could not completely close their eyes to the constant breakdowns caused by defects in the design and manufacture of prototypes. The test range testing report reflected a fairly large list of major defects of the BT-20 (A-20) and T-32 (A-32). In a document prepared for Moscow, the members of the Special Testing Commission formulated a strict requirement for the management of Factory No. 183 (Kharkov): 'All the shortcomings noted in the report must be eliminated, for which a list of works with deadlines must be urgently submitted to ABTU for approval.'[43]

Koshkin and Maksarev reacted very emotionally to the comments mentioned in the Special Testing Commission report. They had reasonable objections regarding the defects found during the tank range testing. Based on the fact that the Head of the Special Testing Commission was Major Evgeny Kulchicky, a long-time enemy of the factory management, Koshkin and Maksarev were preparing for a new round of confrontation with Moscow. However, as noted above, Pavlov had his own plans for using the test results of the BT-20 and T-32 prototypes. Under these conditions, the new conflict between Kharkov and Moscow had no further development.

How Can the Results of the Range Testing be used to Influence Stalin?

The report on the results of the testing was prepared by Pavlov's subordinates, and he had the opportunity to influence its content and conclusions. The Head of the ABTU was well aware that although the report on the BT-20 (A-20) and T-32 (A-32) prototypes was addressed to Voroshilov, it would definitely fall into the hands of Stalin. This gave him another chance to influence the decision that the 'Master' had persistently postponed.

The data obtained during the tests of the two variants of the 'Super BT' gave Head of the ABTU new arguments to convince Stalin of the need to increase the thickness of the tracked tank armour. The following was noted in the test range testing report specifically for the 'Master': 'The T-32 (A-32) tank, as it has a margin for weight gain, it is advisable to protect with more powerful armour, respectively increasing the strength of individual parts and strengthening transmission. At the same time, the reinforced parts of the T-32 (A-32) tank should be used as much as possible on the BT-20 (A-20).'[44] The report emphasised that the BT-20 (A-20) wheel-and-track tank is unable to increase the thickness of the reservation due to the overload of the running gear. This circumstance was used as one of the main arguments for the subsequent abandonment of mass production of the BT-20 (A-20) tank.

Pavlov's efforts were not in vain, and the 'Master' almost agreed with the proposal of the Head of the ABTU to increase the thickness of the tank's armour to 45mm. However, the suspicious Stalin demanded that Pavlov conduct special tests of the tank's capabilities with thicker armour. There was an objective risk that the situation with the BT-7 would repeat, when some components and assemblies could not cope with the additional weight. Thanks to a preliminary agreement with Koshkin, the Head of the ABTU was ready to conduct such tests of the T-32 (A-32).

According to the calculations of the Design Bureau '520' designers, if the thickness of the armour plates was increased to 45mm, the mass of the T-32 (A-32) increased to 24–25 tons. Thus, the weight of this descendant of the Christie tank increased 2.5 times compared to its ancestor. It should be noted that the tendency to increase weight was observed in all BT series tanks. This caused significant problems for the basic design of the tank, which was designed for 10 tons. In particular, the reserves for upgrading the BT running gear were exhausted already on the BT-7. The last Soviet descendants of the Christie tank actually lost the ability to move using wheeled drive.

Although most of the elements of the T-32 (A-32) tracked tank's running gear were unified with the BT-20 (A-20) wheel-and-track tank, Koshkin wisely incorporated a number of important design differences into its design. In addition to the absence of a wheeled drive on the T-32 (A-32), it also had five road wheels on each side, unlike the traditional four of the BT family. Koshkin hoped that these features of the tracked tank would allow it to withstand the additional weight of 45mm of armour. However, in order to test in practice the degree of influence of thick armour on the mobility of the tank, as well as on the reliability of the T-32 (A-32) units and mechanisms, special tests were needed, which Stalin insisted on.

Experiment to Increase the Thickness of the T-32 (A-32) Armour to 45mm

The planning of special tests of the T-32 (A-32) took place in a feverish hurry. Pavlov originally wanted to report the results to the 'Master' at a presentation in September 1939, where Stalin never arrived. However, this plan naturally failed. The first prototype of the T-32 (A-32) was not available for special testing, as it was undergoing range testing in August 1939.

Fortunately, Pavlov and Koshkin had a second copy, which, due to the failure of production dates, did not get to the test range testing. It was this prototype T-32 (A-32) No. 2 that was decided to be loaded to the above-mentioned design weight of 24 tons and subjected to special tests. It was supposed to compare the test results of prototype No. 2 loaded with up to 24 tons with the test results of the T-32 (A-32) in normal weight. The tests were supposed to be carried out at the Factory No. 183 landfill near Kharkov.

On the afternoon of 23 August 1939, after passing factory testing at normal weight, the T-32 (A-32) tank No. 2 returned to the Mechanical Workshop '530' Factory No. 183. In the afternoon of the same day, 5 tons of cargo (cast-iron blocks) was loaded onto the tank, after which it returned to the test site to complete a special testing programme. In total, during the special tests, the 19-ton tank, loaded to 24 tons, travelled 1,534km at an average speed of 28.2km/h. Depending on the road conditions, there was enough fuel for 235-333km. In general, the significantly heavier tank broke down about as often during the tests as its lighter version. The engine, the running gear, and, most importantly, the gearbox, upgraded under the leadership of Morozov, could work for about the same time before a significant breakdown.

The conclusions of the report on the special testing of the T-32 (A-32) tank stated the following: 'It is advisable to manufacture prototypes based on the T-32 (A-32) tank with an increase in total weight to 24 tons due to thickening of armour protection.'[45] Pavlov now had reliable arguments to persuade Stalin to increase the tank's armour protection to 45mm. However, due to the feverish haste, the special tests were conducted according to a shortened programme. This did not allow the identification of all the hidden defects in the tank's design caused by the additional weight. These defects became particularly acute already during the mass production of the T-34 tank. The elimination of these fundamental defects continued with varying success for almost the entire existence of this 'wonder tank'.

Special Operation to Cancel the BT-20 (A-20)

In the autumn of 1939, even before the end of the trials of tanks of the 'New Type', it became clear to the new tank industry bosses that the production of tanks of the 'Old Type' would soon be discontinued. In Moscow, Kharkov and Leningrad, managers were feverishly preparing for the production of the 'New Type'. The approach of this moment caused genuine horror among the managers of tank factories.

It was for the failure of development and the disruption of mass production of new tanks that their predecessors were executed. For the archaic and inefficient Soviet military industry, the transition to the production of new models of military equipment had always been extremely painful. The probability of failure in the organisation of mass production has always been extremely high.

The main concern of the managers of tank factories was the lack of necessary equipment for the production of new tanks. Due to the use of equipment by low-skilled workers in conditions of constant haste caused by the need to fulfil unrealistic plans, scarce foreign machines and equipment bought for gold were broken or badly worn by the end of the 1930s. It was extremely difficult to obtain new foreign machines. Stalin personally supervised the spending of money on equipment purchases abroad. However, realising the inevitability of fulfilling Stalin's decision, the directors of the largest tank factories tried to somehow alleviate their sad fate.

The factory director's only salvation from arrest and imminent execution was to receive an order for the production of a tank of the 'New Type', which could be produced using existing equipment. However, Moscow had its own plans for placing orders at tank factories. These plans often contradicted the wishes of the plant directors. In addition, the military from the Tank-Automotive Directorate of the Red Army (ABTU) had their own preferences on this important issue. As a result, the distribution of lucrative orders for the production of tanks of the 'New Type' was accompanied by the usual intrigues for the Stalinist regime. This has caused new acute conflicts between factory directors, bosses of the military industry and the military.

Fortunately for all employees of Factory No. 183, Pavlov managed to postpone the decision on the organisation of mass production of the highly complex BT-20 (A-20). The painful illness of the 'Master' played a role in this, which, in his opinion, was caused by numerous attempts by 'enemies' to poison him. Stalin, who turned 60 in 1939, could no longer constantly monitor all the details of the implementation of production plans for tanks of the 'New Type' due to age and illness. Eventually, Pavlov managed to convince Stalin not to rush into making a decision on mass production of the BT-20 (A-20). Wheel-and-track tanks were no longer relevant at that time. The experimental BT-20 (A-20) tank was no longer mentioned at numerous meetings, and it gradually disappeared from production plans in 1940.

At a meeting of the Main Military Council of the Red Army held on 21 November 1939, the following decision was made: 'To have in the Red Army, instead of the existing tank corps and separate tank brigades, the same type of separate tank brigades of BT and T-26 tanks, consisting of four tank battalions armed with T-26 and BT tanks. In the future, it is planned to rearm the separate tank brigades with T-34 tanks.'[46] Thus, the BT-20 (A-20) wheel-and-track tank project was effectively closed.

The Birth of the T-34

On 28 September 1939, preparations for the production of two prototypes of the T-34 (A-34) tank began in Kharkov. These works were to be performed on the basis of contract No. 8/678, concluded by the factory with the Tank-Automotive Directorate of the Red Army (ABTU). In strict accordance with Soviet traditions, the order was extremely urgent. According to the terms of the contract, the production of two prototypes was to be completed on 15 January 1940.

Contrary to initial calculations, when the reservation was increased to 45mm, the weight of the T-34 (A-34) tank, compared with its predecessor, the T-32 (A-32), increased not by five tons, but by about six and a half tons. Consequently, the designers needed to recalculate the entire tank structure as soon as possible. Based on the new calculations, the designers of the Design Bureau '520' needed to significantly strengthen many tank units again. Next, it was necessary to re-produce a complete set of production drawings for the T-34 (A-34) tank. This was a new challenge for the Kharkov designers.

To carry out this responsible and time-consuming work on schedule, eight groups of designers were organised in the Design Bureau '520'. Each design group developed drawings for a new tank in accordance with its business profile. In the conditions of feverish haste, the engineers could not do this job efficiently. Despite the reinforcement of many units, including the gearbox, the subsequent operation of tanks in the Red Army showed that many critical elements of the serial

T-34 tanks could not withstand the increased load. Endless work to eliminate these design flaws continued during the serial production of Stalin's 'wonder tank'.

On 19 December 1939, a tracked tank with an armour thickness of 45mm was adopted for service by the Red Army and received the official designation T-34.[47] This decision was an undoubted victory for Pavlov and Koshkin at the end of the long journey of creating the medium tank of the 'New Type'. It took the new Head of the ABTU more than two years to completely get rid of the development of wheel-and-track tanks. However, in the future great war in Europe, which did not begin according to Stalin's plans, wheel-and-track tanks, which accounted for more than 30 per cent of the total number of Red Army tanks, would play a bright but short-lived role.

'We will have to fight Finland!'[48]

Meanwhile, in the autumn of 1939, the 'Great Strategist' began to cautiously implement his plans for the enslavement of Europe. He launched the 'liberation campaigns' of the Red Army with the aim of seizing lands that once belonged to the Russian Empire. This was the final test of the aggressive potential of the Red Army before execution the ambitious future mission to take over the whole of Europe. The implementation of these plans became possible with the forced consent of another 'Great Strategist' Adolf Hitler.

In 1939, Hitler and Stalin developed a 'strong' mutual friendship. The two criminal regimes decided to join forces to defeat their common enemy, Poland. Having shared Polish territory with 'friendly' Germany, the Red Tsar wanted an equally brilliant continuation of the restoration of the lands of the former Russian Empire. Soon, the Red Army's aggression continued. Huge columns of tanks of the 'Old Type' (BT and T-26) were rapidly advancing, capturing vast territories with almost no resistance. The ease with which Stalin captured eastern Poland turned his head. Everything happened in accordance with the scenario according to which the late Tukhachevsky described to Stalin the future lightning war of the Red Army.

After the Baltic States (Estonia, Latvia, and Lithuania) found themselves in the Soviet zone of influence in October 1939, it was Finland's turn. This sparsely populated northern country, which was once part of the Russian Empire, was supposed to fall at the feet of the Red Army soldiers without significant resistance according to the plan of the Soviets. Although Stalin did not expect any significant obstacles along the way, he nevertheless acted with his usual caution.

At first, the Soviet Union, in an ultimatum, demanded that the Finnish government conclude a so-called 'mutual assistance agreement', which in fact meant a peaceful occupation. And then, 'for the sake of Leningrad's security', he demanded that a significant part of Finnish territory be given to the USSR.

However, to Stalin's great surprise, the Finns refused him! Enraged, the 'Red Dictator' ordered the Red Army to seize obstinate Finland with a swift blow. On 30 November 1939, Soviet troops crossed the border, and high-speed SB bombers and long-range Ilyushin DB-3 bombers launched air raids on several Finnish cities, including the capital Helsinki.

As in the operations to occupy eastern Poland, tanks were to play a major role in the Red Army offensive. However, the natural conditions of Finland, saturated with rivers, lakes and swamps, made the terrain almost impassable for tanks. Only in winter, when all the water barriers were frozen, did the tanks have the opportunity to move. It is for this reason that the Red Army struck its blow in the cold winter.

By the beginning of the special military operation to capture Finland, the Soviets had concentrated about 450,000 soldiers, 2,000 artillery pieces, about 1,000 aircraft, and 2,000 tanks from the Leningrad Military District near its borders. They were opposed by Finnish troops numbering up to 340,000, armed with up to 900 guns, 270 aircraft and 60 tanks. Officially, the USSR did not declare war on Finland. The invasion was masked by friendly assistance to the puppet Finnish government created by the Soviets in a small piece of occupied territory.

However, the 'Finnish special military operation' (FSVO) did not immediately go according to plan. The incompetent leadership of the Red Army proved unable to withstand the skilful and courageous actions of the Finnish troops. Further events led the Soviets to a full-scale catastrophe. The gigantic Soviet Union proved to be completely helpless against the fiercely defending soldiers of the small Finnish army. A huge number of Soviet soldiers, in the absence of supplies, died of hunger and disease or went missing, frozen in the dense Finnish forests. During the FSVO, which lasted from 30 November 1939 to 12 March 1940, the Red Army lost 122,000 men killed!

Armoured fighting vehicles also failed to meet the expectations of the Red Army leadership. Stalin's pride, the T-37A and T-38 light amphibious tanks, performed very poorly. They were destroyed even by anti-personnel mines, their armour was penetrated by the fire of anti-tank rifles, and their weapons turned out to be completely ineffective. The engine of the T-37A and T-38 tanks was not powerful enough, and the traction of the tracks with the ground was weak. Amphibious tanks could not move through deep snow.

Other types of tanks, including the T-26, BT and the three-turret T-28, also showed all their shortcomings in the battles. During the FSVO, Finnish gunners destroyed 955 Soviet tanks, 426 tanks burned out (some probably due to technical defects causing fire in the engine compartment), 378 tanks were blown up by mines and land mines, 110 were lost in swamps and 35 were missing.[49]

On 12 March 1940, as a result of the signing by the parties of the Moscow Peace Treaty, hostilities ceased. Finland lost about 10 per cent of its territory, but retained its independence. It was an undoubted victory of little Finland over the gigantic USSR. For the first time, an insurmountable obstacle stood in the way of implementing Stalin's aggressive plans. The unprecedented failure of the Red Army clearly showed Hitler, who was plotting an attack on the 'friendly' USSR, the incredible weakness of the armed forces of the Soviet Union. Stalin, shocked by the failure, hoped that the Red Army would soon receive thousands of tanks of the 'New Type', which could at least partially restore the shaken military might of the 'Red Empire'.

The 'Twins' are Ready!

Meanwhile, the delivery dates for the two T-34 prototypes were again missed. Moscow demanded that Factory No. 183 complete its work as soon as possible. In Directive No. 135669, Stalin ordered the Military Council of the Kharkov Military District, the heads of the Main Tank-Automotive Directorate of the Red Army (GABTU) and the Artillery Directorate of the Red Army (AU) 'in the period from 25 January to 25 March 1940, to conduct range testing of T-34 tanks according to the attached programme in the Kharkov Military District, at the test range at Factory No. 183.'[50]

However, it was not possible to follow the instructions of the 'Master' and start testing within the specified time frame. The first T-34 tank, factory number 311-11-3, was ready only on 6 February 1940. On the same day, it began making his first trips around the factory, which revealed the first defects. Teams of technicians from Experimental Workshop 500 began urgent repairs. At the same time, the assembly of the second prototype of the T-34, factory number 311-18-3, continued. These two completely identical tanks were informally called the 'Twins' by the workers and engineers of Factory No. 183.

Finally, on 10 February 1940, the first prototype was sent for range testing. On 12 February 12, the second prototype, factory number

311-18-3, followed it to the Test Range in the suburb of Kharkov.[51] The strict protocols developed at GABTU required tanks to undergo a full test cycle. A particularly important indicator of compliance with specifications was the ability of tanks to make long marches without significant breakdowns. The test programme stipulated that each tank had to travel at least 2,500km, including 300km on highways, 1,000km on unpaved roads, and 1,200km off road.

Meanwhile, the deadline for showing the 'Twins' to Stalin was approaching. The presentation was scheduled for the first half of March 1940. The 'Master' wanted to personally observe Pavlov's promised outstanding fighting qualities of the new 'wonder tank'. To carry out this pompous performance, Voroshilov ordered the preparation of T-34 tanks to be sent to Moscow. It was assumed that after this 'sacred' ritual, the serial production of T-34 tanks was to officially begin.

It was obvious to everyone who followed the prototype tests that it was impossible to complete the approved test programme before demonstrating the tanks to Stalin. This caused the bosses of the military industry and the management of Factory No. 183 genuine horror. It was impossible to arrange a presentation to Stalin of tanks that had not even formally passed the established test programme. In this critical situation, the experienced Mikhail Koshkin suggested sending the tanks to Stalin to be shown not on flat wagons, but on their own tracks. Thus, the total number of kilometres travelled during the tests could formally include the route from Kharkov to Moscow (approximately 744km) and back. The bosses of the military industry and the military immediately agreed to his proposal.

Koshkin's Tank Trip to Moscow

On 6 March 1940, in Kharkov, the technical specialists of the Mechanical Workshop '530' began preparing the T-34 tanks for their upcoming display to Stalin. Despite the large volume of work, they had to finish it in just a few days. The main problem was the diesel engines. In the few dozen hours that they worked on the tanks on the test range, they were completely out of order. So, on the tank No. 1, the diesel engine V-2 with serial number No. 1015-20 worked for 71 hours and 47 minutes, and on the T-34 tank No. 2, the diesel engine V-2 with serial number No. 1030-13 worked for 76 hours and 26 minutes. It was necessary to install new engines in both.

Despite the large number of diesel engines produced after the official launch of mass production, the search for two new engines without serious defects proved to be a very difficult task. Factory No. 183 specialists selected the best of several hundred diesel engine technicians to install on the T-34 prototypes for Stalin's demonstration. However, even careful selection and tuning of diesel engines did not save the technicians of Mechanical Workshop '530' from an unfortunate setback. On the last day of preparation, during a test trip around the factory, new problems were discovered on the T-34 tank No. 1. It took extra time to fix them. As a result, the start of the tank march to Moscow was postponed for several hours.

In addition to the tanks, a special team of drivers and technical specialists from Factory No. 183 was preparing for the trip. They were led by Mikhail Koshkin, who decided to personally participate in the trip from Kharkov to Moscow and back. Although experimental BT family tanks had previously made trips from Kharkov to Moscow, winter conditions and the novelty of the 'wonder tanks' design made the nearly 750km trip an extremely risky operation. The main danger was the high probability of a serious breakdown en route. In order to increase the possibilities for operational repairs en route, two 'Voroshilovec' artillery tractors were included in the convoy. They were carrying spare diesel engines, gearboxes and other spare parts for tanks in their bodies.

At 16:00 on 12 March 1940, the tank convoy set off. The tanks' trip from Kharkov to Moscow was not without the intervention of NKVD agents, who saw foreign 'spies' everywhere. Because of the stupid Stalinist secrecy, the tank convoy avoided highways and moved along country roads and off-road. Despite the risky adventures and the loss of the ability of one of the tanks to move independently, the trip was successful.

On 16 March the tanks arrived in Moscow at Tank Factory No. 37 'Ordzhonikidze' for major repairs, which they badly needed. One of the T-34s arrived under tow by one of the artillery tractors due to a serious breakdown. The repairs lasted for several days. Next, the tanks were planned to be sent for testing at the Scientific and Testing Tank-Automotive Test Range (NIABP) near Kubinka railway station. These tests were purely a formality and were conducted in extreme haste. Dmitry Pavlov was appointed head of the T-34 tank testing commission.

Pavlov Hurries and Receives a New Military Rank from Stalin for his Efforts

In the early morning of 24 March 1940, both T-34s left Tank Factory No. 37 'Ordzhonikidze' for Kubinka. The testing programme provided for determining the durability of the tank's armour when fired at by an anti-tank gun. Usually, a tank hull specially made for these purposes was used for such potentially destructive testing. However, due to the haste caused by the failure of all planned deadlines, they could not produce such a special target for the Test Range. In order to complete the test programme and send an optimistic report to Stalin, a risky decision was made to shoot at one of the existing prototypes.

By Pavlov's order, tank No. 1 was selected for testing with anti-tank gun fire. To check the impact of the shelling on the crew, a dummy was placed in the turret in place of the tank commander. The shelling was carried out by a well-trained crew with a British anti-tank gun. This weapon, unlike Soviet guns, was distinguished by its phenomenal accuracy. This was the only way to ensure that the tank would remain intact after the shelling and could be demonstrated to Stalin.

On 26 March 1940, following the tests of the T-34 against anti-tank gun fire, Pavlov reported to Stalin:

> The tank was fired at by an armour-piercing shell at a distance of 100m from an English long-barrelled 37mm gun manufactured in 1940. 2 shots were fired – 1 at the centre of the turret 4-5 cm from the pistol port and 1 shot at the centre of the tank's side. Armor-piercing shells bounce off, leaving traces up to 10mm deep on the tank's armour, and they do not produce any destructive effects on the tank. The periscopes viewing mirrors burst from the concussion, and they can be replaced immediately. The dummy planted in the tank remained intact.
>
> The tank's armour is not penetrated by 37mm and 45mm armour-piercing shells, and after hitting them in the tank, it continues to work normally. The tank has a cross-country capability that is much higher than that of all existing types of tanks and tractors.
>
> Main Tank-Automotive Directorate of the Red Army (GABTU) is taking measures to launch serial production of the tank as soon as possible.[52]

In this report, Pavlov significantly exaggerated the actual parameters of armour durability and cross-country capability of the T-34 tank. All test protocols were grossly violated and the results in the report did not correspond to reality. However, the incompetent Stalin did not notice or did not want to notice the obvious lies of his favourite. The day after this report, on 27 March 1940, the Head of the Tank-Automotive Directorate of the Red Army (ABTU) Komkor Dmitry Pavlov was awarded a military rank – Komandarm 2nd Rank (General of the Army).

Pavlov and Koshkin Demonstrate the T-34 to Stalin

Due to ongoing health problems and the increased fear of attempts on his life, Stalin again refused to go to Kubinka. After the execution of the members of 'Tukhachevsky's Group', the 'Master' was very afraid of revenge from his 'enemies' and significantly restricted travel even to the Moscow region. For this reason, Pavlov had to organise a special military operation to present T-34 tanks in the Kremlin.

In the early morning of 30 March 1940, when the streets of the capital were completely empty, tanks drove 11km from Tank Factory No. 37 'Ordzhonikidze' to the centre of Moscow. This was done to preserve idiotic secrecy. All this time, NKVD agents strictly ensured that random passers-by did not appear as the secret tanks passed. Before allowing the tanks to enter the Kremlin, NKVD officers carefully examined them, and the tank crews were searched. Koshkin was not in the tank, arriving at the Kremlin in a car, and was also forced to undergo a thorough NKVD check. Apart from Mikhail Koshkin, only two employees of Factory No. 183 were allowed to meet with Stalin.

Alexander Vetrov, representative of the Military Department of the Council of People's Commissars of the Soviet Union, who witnessed the display of the T-34s to Stalin, recalled:

> Putting aside all urgent and urgent matters, I hurried to the place of the scheduled presentation. After leaving the wide metal gates separating the government buildings from the off-duty territory, we walked along the paving stones of Ivanovskaya Square.
>
> It was a normal work day, so the wide Square was almost deserted. And only near the Kremlin Senate Palace building were two dark green tanks of a familiar streamlined shape, near which tank crews in black leather suits were lined up, and two small groups of military and civilians were located on the sidewalk.
>
> I went to the corner of the Kremlin Senate Palace, from where the entire Square was clearly visible, and joined the Kremlin security officer on duty.
>
> Soon, an exclamation was heard:
> - They're coming!
>
> Indeed, a group was approaching from the gate of the Troitskaya Tower, in the centre of which, somewhat moving forward, went Joseph Stalin, Mikhail Kalinin[53] and Kliment Voroshilov. Talking about something, they crossed the Square and headed straight for the tanks.
>
> After the report of the senior military officer, Stalin and his entourage approached the nearest tank. Explanations began to be given by Mikhail Koshkin and Military Engineer of the 3rd Rank (Captain) Petr Voroshilov.[54] Then a lively conversation ensued. Being at a distance,

I, of course, could not hear what the government members were asking the speakers, but I saw how Voroshilov soon climbed onto the tank, and Malyshev[55] even climbed inside the tank.

A little later, one of the witnesses of the conversation told me that the leaders of the Communist Party and the government showed great interest in the new tanks, knowledgably and meticulously questioned the designer Koshkin and Petr Voroshilov about their specifications, while expressing a number of significant comments and suggestions.

But now the presentation was over, and all the participants, still talking animatedly, followed Stalin away from the new tanks. A short command immediately followed, and the tank crews quickly took their places in the tanks.[56]

Other eyewitnesses of the T-34 presentation describe further events as follows:

With a roar of engines, the tanks turned around and raced in opposite directions. One is for the gate of Spasskaya Tower, the other is for the gate of the Troitskaya Kremlin Tower. Before reaching the gate, they turned sharply and raced towards each other, effectively striking sparks from the paving stones. After completing several laps with turns in different directions, the tanks stopped at the same place on command.

Stalin liked the tanks.

'This will be the "swallow bird" of our Tank-Automotive Troops', – Stalin said, referring to Koshkin. – 'Convey our congratulations to all the staff of Factory No. 183. It will be necessary to take into account the comments on the test results, finalise the design and immediately launch the tank into mass production.'[57]

The ritual performance of the 'wonder tank' for Stalin was over. The 'Master' was pleased with the efforts of his servants and graciously decided to mass-produce the T-34 tanks. The next day, numerous meetings began to process the bureaucratic documents required to begin mass production of the T-34 tank at Soviet tank factories.

Accelerate Preparations for the Serial Production of the T-34 tank!

Although testing of the two prototypes of the T-34 tank continued and were still far from complete, Stalin's order forced the bosses of the military industry to break all the rules. Contrary to common sense, they began preparations for the serial production of the defective T-34 tank at Factory No. 183 (Kharkov). To this end, on 29 March 1940, the

military and the bosses of the military industry issued a joint order
No. P-12/016s as follows:

1. To accelerate the mass production of T-34 tanks at Factory No. 183, immediately launch full preparations for the mass production of the T-34
   tank. As the development of technology and devices is completed, it is
   necessary to immediately start production of tank parts and assemblies.
   All this needs to be done without waiting for the end and conclusion
   based on the results of troop testing.
2. The prototypes previously produced by the factory should be considered the standard of the 1940 serial batch of tanks, taking into account
   the additional changes that were identified during testing.
3. Production drawings should be approved immediately after determining the suitability of the components and mechanisms of the tank. The
   deadline for approval of the drawings is 7 April 1940.[58]

After Stalin blessed the production of the T-34, the usual feverish rush
for Soviet military factories began (Shturmovshchina). To make up for
lost time, employees had to combine several interrelated processes.
Simultaneously with the development of production drawings, the
process of developing technology for the serial manufacture of
individual components of the T-34 tank was underway. At the same
time, throughout 1940, Factory No. 183 hastily repaired numerous
defects in the design of the T-34, identified during testing. However,
despite all efforts, the start of mass production of the T-34 was
constantly postponed. No preliminary preparation for the mass
production of T-34 tanks helped again.

By the end of 1940, Military Representatives of the Military Quality
Control System for Weapons had accepted a total of 115 T-34 tanks
from Factory No. 183. However, the first mass-produced T-34 tanks,
assembled with great effort, could not be called combat-ready. In order
to eliminate endless defects, teams of factory mechanics had to travel
to military units and carry out repairs on the spot.

Gradually, the number of tanks produced grew. In the first six
months of 1941, another 816 medium tanks of the 'New Type' were
produced. However, the quality of the tanks continued to be poor.
Stalin, who believed Pavlov's optimistic reports about the 'wonder
tank', ordered the mass production of T-34 tanks to be launched at the
Stalingrad Tractor Plant in addition to the Kharkov.[59]

Death of Koshkin and Pavlov

Against the background of the success of the T-34 tank, a banal
domestic drama unfolded in Mikhail Koshkin's life. The trip of the

T-34 tank prototypes from Kharkov to Moscow to be shown to Stalin proved fatal for Chief Designer of the Factory No. 183. Koshkin returned from Moscow to Kharkov seriously ill. Stalin's idiotic secrecy, which forced tanks to move off-road in winter conditions and cross rivers away from bridges, led to one of the tanks tipping over into the water. All the participants of the trip, including Koshkin, participated in its rescue. Soviet sources give different versions of when Koshkin's fatal bathing in icy water happened. Some claim that it happened on the way to Moscow and Koshkin, presenting tanks to Stalin at Red Square, was already ill. Other sources claim that the creator of the T-34 fell ill on the way back from Moscow to Kharkov. In any case, the presentation of the tank to Stalin turned out to be his last.

Against the background of constant nervous and physical overstrain, Koshkin's disease progressed. Despite all the efforts of doctors, a common cold, which turned into pneumonia, could not be cured. On 26 September 1940, Koshkin died. During his illness and after his death, all work on the modification of the T-34 was led by Aleksander Morozov. He remained the chief designer of Soviet medium tanks until his retirement in 1976.

The fate of another creator of the T-34 was also even more dramatic. On 7 June 1940, Stalin appointed Dmitry Pavlov to the post of commander of the Belorussian Special Military District. This appointment meant for him a meteoric rise in his military career. However, the former head of the Main Tank-Automotive Directorate of the Red Army (GABTU) was not among the top commanders of the Red Army for long. Dmitry Pavlov outlived Mikhail Koshkin by less than a year. On 22 July 1941, exactly one month after the beginning of the German invasion of the USSR, Pavlov was shot on Stalin's orders. The bloodthirsty 'Master' shifted the blame for his own crushing failure in the war with Hitler onto him.

Koshkin and Pavlov were forgotten in the USSR for many years. Meanwhile, their brainchild, the T-34 tank, outlived its creators and became the most numerous medium tank of the Second World War. The disclosure of the further history of this tank and its creators, the features of combat use and the analysis of the modifications created requires several separate books.

CONCLUSION: AND WHAT DOES STALIN HAVE TO DO WITH ALL THIS?

The ugliness of the character of one man, Stalin, completely determined the features of the history of the USSR for almost 30 years. His pathological features formed a black indelible stain on all the events that took place at that time.

Behind the beautiful slogans of the Bolsheviks, the inhuman essence of the criminal Soviet regime was hidden. The state created by the monstrously cruel Lenin to enslave the peoples of Europe, under Stalin's leadership, concentrated all its forces for more than 20 years to realise the Bolsheviks' dream of world domination. By the early 1940s, the Red Army had become one of the most powerful armies in the world. The strategy of using tank forces as the tip of the spear of total aggression has given rise to the most numerous tank forces in the world. By the end of the 1930s, the Red Army had more than 20,000 tanks of various types.

The gigantic Industrialisation programme, for which Stalin condemned millions of Soviet citizens to starve to death, provided potential opportunities for their production. However, the large number of Soviet tanks could not compensate for their dubious combat qualities. The Soviet tank industry, created on the basis of Western equipment and technology, tried in vain to fulfil fantastic plans for the production of tens of thousands of defective copies of British and American tanks. However, despite all efforts, the archaic tank factories could not fulfil all of Stalin's wishes. What was produced was of abominable quality. The predominance of quantitative indicators of production over their quality became an integral characteristic of tank production in the USSR. No positive or negative incentives applied by Stalin's servants could change this trend. Even after the collapse of the Soviet Union, terrible design and manufacturing defects constantly plagued Soviet and later Russian tanks.

Despite the fact that Stalin possessed no technical or military competencies, he exerted total influence on the creation of Soviet tanks until his death in March 1953. This trend, reflecting the constant strengthening of Stalin's absolute power, manifested in the beginning of the 1930s, became dominant by the end of the 1930s. After the execution of Tukhachevsky in 1937, Stalin effectively assumed the role of Technical Leader of the Red Army.

The 'Master' constantly interfered not only in the strategy and tactics of using tanks, but also in the smallest details of tank design. It was his pathological personality traits, often dominating other rational factors, which determined the appearance and technical characteristics of Soviet tanks. All the key decisions about the production of one type or another of armoured fighting vehicles were made by him. During this period, numerous technical and military specialists were used by him only as advisers. The pathological fear of an attempt on his life forced Stalin to give preference to young and executive advisers. More and more often, mature favourites executed on absurd charges were replaced by very young people who were very well suited to the role of 'sons' of the 'Master'.

After the execution of Tukhachevsky, Stalin's pathological distrust of the new favourites was constantly increasing. Their time spent near the throne of the 'Red Emperor' was also constantly decreasing. Any suspicion, real or imaginary mistake of the favourite could lead to arrest and death. The scale of the personality of the new generation of favourites has also significantly decreased. Compared to Tukhachevsky, even Pavlov, who was very competent in the development of tank forces, was perceived as a pygmy against the background of a giant. Further, the situation of a steady decline in the competence of the leaders of the tank forces only intensified. The heads of the Main Tank-Automotive Directorate of the Red Army (GABTU) who followed Pavlov were diligent executors of Stalin's will. They were 'biorobots' almost devoid of their own individuality. In the end, Stalin's opinion alone determined not only the fate of a particular new tank, but also the fate of their creators, up to and including deciding on their life or death.

In addition to his constant interference in the technical issues of tank construction, Stalin exerted total influence on the Soviet state and society. The two waves of repression unleashed by him in 1929–30 and 1937–8 turned into a catastrophe. Most of the most professional managers of the tank industry and almost all competent tank designers of the older generation were destroyed. As in the case of the extermination of the progressive elite of the Red Army command, the shortage of professionals was compensated by young specialists, of whose loyalty Stalin had no doubt. Despite their youth, most of these people were formally able to replace the destroyed older generation of specialists. Moreover, the Koshkin and Morozov mentioned in this book have become real 'diamonds' of the younger generation of Soviet designers. The ideas and technical solutions they borrowed from the West determined the development of Soviet tanks for several decades. However, as with the new generation of Red Army commanders, the lack of experience could not be fully compensated for by the energy and dedication of the young engineers.

The Great Terror of 1937–8 completely halted the technical development of the Soviet tank forces for two years. The main tank factories of Kharkov and Leningrad stopped for several months, apathy reigned in design bureaus, and many promising experimental work was stopped. The archaic design of Soviet tanks became a direct consequence of the repression. Innovations that were widespread in the West were either ignored (epicyclic gear train) or painfully slow to implement (torsion bar suspension). The advantages widely advertised by Soviet propaganda, borrowed from the West by the heavily sloped armour, wide tank tracks and the diesel engine used on the T-34 were offset by the total defects of the tanks of the 'New Type'. The bloody repressions caused by Stalin's pathological fear of a non-existent opposition had a negative impact on the development of the Soviet tank forces over the next few decades.

As a result of Stalin's stupid decisions, the first (T-18 (MS-1), T-24) and the second generation of Soviet tanks (BT, T-26) turned out to be not combat-ready by the end of the 1930s. They were produced in a hurry in huge numbers by unskilled workers from low-quality materials. Stalin realised these obvious problems only after the failure of the BT-5 and T-26 in the Spanish Civil War. Wheel-and-track and amphibious tanks, which were the pride of Stalin's parades, were considered obsolete by the early 1940s, and their design was considered 'wrecking'. The huge resources spent on building these tanks turned out to be rusty and immobile scrap metal. Stalin's former favourites were blamed for mistakes in the strategic selection of these types of tanks.

Pavlov, who replaced the executed Tukhachevsky, Uborevich and Khalepsky, took a long time to correct the 'mistakes' of his predecessors in the face of unprecedented repression. He diligently tried to destroy what had been so painstakingly created for many years. The new

Stalinist favourite threw all the forces of the military industry into the creation of the third generation of Soviet tanks. According to Pavlov, tanks of the 'New Type' were supposed to have thick armour, a diesel engine and tracked drive. However, they also failed to meet the optimistic expectations of the 'Master'.

The most famous third-generation tanks (T-34s and KVs) turned out to be full of design flaws. The incredible rush to create tanks of the 'New Type', the shortage of professional engineers and workers caused by the consequences of the repression did not go unnoticed. New problems have been added to the technical shortcomings of its predecessors, the direct descendants of which were tanks of the 'New Type'. The thick well-sloped armour and cramped turret created poor working conditions for the crew, and the defective diesel engine was constantly failing.

As the first months of the rapid Wehrmacht invasion in the summer of 1941 showed, the tanks of the 'New Type' (T-34 and KV) proved to be as useless as declared by Stalin the obsolete tanks of the 'Old Type' (BT, T-26 and T-28). Despite the enormous resources devoted to preparing for total war in Europe, the Red Army and Stalin's tank industry suffered a terrible defeat in 1941. Under the blows of the German Blitzkrieg, the Soviet front was rapidly collapsing. The soldiers of the Red Army did not want to defend the bloody dictatorship of Stalin from the enemy. The tank armada of 12,000 tanks, created by the enormous exertion of the forces of the Soviet people to enslave Europe, was abandoned on the side of the roads under the lightning strike of the Wehrmacht.

NOTES

Introduction

1   Vyacheslav Malyshev (1902–57) was a young favourite of Stalin. On 11 September 1941 Malyshev was appointed to the position of People's Commissar of the Tank Industry of the USSR.

Chapter 1: Stalin's Militarism

1   The Stalinist Secret Police (OGPU) had in its structure quite a large number of troops designed to suppress uprisings within the USSR.

2   Kuzma Minin and Prince Pozharsky are historical figures of the early seventeenth century, elevated by Russian propaganda to the rank of national heroes. The Monument to Minin and Pozharsky was built in 1818 by architect Ivan Martos.

3   In Tolkien's legendarium, Morgoth is the embodiment of evil. The servant of Morgoth, Sauron, took his place after the fall of his Master.

4   Andrei Snesarev (1865–1937) voluntarily joined the Red Army in April 1918. On 28 January 1930, Snesarev was arrested on charges of participating in a military conspiracy and sentenced to death by firing squad. On Stalin's instructions, the execution was commuted to 10 years in Gulag labour camps. On 27 September 1934, Snesarev was released due to a serious illness. On 4 December 1937, he died in complete obscurity in Moscow.

5   Mikhail Tukhachevsky (1893–1937), nobleman, graduate of the Moscow Cadet Corps of Empress Catherine II and Alexander Military College. In 1912, Tukhachevsky joined the Russian Imperial Army. In the First World War, as an officer of the 1st Guards Division, he took part in battles with Triple Alliance troops. Tukhachevsky was decorated five times for his bravery. On 19 February 1915, he was captured by the Germans. After four unsuccessful attempts to escape from captivity, Tukhachevsky was sent to a camp for incorrigible fugitives in Ingolstadt, where he met Charles de Gaulle. In September 1917, Tukhachevsky made his fifth escape, which became successful. In October 1917, he returned to Russia. In March 1918, Tukhachevsky voluntarily joined the Red Army.

6   N.S, Simonov, *The Military-Industrial Complex of the USSR in the 1920s–1950s: Economic Growth Rates, Structure, Organisation of Production and Management*, Moscow, 1996. p. 65.

7   The Battle of Warsaw ('the Miracle on the Vistula') was the most important battle of the Soviet-Polish War of 1919–21. As a result of Pilsudski's victory, Lenin's attempts to turn Poland into a Soviet republic and invade Germany to provoke a Bolshevik revolution there completely failed.

8   As Stalin was unofficially called by his entourage.

9   The sarcastic expression of the French King Louis XVI about his younger brother Charles Philippe (the future King Charles X of France), who fiercely defended the rights of the monarchy.

10 Lennart Samuelson, *The Red Colossus. The formation of the military-industrial complex of the USSR 1921-1941*, Moscow, AIRO-XX, 2001, pp. 70–5.

11 Ibid.

12 Ibid.

13 O.N. Ken, *Mobilisation Planning and Political Decisions (late 1920s–mid-1930s)*, Saint-Petersburg., European University Press, 2002, p. 55.

14 Boris Shaposhnikov (1882–1945) graduated from Aleksey Military College (Moscow) and Imperial Nicholas Military Academy (Saint Petersburg). From August 1914, as a staff officer of the Russian Imperial Army, he participated in the First World War. In September 1917, Shaposhnikov received the military rank of Colonel. On 22 May 1918, he voluntarily joined the Red Army.

15 The Red Army leadership showed great interest in British tanks, including the Vickers Medium Mk-I/Mk-II. Since September 1925, the Soviets made a number of attempts to buy several tanks from Vickers for testing. The British categorically refused.

16 Three FIAT 3000 tanks were bought by the Soviets in December 1926. In November 1927, Italian tanks arrived in the USSR and became a model for copying when creating a new light infantry tank.

17 Until 1922, Factory No. 232 'Bolshevik' was called the Obukhov State Factory. It had been founded on 4 May 1863 by order of Emperor Alexander II.

18 Until 1922, the 'Krasny Putilovets' Factory was called the Putilov State Factory. It had been founded in 1801 by order of Emperor Paul I.

19 Izhorsky steel mill was founded in 1722 by order of Emperor Peter the Great.

20 From 1924 to 1931, the Kharkov Locomotive Factor produced a copy of the German Hanomag WD Z 50 'Kommunar' tractor. A total of 3,900 'Kommunar' tractors units of various modifications were produced.

Chapter 2: Vickers and Christie

1   Later, this plant, bought by Khalepsky, was named the Gorky Automobile Plant 'Molotov' (GAZ). You can read more about it in Dmitry Degtev, and Dmitry Zubov, *Hitler's Strategic Bombing Offensive on the Eastern Front: Blitz Over the Volga, 1943*, Barnsley: Pen & Sword Air World, 2021.

2   Praporshchik is the lowest officer rank in the Russian Imperial Army.

3   RGVA. Foundation 41132. Inventory 1. Case 3. Sheet 4.

4   RGVA. Foundation 41132. Inventory 1. Case 3. Sheet 26.

5   Alexander Yegorov (1883–1939) was a former tsarist Lieutenant Colonel. In January 1918, he voluntarily joined the Red Army. In June 1931, Yegorov was appointed by Stalin to the post of Chief of Staff of the Red Army. On 27 March 1938, he was arrested on Stalin's orders. On 23 February 1939, Yegorov was shot.

6   RGASPI. Foundation 17. Inventory 162. Case 8. Sheets 18–19.

7   RGVA. Foundation 31811. Inventory 1. Case 38. Sheets 2–3.

8   Yan Berzin (1889–1938) – real name Pēteris Ķuzis – was the creator of Soviet military intelligence. On 27 November 1937, he was arrested on Stalin's orders. Berzin was accused of anti-Soviet nationalist activities and was shot on 29 July 1938.

9   The Military-Industrial Directorate of the Supreme Soviet of the National Economy (VSNKh) was established on 24 November 1925 by order of Stalin to strengthen control over all structures of the military industry.

10   RGVA. Foundation 4. Inventory 18. Case 15. Sheets 190–203.

11   RGASPI. Foundation 74. Inventory 2. Case 105. Sheet 49.

12   RGVA. Foundation 31811. Inventory 1. Case 38. Sheet 2.

13   Ibid. Sheet 4.

14   Ibid. Sheet 38.

15   Ibid.

16   Ibid. Sheet 304.

17   The Amtorg Trading Corporation was established by the Bolsheviks in 1924 to trade with US commercial firms in the absence of official diplomatic relations between the countries.

18   RGVA. Foundation 31811. Inventory 1. Case 38. Sheets 306–307.

19   Ibid. Case 38. Sheet 309.

20   EKU OGPU was the OGPU economic directorate, created by the Bolsheviks on 25 January 1921 for total control over the economy. In 1928, enterprising OGPU officers created special prisons (Sharashkas) to exploit the labour of high-value 'wreckers'.

21   RGASPI. Foundation 17. Inventory 162. Case 9. Sheets 151–156.

22 It is likely that Dyrenkov took the prototype wheel-and-track tank by German designer Joseph Vollmer as the basis of his 'project'.

23 RGVA. Foundation 4. Inventory 18. Case 15. Sheet 248.

24 RGVA. Foundation 31811. Inventory 1. Case 38. Sheets 39–53.

25 The thickness of the 12-ton Vickers Medium Mark II's armour was 14mm (front, side). However, the British pledged to protect tanks made for the Bolsheviks with a special type of particularly durable armour – S.T.A.Plat. They ensured that the durability of the S.T.A.Plat armour significantly exceeded the characteristics of conventional 14mm-thick armour steel.

26 RGVA. Foundation 4. Inventory 18. Case 20. Sheets 83–86.

27 The passage of the Medium Mark II tank through Red Square is recorded on Soviet newsreel footage.

28 S.T. Minakov, *Behind the Lapel of a Marshal's Greatcoat*, Orel: Orelizdat, 1999, p. 200.

29 S.T. Minakov, *The Soviet Military Elite of the 1920s*, Orel: Orelizdat, 2000, p. 526.

Chapter 3: The American Ancestor of the T-34

1 Tukhachevsky, who was well aware of Ordzhonikidze's military abilities, believed that he was a much more suitable candidate for the role of Minister of War than the incompetent Voroshilov.

2 M.N. Svirin, *The Armour is Strong. The History of the Soviet Tank, 1919-1937*, Moscow, 2005, p. 193.

3 RGVA. Foundation 31811. Inventory 1. Case 340. Sheet 21.

4 Svirin, *The Armour is Strong*, p. 164.

5 RGVA. Foundation 4. Inventory 18. Case 20. Sheets 38–39.

6 Yan Gamarnik (1894–1937), Head of the Political Directorate of the Red Army, led the political supervision in the military. In 1934–7, he served as Voroshilov's deputy. On 20 May 1937, Gamarnik was removed from his post at the Political Directorate. Realising the inevitability of his arrest and execution, he committed suicide on 31 May 1937.

7 Iona Yakir (1896–1937) was arrested on 28 May 1937 in the case of the 'Military-Fascist Conspiracy in the Red Army'. He was shot on Stalin's orders on 11 June 1937.

8 Romuald Muklevich (1890–1938) oversaw the development of the Soviet Navy. He was arrested on 28 May 1937. After severe torture, he confessed to 'espionage' and 'wrecking'. On 8 February 1938, on Stalin's orders, Muklevich was sentenced to death and shot the next day.

9 Pyotr Baranov (1892–1933) oversaw the development of the Soviet aviation industry. He was the initiator of the purchase of licences for

the production of German and American aircraft engines in the USSR. Baranov died on 5 September 1933 in the crash of a Tupolev ANT-7 bomber near Podolsk.

10   Semyon Budyonny (1883–1973) was a former non-commissioned officer in the Tsarist army who joined the Bolsheviks. During the Russian Civil War, he commanded the 1st Cavalry Army. Budyonny was known for his doglike devotion to Stalin. Despite his complete incompetence, Budyonny received from Stalin the rank of Marshal and held many high positions in the Red Army.

11   RGAVMF. Foundation r-360. Inventory 2. Case 196. Sheet 32.

12   Leonid Vladimirov (1895–1938) served as director of KhPZ from 1930 to 1933. On 29 November 1933, he was appointed director of Ural Heavy Machinery Plant (Uralmash) in Sverdlovsk by order of Ordzhonikidze. On 1 September 1937, he was arrested and charged with participating in the 'Anti-Soviet and Terrorist Organization' in a fabricated NKVD case. On 14 January 1938, Vladimirov was shot in Sverdlovsk.

13   RGVA. Foundation 4. Inventory 18. Case 21. Sheet 117.

14   The production plan for 1932 envisaged the production of 10,000 tanks: tankettes – 5,000, light tanks – 3,000, and medium tanks 2,000. By the beginning of 1932, by limiting the order for tankettes from 5,000 to 3,100, the Tank Programme for the year was reduced to 8,100.

15   Ivan Bondarenko (1894–1938) held the position of Chief Engineer of the Kharkov Locomotive Factory (KhPZ) from 1931. On 1 January 1934, he was appointed director. Bondarenko was arrested by NKVD investigators on 25 May 1938, and shot on 28 July 1938.

16   The 45mm gun was a low-quality upgrade of the German 3.7cm Pak 35/36. The 37mm barrel was replaced with a 45mm barrel. It was planned to be mass-produced by Gun Factory No. 8.

17   GARF. Foundation R-8418. Inventory 8. Case 44. Sheets 20-43.

18   A similar correction of Stalin's fantastic plans was carried out across the entire range of military products. The double decrease in the planned figures in 1933 compared with the 1932 plan allowed Stalin to boastfully declare the victory of Industrialisation.

19   The rapid increase in the number of defective tanks by the end of the year was simply caused by the desire of KhPZ management to fulfil the annual plan at any cost. The feverish rush (Shturmovshchina) of the end of the year led to a huge number of defects in the production of tanks.

20   RGVA. Foundation 31811. Inventory 3. Case 186. Sheets 193–195.

21   The 76mm M1927/32 KT-28 tank gun was created in 1932 in Leningrad by modifying the 76mm M1927 regimental gun. This gun was chosen as a temporary solution during the waiting period for the completion of the 76mm tM1933 PS-3. The M1927/32 KT-28 was produced in Leningrad at the Krasny Putilovets Factory (since 1934 'Kirov' Factory). In addition to

the BT-7A, this gun was installed on the T-28, T-35 and the SU-12 self-propelled gun (gun truck).

22   RGVA. Foundation 3. Inventory 46. Case 383. Sheets 6–10.

23   Pavel Syachintov, chief designer of the 76mm M1933 PS-3 gun, was arrested by the NKVD on 31 December 1936. He was accused of 'espionage' and 'wrecking', and was executed on 6 May 1937.

24   The PT-1 wheel-and-track amphibious tank was another of Stalin's 'wonder tanks'. Based on the design of the Christie tank, it had the ability to float. The monstrous complexity of the PT-1's design and chronic defects made it impossible to hope for mass production of this tank.

25   GARF. Foundation R-8418. Inventory 28. Case 6. Sheets 230–232.

26   GARF. Foundation 3. Inventory 46. Case 383. Sheets 6–10.

27   Ibid.

28   More information about these aircraft designers can be found in Dmitry Zubov, *Stalin's Falcons: Exposing the Myth of Soviet Aerial Superiority over the Luftwaffe in WW2*, Barnsley, UK: Air World / Pen & Sword, 2024.

29   RGASPI. Foundation 17. Inventory 166. Case 565. Sheets 63–67.

30   More information about the participation of Soviet aircraft in the Spanish Civil War can be found in Zubov, *Stalin's Falcons*.

31   RGASPI. Foundation 85. Inventory 29. Case 156. Sheets 1–11.

Chapter 4: The T-34 is a by-product of Stalin's repressions

1   In November 1935, Stalin awarded Tukhachevsky the highest military rank of Marshal of the Soviet Union.

2   Vitaliy Primakov (1897–1937) was a professional military man, who fought in the Russian Civil War. For a long time he was a Military Attache in Afghanistan and Japan. In 1931–2, Primakov studied at the German War Academy (Kriegsakademie). Primakov was executed on Stalin's orders on 12 June 1937.

3   Vitovt Putna (1893-1937) was a professional military man, fighting in the First World War and the Russian Civil War. For a long time he was a Military Attache in Japan, Finland, Germany and the UK. Putna was executed on Stalin's orders on 12 June 1937.

4   In 1936, Tukhachevsky met with Stalin nine times in the Kremlin; in 1937 this meeting was the first.

5   RGASPI. Foundation 558. Inventory 11. Cases 408-411.

6   On 20 June 1934, the Revolutionary Military Council (RVS), created by Trotsky during the Russian Civil War, was abolished by Stalin. Instead, on 22 November 1935, the Military Council of the Red Army was created. Compared to the RVS, the number of its participants increased to eighty. All these people were personally selected by Stalin from among the top

commanders of the Red Army. Thus, Stalin eliminated the last remnants of the independence of the Soviet military.

7   RGASPI. Foundation 558. Inventory 11. Case 1120. Sheets 28–44, 48–57.

8   Ibid.

9   Ibid.

10   Along with Marshal Mikhail Tukhachevsky, Komandarms 1st rank (General of the Army) Ieronim Uborevich, Iona Yakir, Komandarm 2nd rank August Kork, Komkors Vitaliy Primakov, Vitovt Putna, Boris Feldman and Robert Eideman were tried on Stalin's orders.

11   The Special Military Tribunal consisted of Chairman Vasily Ulrikh and members of the Tribunal: Yakov Alksnis, Vasily Blyukher, Semyon Budyonny, Boris Shaposhnikov, Ivan Belov, Pavel Dybenko, Nikolai Kashirin and Yelisey Goryachev. After the Great Terror, only Ulrikh, Budyonny and Shaposhnikov survived from the members of the Tribunal.

12   RGVA. Foundation 4. Inventory 15. Case 13. Sheet 263.

13   At the end of 1936, the Kharkov Locomotive Factory (KhPZ) was renamed Factory No. 183.

14   A.V. Zabaykin, 'Metallurgists and the legendary T-34 tank', *Tagil Local Historian* No. 15, 1995.

15   RGVA. Foundation 4. Inventory 14 . Case 1272. Sheet 21.

16   RGVA. Foundation 33987. Inventory 3. Case 1362. Sheets 1–2.

17   GARF. Foundation R-8418. Inventory 28. Case 6. Sheets 230–232.

18   GARF. Foundation R-8418. Inventory 28. Case 2. Sheets 72–79.

19   RGVA. Foundation 33987. Inventory 3. Case 1362. Sheets 1–2.

20   RGVA. Foundation 4. Inventory 14. Case 1826. Sheets 5–22.

21   RGVA. Foundation 31811. Inventory 3. Case 975. Sheets 5–26.

22   RGVA. Foundation 31811. Inventory 3. Case 760. Sheet 21.

23   Colonel Pols Armans was killed by a bullet from a German sniper on 7 August 1943 in a battle near the village of Porechye in the Mginsky district of the Leningrad region. For the fighting in the Leningrad area, see Dmitry Degtev and Dmitry Zubov, *Air Battle for Leningrad, 1941-1944* Barnsley: Air World/Pen & Sword Books, 2023.

24   RGVA. Foundation 31811. Inventory 3. Case 975. Sheets 73–74.

25   RGVA. Foundation 31811. Inventory 3. Case 974. Sheets 57–58.

26   T-46-5 – a top-secret experimental medium tank. Weighing 28–32 tons, the tank had 60mm thick armour. The T-46-5 was armed with a 45mm gun mounted in a conical cast turret.

27 The 76.2mm L-10 tank gun was developed and produced at the 'Kirov' Factory (Leningrad). After numerous improvements, it was adopted for service by the Red Army in 1938 and was produced in a limited series. It was installed on T-28 tanks.

28 RGVA. Foundation 4. Inventory 14. Case 1897. Sheets 87–92.

29 RGAE. Foundation 7515. Inventory 1. Case 11. Sheet 101.

30 In 1935, Stalin awarded Voroshilov and Tukhachevsky the title of Marshal of the Soviet Union. If Tukhachevsky fully deserved this title, Voroshilov received it only because of his doglike devotion to Stalin.

31 Josef Kotin (1908–79) was a Soviet heavy tank designer. In 1932, he graduated from the Red Army's Military-Technical Academy 'Dzerzhinsky'. In 1932–7, Kotin served as an engineer and then Head of the Design Bureau Research Department of the Military Academy of the Red Army 'Stalin' (VAMM).

32 Petr Voroshilov (1914–84) graduated from the Military Academy of Mechanisation and Motorisation of the Red Army 'Stalin' (VAMM) in 1938, then worked at ABTU.

33 Ivan Lebedev (1899–1982) was a former Feldwebel (non-commissioned officer) of the Russian Imperial Army. He voluntarily joined the Red Army in May 1919. In 1922, Lebedev graduated from the Higher Military Automobile and Armor School in Petrograd. From June 1936 to October 1939, Lebedev served as Head and Military Commissar of the Military Academy of Mechanisation and Motorisation of the Red Army 'Stalin' (VAMM).

34 RGVA. Foundation 31811. Inventory 3. Case 760. Sheets 85–87.

35 The Mennonites are one of the branches of Christianity that appeared in Western Europe in the sixteenth century. Mennonites, according to their religious beliefs, refuse to take up arms. Mennonites, mostly Germans, arrived in the Russian Empire in 1789 at the invitation of Empress Catherine II.

36 RGVA. Foundation 31811. Inventory 3. Case 760. Sheets 57–64.

37 RGVA. Foundation 31811. Inventory 3. Case 760. Sheet 56.

38 RGVA. Foundation 31811. Inventory 3. Case 974. Sheets 97–98.

39 For Mikhail Kaganovich see Zubov, *Stalin's Falcons*.

40 RGVA. Foundation 31811. Inventory 3. Case 974. Sheets 110 – 111.

41 Ibid.

42 TsAGI – Central Aerohydrodynamic Institute.

43 NATI – Tractor Research Institution.

44 Design Bureau '35' was engaged in supporting of mass production and improvement of the design of the five-turret T-35 heavy tank.

Chapter 5: Tank of the 'New Type'

1   RGASPI. Foundation 17. Inventory 166. Case 565. Sheets 63–67.

2   RGASPI. Foundation 558. Inventory 11. Case 1120. Sheets 28–44, 48–57.

3   Ibid.

4   The second Battle of Madrid. As a result of the battle, the advancing Franquistas were stopped literally on the very outskirts of the capital, at the Majadahonda River. Soviet T-26 tanks played a significant role in the battle.

5   The third Battle of Madrid.

6   The fourth Battle of Madrid. The battle began with an offensive by the Franquistas with the participation of the Italian army and ended with a subsequent counteroffensive by the Republicans.

7   GARF. Foundation R-8418. Inventory 28. Case 27. Sheets 80–89.

8   TSAMO RF. Foundation 363. Inventory 6208. Case 18. Sheet 178.

9   Transbaikal is a vast region of Russia located in the south-east of Eastern Siberia and the south-west of the Far East, south and east of Lake Baikal.

10   RGVA. Foundation 4. Inventory 19. Case 55. Sheets 2–4.

11   GARF. Foundation R-8418. Inventory 28. Case 27. Sheets 80–89.

12   RGVA. Foundation 4. Inventory 19. Case 55. Sheet 1.

13   GARF. Foundation R-8418. Inventory 28. Case 35. Sheets 215–225.

14   RGVA. Foundation 31811. Inventory 2. Case 745. Sheet 38.

15   Nikolai Gikalo (1897–1938) was a high-ranking Bolshevik functionary. On 11 October 1937, he was arrested on Stalin's orders and was shot on 25 April 1938.

16   RGAE. Foundation 7515. Inventory 1. Case 4. Sheets 9–12.

17   K.M. Slobodin and V.D. Listrovy, *T-34: the Path to Victory: Memoirs of Tank Builders and Tankmen*, Publishing House of Political Literature of Ukraine, 1989, p. 42.

18   RGVA. Foundation 31811. Inventory 2. Case 842. Sheets 263–315.

19   RGAE. Foundation 7515. Inventory 1. Case 231. Sheet 46.

20   RGVA. Foundation 31811. Inventory 2. Case 842. Sheets 312–314.

21   TSAMO RF. Foundation 38. Inventory 11355. Case 931. Sheet 3.

22   N.A. Sobol, *Memoirs of the Director of the Factory*, edited by A.S. Epstein, H.: Prapor, 1995, p. 43.

23   Stalin's words, according to eyewitnesses, allegedly said by him during a review of the technical design of the BT-20 (A-20) tank.

24   Leon Mekhlis (1889–1953) was a former non-commissioned officer in the Russian Imperial Army. In 1918, Mekhlis voluntarily joined the Red Army and participated in the Russian Civil War. In 1918, he joined

the Bolshevik Party. In 1922–6, he was Stalin's personal secretary. In 1937, after the execution of Tukhachevsky, he received the position of Voroshilov's deputy. Mekhlis was one of the organisers of mass repressions in the Red Army.

25   Yefim Shchadenko (1885–1951), a former tailor, joined the Bolshevik Party in 1906. Shchadenko met Stalin and Voroshilov during the defence of Tsaritsyn. From November 1937, Shchadenko served as Deputy People's Commissar for Defence of the Soviet Union.

26   Grigory Kulik (1890–1950) was a former non-commissioned officer in the Russian Imperial Army. In 1918, Kulik voluntarily joined the Red Army. He met Stalin and Voroshilov during the defence of Tsaritsyn. In 1936, as a military adviser, he took part in the Spanish Civil War. On 23 May 1937, at the suggestion of Stalin, Kulik took the post of Head of the Artillery Directorate of the Red Army.

27   Aleksandr Loktionov (1893–1941) was a former non-commissioned officer in the Russian Imperial Army. In 1918, Loktionov voluntarily joined the Red Army. In November 1937, he was appointed Chief of the Air Force of the Red Army. Loktionov was shot on 28 October 1941, along with a group of other Soviet generals, without trial on Beria's orders.

28   The experimental T-100 heavy tank had 76mm and 45mm guns in two turrets. The maximum thickness of the tank's armour was 60mm, and it weighed 58 tons.

29   The experimental SMK heavy tank had 76mm and 45mm guns in two turrets. The maximum thickness of the tank's armour was 75mm, weighing 55 tons.

30   The T-40 light amphibious tank was armed with a 20mm ShVAK-T gun. Weighing 5.5 tons, the maximum thickness of the tank's armour was 20mm.

31   GARF. Foundation R-8418. Inventory 23. Case 512. Sheets 3, 4.

32   RGVA. Foundation 31811. Inventory 3. Case 1633. Sheet 178.

33   Nikolai Voznesensky (1903–50) was the main young Stalinist economist who succeeded his executed predecessors. On 27 October 1949, Voznesensky was arrested on charges of responsibility for the disappearance of secret documents and on 30 September 1950, he was shot on Stalin's orders.

34   Anastas Mikoyan (1895–1978) was a professional revolutionary who joined the Bolshevik Party in 1915. Mikoyan was one of Stalin's closest servants.

35   Andrei Zhdanov (1896–1948), Stalin's closest servant, became the leader of the Leningrad Bolsheviks after Kirov's assassination.

36   Ivan Likhachev (1896–1956) was a former locksmith at the Putilov State Factory. In June 1917, he joined the Red Army, then worked in the Bolshevik secret police until 1921. In 1926, Likhachev was appointed

director of the Moscow Automobile Plant. On 5 February 1939, Likhachev was appointed by Stalin to the post of People's Commissar for Medium Machine Building, and his powers extended to the tank industry.

37 Aleksandr Vetrov (1907–93) was a military engineer who graduated from the Military Academy of Mechanisation and Motorisation of the Red Army 'Stalin' (VAMM) in 1934. Vetrov participated in the Spanish Civil War as Deputy Commander of the International Tank Regiment on the technical side.

38 Nikolai Barykov (1900–67) was a follower and deputy of Edward Grote. In 1933, Barykov was appointed director of Factory No. 185 'S. M. Kirov' (Leningrad).

39 Nikolai Dukhov (1904–64), Soviet designer of armoured vehicles, one of the creators of the heavy tank KV.

40 A.A. Vetrov, *That's How It Was*, Moscow: Voenizdat Publisher, 1982. (Military memoirs), pp. 31–4.

41 RGVA. Foundation 31811. Inventory 3. Case 1633. Sheet 376.

42 RGVA. Foundation 31811. Inventory 3. Case 1606. Sheet 35.

43 Ibid.

44 Ibid.

45 RGVA. Foundation 31811. Inventory 3. Case 1672. Sheet 16.

46 RGVA. Foundation 4. Inventory 18. Case 49. Sheets 6–7.

47 GARF. Foundation R-8418. Inventory 28. Case 92. Sheets 121–129.

48 A statement attributed to Stalin.

49 M.V. Kolomiets, *Soviet Armored Troops in the Winter War*, Tankmaster No. 2, 1997.

50 RGVA. Foundation 31811. Inventory 2. Case 1181. Sheet 13.

51 RGVA. Foundation 31811. Inventory 2. Case 1181. Sheet 22.

52 RGVA. Foundation 4. Inventory 14. Case 2831. Sheets 14–15.

53 Mikhail Kalinin (1875–1946), Stalin's closest servant and puppet. In 1940, he served as Chairman of the Presidium of the Supreme Soviet of the Soviet Union.

54 Petr Voroshilov – adopted son of Marshal Kliment Voroshilov.

55 Vyacheslav Malyshev – People's Commissar for Heavy Machine Building (Minister).

56 Vetrov, *That's How It Was*, pp. 303–06.

57 K.M. Slobodin, *The Design Bureau Accepts the Challenge*, Yaroslavl: Verkhnevolzhskoe Publishing House, 1987. p. 109.

58 RGVA. Foundation 31811. Inventory 2. Case 1181. Sheet 62.

59 GARF. Foundation R-5446. Inventory 1v. Case 523. Sheets 216–224.

BIBLIOGRAPHY

Archives

Russian State Archive of Economics (RGAE)
RGAE. Foundation 2097. Inventory 1. Case 1051. Sheet 35.
RGAE. Foundation 4372. Inventory 91. Case 902. Sheets 57–56.
RGAE. Foundation 7515. Inventory 1. Case 11. Sheet 101.
RGAE. Foundation 7515. Inventory 1. Case 4. Sheets 9–12.
RGAE. Foundation 7515. Inventory 1. Case 231. Sheet 46.
RGAE. Foundation 7719. Inventory 2. Case 235. Sheets 5, 6.
RGAE. Foundation 7719. Inventory 2. Case 235. Sheet 7.
RGAE. Foundation 8122. Inventory 1. Case 31. Sheet 599.

State Archive of the Russian Federation (GARF)
GARF. Foundation 3. Inventory 46. Case 383. Sheets 6–10.
GARF. Foundation 3. Inventory 24. Case 332. Sheets 61, 71–86.
GARF. Foundation R-5446. Inventory 1v. Case 523. Sheets 216–224.
GARF. Foundation 8418. Inventory 17. Case 2. Sheets 252–257.
GARF. Foundation 8418. Inventory 5. Case 59. Sheets 36–37.
GARF. Foundation R-8418. Inventory 6. Case 45. Sheets 141–145.
GARF. Foundation R-8418. Inventory 8. Case 44. Sheets 20–43.
GARF. Foundation R-8418. Inventory 28. Case 126. Sheets 33–34.
GARF. Foundation R-8418. Inventory 28. Case 6. Sheets 230–232.
GARF. Foundation R-8418. Inventory 28. Case 2. Sheets 72–79.
GARF. Foundation R-8418. Inventory 28. Case 27. Sheets 80–89.
GARF. Foundation R-8418. Inventory 28. Case 35. Sheets 215–225.
GARF. Foundation R-8418. Inventory 23. Case 512. Sheets 3, 4.
GARF. Foundation R-8418. Inventory 28. Case 92. Sheets 121–129.

Russian State Military Archive (RGVA)
RGVA. Foundation 3. Inventory 46. Case 383. Sheets 6–10.
RGVA. Foundation 4. Inventory 18. Case 15. Sheets 190–203.
RGVA. Foundation 4. Inventory 18. Case 15. Sheet 248.

RGVA. Foundation 4. Inventory 18. Case 20. Sheets 83–86.

RGVA. Foundation 4. Inventory 18. Case 20. Sheets 38–39.

RGVA. Foundation 4. Inventory 18. Case 21. Sheet 117.

RGVA. Foundation 4. Inventory 15. Case 13. Sheet 263.

RGVA. Foundation 4. Inventory 14. Case 1272. Sheet 21.

RGVA. Foundation 4. Inventory 14. Case 1826. Sheets 5–22.

RGVA. Foundation 4. Inventory 14. Case 1897. Sheets 87–92.

RGVA. Foundation 4. Inventory 14. Case 1897. Sheets 93–94.

RGVA. Foundation 4. Inventory 19. Case 55. Sheets 2–4.

RGVA. Foundation 4. Inventory 19. Case 55. Sheet 1.

RGVA. Foundation 4. Inventory 18. Case 49. Sheets 6–7.

RGVA. Foundation 4. Inventory 14. Case 2831. Sheets 14–15.

RGVA. Foundation 31811. Inventory 1. Case 38. Sheets 2–3.

RGVA. Foundation 31811. Inventory 1. Case 38. Sheet 2.

RGVA. Foundation 31811. Inventory 1. Case 38. Sheets 3, 23–24.

RGVA. Foundation 31811. Inventory 1. Case 38. Sheet 4.

RGVA. Foundation 31811. Inventory 1. Case 38. Sheet 38.

RGVA. Foundation 31811. Inventory 1. Case 7. Sheet 41.

RGVA. Foundation 31811. Inventory 1. Case 38. Sheet 38.

RGVA. Foundation 31811. Inventory 1. Case 38. Sheet 304.

RGVA. Foundation 31811. Inventory 1. Case 38. Sheets 306–307.

RGVA. Foundation 31811. Inventory 1. Case 38. Sheet 309.

RGVA. Foundation 31811. Inventory 1. Case 245. Sheets 204–211.

RGVA. Foundation 31811. Inventory 1. Case 38. Sheets 39–53.

RGVA. Foundation 31811. Inventory 1. Case 38. Sheet 231.

RGVA. Foundation 31811. Inventory 1. Case 340. Sheet 21.

RGVA. Foundation 31811. Inventory 2. Case 77. Sheet 3.

RGVA. Foundation 31811. Inventory 2. Case 77. Sheet 6.

RGVA. Foundation 31811. Inventory 2. Case 77. Sheet 3.

RGVA. Foundation 31811. Inventory 2. Case 54. Sheets 65–66.

RGVA. Foundation 31811. Inventory 2. Case 54. Sheets 40–41.

RGVA. Foundation 31811. Inventory 3. Case 186. Sheets 193–195.

RGVA. Foundation 31811. Inventory 3. Case 975. Sheets 5–26.

RGVA. Foundation 31811. Inventory 3. Case 760. Sheet 21.

RGVA. Foundation 31811. Inventory 3. Case 975. Sheets 73–74.

RGVA. Foundation 31811. Inventory 3. Case 974. Sheets 57–58.

RGVA. Foundation 31811. Inventory 3. Case 760. Sheets 85–87.

RGVA. Foundation 31811. Inventory 3. Case 760. Sheets 57–64.

RGVA. Foundation 31811. Inventory 3. Case 760. Sheet 56.

RGVA. Foundation 31811. Inventory 3. Case 974. Sheets 97–98.

RGVA. Foundation 31811. Inventory 3. Case 974. Sheets 110–111.

RGVA. Foundation 31811. Inventory 2. Case 773. Sheet 156.

RGVA. Foundation 31811. Inventory 2. Case 745. Sheet 38.

RGVA. Foundation 31811. Inventory 2. Case 842. Sheets 263–315.

RGVA. Foundation 31811. Inventory 2. Case 842. Sheets 312–314.

RGVA. Foundation 31811. Inventory 3. Case 1633. Sheet 178.

RGVA. Foundation 31811. Inventory 3. Case 1633. Sheet 376.

RGVA. Foundation 31811. Inventory 3. Case 1606. Sheet 35.

RGVA. Foundation 31811. Inventory 3. Case 1672. Sheet 16.

RGVA. Foundation 31811. Inventory 2. Case 1101. Sheets 139–140.

RGVA. Foundation 31811. Inventory 2. Case 1181. Sheet 13.

RGVA. Foundation 31811. Inventory 2. Case 1181. Sheet 22.

RGVA. Foundation 31811. Inventory 2. Case 1181. Sheet 62.

RGVA. Foundation 33987. Inventory 3. Case 1362. Sheets 1–2.

RGVA. Foundation 33987. Inventory 3a. Case 1060. Sheets 2, 4.

RGVA. Foundation 33987. Inventory 3. Case 1026. Sheets 10–37.

RGVA. Foundation 35082. Inventory 1. Case 78. Sheets 926–941, 946.

RGVA. Foundation 35082. Inventory 1. Case 412.

RGVA. Foundation 41132. Inventory 1. Case 3. Sheet 4.

RGVA. Foundation 41132. Inventory 1. Case 3. Sheet 26.

Russian State Archive of Socio-Political History (RGASPI)

RGASPI. Foundation 74. Inventory 2. Case 105. Sheet 49.

RGASPI. Foundation 85. Inventory 29. Case 156. Sheets 1–11.

RGASPI. Foundation 558. Inventory 11. Cases 408–411.

RGASPI. Foundation 558. Inventory 11. Case 1120. Sheets 28–44, 48–57.

RGASPI. Foundation 17. Inventory 162. Case 8. Sheets 18–19.

RGASPI. Foundation 17. Inventory 162. Case 7. Sheet 192.

RGASPI. Foundation 17. Inventory 162. Case 8. Sheets 85–91.

RGASPI. Foundation 17. Inventory 162. Case 9. Sheets 151–156.

RGASPI. Foundation 17. Inventory 166. Case 565. Sheets 63–67.

Russian State Archive of the Navy (RGAVMF)

RGAVMF. Foundation r-360. Inventory 2. Case 196. Sheet 32.

Central Archives of the Ministry of Defence of the Russian Federation (TSAMO RF)

TSAMO RF. Foundation 38. Inventory 11355. Case 931. Sheet 3.

TSAMO RF. Foundation 363. Inventory 6208. Case 18. Sheet 178.

Published Works

Bystrova I.V., *The Soviet Military-Industrial Complex: Problems of Formation and Development (1930s-1980s)*, Moscow: IRI RAS, 2006.

Ermolov, A.Y., *State Management of the Military Industry in the 1940s: Tank Industry*, St. Petersburg, 2013.

Golubev, A.V., 'Soviet society and the "military troubles" of the 1920s', *National History* 2008, No. 1, pp. 49–50.

Hofmann, G.F., 'A Yankee Inventor and the Military Establishment: The Christie Tank Controversy', *Military Affairs* 1975, Vol. 39, No. 1, pp. 12–18.

Hofmann, G.F., 'The United States Contribution to Soviet Tank Technology', *Journal of the RUSI* 1980, Vol. 125, No. 1, pp. 63–8.

Hofmann, G.F., 'Doctrine, Tank Technology, and Execution: I.A. Khalepskii and the Red Army's Fulfillment of Deep Offensive Operations', *The Journal of Slavic Military Studies* 1996, Vol. 9, No. 2, pp. 283–334.

Ken, O.N., *Mobilisation Planning and Political Decisions (late 1920s–mid-1930s)*, St Petersburg: European University Press, 2002.

Kilichenkov, A.A., 'Joseph Stalin and the development of Tank Forces of the Red Army in the 1930s – early 1940s', *RUDN Journal of Russian History* 18, no. 4 (2019), pp. 962–84.

Kilichenkov, A.A., 'Marshal Mikhail Tukhachevsky and the Development of the Red Army's Armored Forces in the 1930s', *The New Historical Bulletin* No. 2 (60) (2019), pp. 138–87.

Kilichenkov, A.A., 'Tanks designed by J. Christie and their fate in the USA and the USSR (1930s)', *The New Historical Bulletin* 2018, No. 2, pp. 139–54.

Kolomiets, M.V., *Soviet Armored Troops in the Winter War*, Tankmaster, No. 2/1997.

Kolomiets M.V., *Soviet Medium Tank T-34. The Best Tank of the Second World War* Moscow, 2017.

Kondrashin, V.V., Kornilov, G.E., Melnikov N.N. and Mozokhin, O.B., 'Soviet tank building in 1930s: problems of serial production establishment', *University Proceedings*. Volga region № 1 (41), 2017.

Malyshev, G.N., *Tanks of the Factory 'Kirov'. Production activity of the factory in the period from 1934 to 1941 (in documents): the manuscript* St. Petersburg, 2005.

Minakov, S.T., *Behind the Lapel of a Marshal's Greatcoat*, Orel: Orelizdat, 1999.

Rybalkin, Y.E,. *Operation 'X'. Soviet Military Aid to Republican Spain (1936-1939)*, Moscow, 2000.

Samuelson, L., *The Red Colossus. The Formation of the Military-Industrial Complex of the USSR 1921-1941*, Moscow, AIRO-XX. 2001.

Simonov, N.S., *The Military-Industrial Complex of the USSR in the 1920s and 1950s: Economic Growth Rates, Structure, Organisation of Production and Management*, Moscow: ROSSPEN, 1996.

Slobodin, K.M., *The Design Bureau Accepts the Challenge*, Yaroslavl: Verkhnevolzhskoe Publishing House, 1987.

Slobodin, K.M. and Listrovy, V.D., *T-34: the Path to Victory: Memoirs of Tank Builders and Tankmen*, Publishing House of Political Literature of Ukraine, 1989.

Sobol, N.A., *Memoirs of the director of the factory*, edited by A.S. Epstein, H.: Prapor, 1995.

Sokolov, A.K. '"Militarisation" of the first five-year plan: (Soviet military industry in 1927-1932)', *Proceedings of the Institute of Russian History* Issue 7, Russian Academy of Sciences, Institute of Russian History; ed. by A.N. Sakharov, Moscow, 2008.

Sokolov, A.K., *From the Military Industry to the Military-Industrial Complex: The Soviet Military Industry. 1917 – June 1941*, Moscow: Novy Chronograf, 2012.

Solyankin, A.G., Pavlov M.V., Pavlov I.V. and Zheltov, I.G., *Domestic Armoured Vehicles. The twentieth century. Domestic Armoured Vehicles. 1905-1941*, Moscow: Exprint, 2002.

Svirin, M.N., *The Armour is Strong. The History of the Soviet Tank, 1919-1937*, Moscow, 2005.

Vetrov, A.A., *That's How It Was*, Moscow: Voenizdat Publisher. 1982. (Military memoirs).

Website https://t34inform.ru/.

Zabaykin, A.V. 'Metallurgists and the legendary T-34 tank', *Tagil Local Historian* No. 15, 1995.

Zheltov, I.G., Pavlov, I.V., and Pavlov, M.V. *Tanks BT*, Moscow: Eksprint Publ., 2001.

Zubov, Dmitry, *Stalin's Falcons: Exposing the Myth of Soviet Aerial Superiority over the Luftwaffe in WW2*, Barnsley, UK: Air World / Pen & Sword, 2024.

INDEX

Astrov, Nikolai, tank designer, 95

Barykov, Nikolai, tank designer, 198, 230
Beria, Lavrentiy, People's Commissar (Minister) of Internal Affairs, 100, 120, 188, 228
Berzin, Jan, Head of the Red Army's Fourth Bureau (GRU – Military Intelligence), 48, 75, 222
Big Tank Conference, 175, 176, 184
Bokis, Gustav, Head of Tank-Automotive Directorate of the Red Army (ABTU), 88, 127–31, 134, 139–40, 142, 146, 148–55, 157, 160–1, 165, 167, 171, 173, 175, 184, 196, 199
Bondarenko, Ivan, Director of the Factory No. 183, vii, 84, 94, 140, 149, 150–2, 154, 156, 173, 177–82, 187, 224
BT-2, 4, 7, 84, 86, 87–8, 94, 114, 125, 126, 169
BT-2-IS, 126
BT-5, vii, 4, 7, 86–92, 94–5, 98–9, 122, 126–7, 133, 160–1, 169, 178, 196, 218
BT-5-IS, vii, 126–7, 145–6
BT-7, vi, 90–5, 111–12, 115, 120, 122, 126, 129–31, 141–2, 145, 155, 169, 173, 183, 192, 194, 202
BT-7A, 225
BT-7-B-IS, 133, 135–6, 140, 144–9, 151
BT-7M, 180, 183, 196, 198
BT-9, 129–31, 136, 145, 151
BT-20 (A-20), vii, 151–2, 154–5, 172–3, 175–6, 181–9, 190–6, 198, 201–02, 204–05, 228
BT-IS, 125–7, 131, 134

Carden-Loyd Mk VI tankette, 52–3
Central Committee of the Communist Party of the Soviet Union, 12, 14, 46, 57, 96–7

Christie, Walter, tank designer, 53–4, 75–7
Christie tank, vi, 50, 53–4, 74–9, 81–6, 89, 138, 140, 161, 202, 225
Cyganov, Nikolai, tank designer, 124–7, 131, 134, 137, 142–3, 146, 182

Design Bureau '24', 155–7, 172–3, 176–7, 181–5, 187, 190–2
Design Bureau '35', 155, 227
Design Bureau '190', 115–16, 129–31, 136, 140–50, 155–6
Design Bureau '520', 193, 200, 202, 205
diesel engine V-2 (BD-2), 89, 130, 177–81, 183, 196, 209
Dik, Adolf, tank designer, 141–55, 157, 182
Doroshenko, Vladimir, tank designer, 112
Dukhov, Nikolai, tank designer, 199, 230
Dyrenkov, Nikolai, tank designer, 58–61, 127, 146, 223
Dyrenkov Design Bureau, 60, 61

Experimental Tank Workshop, 114–16, 154
Experimental Workshop '500', 194, 196

Factory No. 185 'S. M. Kirov', 119–20, 125, 230
Factory No. 232 'Bolshevik', 23–7, 29, 46, 56–7, 81, 221
FIAT 3000, tank, 23, 221
Firsov, Afanasii, tank designer, vi, 85–7, 89, 91, 94–5, 111, 113–5, 120, 126, 130, 136, 140, 155, 173, 182
First World War, 8, 24, 29, 41, 43, 64, 117, 162, 168, 220–1, 225

Frunze, Mikhail, Minister of War and
  Commander-in-Chief of the Red
  Army, 13, 43
FT-17, vi, 3, 21–4

Gorky, viii, 222
Great Terror, 14, 30, 101–02, 109, 132,
  137, 161, 171, 177, 183, 186, 188, 195,
  201, 218, 226
Grigorovich, Dmitry, aircraft
  designer, 95
Grote, Edward, tank designer, 55–8,
  123, 230
Grote Design Bureau, 55–6
Gulag, 5, 31, 55, 85, 111, 156–7, 188, 220

Hitler, Adolf, ix, x, 158–9, 206, 208, 215

Industrialisation, 4–6, 20, 70–4, 95,
  216, 224
Izhorsky steel mill, 24, 59–60, 221

Kaganovich, Lazar, People's
  Commissar of Railways of
  the Soviet Union (Minister of
  Transport), 105, 152
Kaganovich, Mikhail, People's
  Commissar of the Defence
  Industry (Minister), 152–5, 184–5,
  187, 227
Khalepsky, Innokenty, Head of the
  Red Army's Mechanization and
  Motorization Directorate (UMM),
  vi, 34–8, 40, 47–8, 51–4, 56, 59–3, 70,
  74–9, 81, 84–8, 90, 109–11, 121, 124,
  127–9, 138, 140, 157, 165, 167, 171,
  183, 196–7, 218, 222
Kharkov Locomotive Factory (KhPZ,
  Factory No. 183), xi, vii, 27–9, 57, 62,
  81–95, 111–16, 120, 125–7, 130–1, 136,
  138, 140–2, 145, 147, 148–56, 175–87,
  190–1, 193–5, 200–1, 203–4, 208–10,
  212–15, 224, 226
Kirov, Sergei, First Secretary of
  the Leningrad City Committee of
  the All-Union Communist Party
  (Bolsheviks), 96–7, 119, 229
'Kirov' Factory, 137–8, 187, 224, 227
Koshkin, Mikhail, tank designer,
  vii, 114–20, 129, 130–1, 133, 135–7,
  140–57, 159, 173, 177, 181–92, 195,
  198–203, 206, 209–10, 212–15, 218

Kotin, Josef, tank designer, 137,
  198–9, 227
Krasnoye Sormovo Shipyard No. 112,
  vi, viii, 21
Kucherenko, Nikolai, tank designer,
  111, 155
Kulchicky, Evgeny, tank tester, 93, 142,
  154, 194–5, 201
KV tank, x, 180, 198, 219, 230

Lebedev, Ivan, Head of Academy
  Mechanization and Motorization
  of the Red Army 'Stalin' (VAMM),
  139–40, 146, 149–51, 199, 227
Lenin, Vladimir, vi, 1–3, 7–13, 15, 17,
  21–2, 42, 66, 69–70, 87, 117, 216, 221

M-17 engine, 89–90
M-17T engine, 90–2
Main Directorate of the War Industry
  (GUVP), 21–2, 26, 28, 34, 38, 47
Main Tank-Automotive Directorate
  of the Red Army (GABTU), 208–09,
  211, 215, 217
Maksarev, Yuri, Director of the
  Factory No. 183, 187, 191, 195–6, 201
Malyshev, Vyacheslav, People's
  Commissar for Heavy Machine
  Building (Minister), viii, 197, 213,
  220, 230
Mariupol steel mill, 87–8, 91, 200
Mechanised Troops, 45, 49, 83, 110, 124,
  158, 161, 164, 170, 174
Mikoyan, Anastas, People's
  Commissar of Foreign Trade
  (Minister), 197, 199, 229
Mikulin, Alexander, engine designer,
  89–90
Military Academy Mechanization
  and Motorization of the Red Army
  'Stalin' (VAMM), vii, 139, 142, 146,
  149, 151, 154, 157, 227, 230
Military Council of the Red Army, 13,
  44, 48, 59, 62–3, 74, 77–8, 82–3, 107–9,
  158–61, 189, 191–2, 205, 208, 225
Military Quality Control System
  for Weapons, 80, 94, 112, 115, 128,
  180, 214
Military Representatives, 80–1, 87,
  112, 214
Moloshtanov, Aleksey, tank
  designer, 181

Molotov, Vyacheslav, Chairman of the
    Council of People's Commissars of
    the Soviet Union (formal Head of
    the Government of the USSR), 70,
    102, 105
Morozov, Aleksander, tank designer,
    112, 154, 155, 190–1, 203, 215, 218
Moscow, vi, vii, x, 1–4, 10–1, 20–1, 24–5,
    28, 34–5, 44, 52, 57, 60–3, 65, 67, 70–2,
    76, 84–5, 87, 90–1, 93–4, 103–06, 112–
    13, 116–18, 126–7, 131, 134, 136–7,
    140, 143–4, 146–54, 157, 172–3, 175–9,
    181–7, 189, 191–2, 194, 196, 201, 204,
    208–10, 212, 215, 220–1

New Design Group, 148–50, 153
NKVD, 7, 12, 31, 61, 81, 90, 92–4, 96,
    99–102, 104–06, 109–14, 122, 127,
    132, 152–3, 155–7, 167, 171, 177, 179,
    180–4, 186–8, 210, 212, 224–5

OGPU, 1, 5, 28, 33, 39, 46, 54–6, 61, 66,
    71, 73, 85, 95, 220, 222
Ordzhonikidze, Gregory (Sergo),
    People's Commissar of Heavy
    Industry (Minister), vi, 64, 68, 69,
    70–4, 79, 85, 87, 96, 99, 100, 113, 114,
    119, 120, 122, 124–6, 128–9, 136–8,
    150, 152, 223–4

Panzerwaffe, x, 170
Pavlov, Dmitry, Head of Tank-
    Automotive Directorate of the Red
    Army (ABTU), vii, 159–76, 183–93,
    196–206, 209, 210–19
Pilsudski, Jozef, Marshal, 16, 221
Polikarpov, Nikolai, aircraft
    designer, 95
PT-1 tank, 91, 143, 225

Red Army, vi, vii, viii, ix, x, 1–4, 7,
    9–28, 31–50, 53–4, 57–69, 71, 74–8,
    80–6, 88–9, 91–5, 103–04, 106–12,
    117–18, 121, 123–5, 127–33, 137–40,
    146, 148–51, 153–4, 157–75, 180–1,
    183, 186, 188, 189, 191–2, 198, 200–01,
    204–08, 211, 215–30
Red Army's Mechanization and
    Motorization Directorate (UMM), vi,
    34–5, 37–8, 40, 44, 48, 56, 60, 62–4, 75,
    77–8, 84, 87, 89, 109–10, 128

Revolutionary Military Council (RVS),
    13, 44, 48, 59, 62, 74, 77–9, 83, 225
Rukhimovich, Moisey, People's
    Commissar of the Defence Industry
    of the Soviet Union (Minister), 136,
    138, 150, 152, 153
Russian Civil War, 3, 8, 9, 11, 14, 17, 24,
    31, 36–40, 42, 58, 64, 69, 71, 104, 117,
    163, 164, 168, 224, 225, 228

Scientific and Testing Tank-
    Automotive Test Range (NIABP),
    194, 196–7, 210
Separate Design Bureau (OKB), 150–1,
    153–5
Shaposhnikov, Boris, Chief of Staff of
    the Red Army, 20, 40, 48, 50, 82, 109,
    129, 221, 226
Shukalov, Sergey, tank designer, 21,
    26, 30–1
SMK, tank, 190, 198, 229
Soviet tank industry, viii, ix, 4, 7, 21, 29,
    38, 76, 83, 121–3, 125, 127–8, 134, 138,
    157, 166, 172, 174, 188, 216
Soviet Tank-Automotive Troops, 111,
    138–40, 160–1, 165, 167–9
Spanish Civil War, 7, 97, 99, 133, 138,
    158, 160–1, 168–9, 200, 218, 225,
    229–30
Special Tank Purchasing Commission,
    45, 47, 50–3, 61, 70
Stalin, Joseph, vii, viii, ix, x, xi, 2–30,
    32–43, 44–8, 50, 52–9, 61–89, 91–114,
    118–25, 127–34, 136–9, 146, 149–50,
    152–3, 155–61, 164–8, 170–93, 195–7,
    199–230
Sviridov, Vasily, Head of 8th Main
    Directorate of the People's
    Commissariat of the Defence
    Industry, 140, 144, 147, 153–4, 157,
    181, 184
System of Tank-Tractor-Automotive
    Vehicles of the Red Army
    (Armament System), 44–5, 48, 19,
    50–1, 62, 74, 83, 88,

T-12, 27–8, 34, 54, 62, 77, 83
T-17, vi, 3, 21, 28, 34, 54, 83
T-18 (MS-1), 23, 25–8, 30, 46, 49, 54, 57,
    77, 81, 166, 218
T-19, 34, 54, 83

T-20, 83

T-23, 28, 54, 83

T-24, vi, 28, 54, 57, 62, 82–4, 218

T-26, 4, 7, 77, 81, 98–9, 132–3, 160–1,
    164–5, 167, 168–9, 174, 192, 198,
    205–06, 208, 218–19, 228

T-27, 4, 164, 169

T-28, 3, 4, 7, 90, 120, 165, 169, 208, 219,
    225, 227

T-29, vii, 120–2, 143, 165–6, 169, 174

T-32 (A-32), vii, 191–6, 198–203, 205

T-34 (A-34), vii, viii, ix, x, xi, 26, 51, 68,
    85, 116–19, 123, 135–6, 139–40, 146,
    157, 172, 174, 180–2, 185, 193, 195,
    204–6, 208–15, 218–19

T-35, 3–4, 7, 120, 169, 225, 227

T-37A, 4, 7, 164, 207, 208

T-38, 169, 207, 208

T-40, 190, 229

T-46, 120–2, 135, 165–6, 174, 226

T-100, 190, 229

Tank Armament System of the Red
    Army, 121, 168, 171–5

Tank Bureau KhPZ (T2K), 28, 85–7, 89,
    92, 94, 111–15, 120, 126, 142

Tank Programme, 28–9, 30, 33, 35, 38,
    45–7, 54, 57, 58, 83, 86, 224

Tank Repair Factory No. 48, 126–7,
    146

Tank-Automotive Directorate of the
    Red Army (ABTU), 110, 112, 124,
    127–9, 131, 133–6, 139–44, 146–54,
    157, 160–1, 165, 167, 169–73, 175, 183,
    184, 186, 188–91, 200–02, 204–06,
    208–09, 211, 227

TG (Tank Grote), vi, 56–8, 82–3

Trotsky, Leon, People's Commissar for
    Military and Navy Affairs (Minister
    of War), 2, 8–14, 37, 42–3, 66–7, 69,
    71, 106, 108–09, 117, 225

Tsaritsyn, 10–11, 32, 229

Tukhachevsky, Mikhail, Head of
    Armaments of the Red Army, vi,
    14–16, 18–20, 32–3, 35, 37, 39, 40–4,
    50, 53–4, 59, 63, 65, 66–8, 74, 77–8,
    82–3, 86, 89, 95, 103–11, 123–4, 127–8,
    138–9, 157–61, 164–5, 168–71, 174,
    190, 206, 212, 217–18, 220, 223, 225–7,
    229

Uborevich, Ieronim, Head of
    Armaments of the Red Army, vi,
    41–5, 48, 50, 54, 56, 59, 62–5, 70, 77–8,
    82, 106, 138, 158–9, 161, 164, 168, 218,
    226

Vickers 6-ton light tank, 52–3, 76–7, 81

Vickers 12-ton Medium Mark II, vi, 52,
    61–3, 223

Vladimirov, Leonid, Director
    of the Kharkov Locomotive
    Factory (KhPZ), 81, 83–4, 224

Voroshilov, Kliment, People's
    Commissar for Defence of the
    Soviet Union (Minister), vii, 2–3, 10,
    13–15, 18–20, 31–2, 40, 44, 48, 55–60,
    66–8, 74, 76–9, 82, 88, 97, 103–05,
    108–10, 123–7, 129, 131–2, 134–40,
    145–7, 149–52, 154–5, 169–70, 175–7,
    180, 182, 189, 193, 197–9, 202, 209,
    212–3, 223, 227, 229

Yakir, Iona, Commander of the
    Ukrainian Military District, 78,
    124, 223

Yezhov, Nikolai, People's Commissar
    for Internal Affairs (Minister), 96–7,
    99–102, 105–07, 110, 112, 120, 152–3,
    157, 188

Zaslavsky, Vladimir, tank designer, 21,
    26, 30, 31